**EXPLORING
THE FAITH**

1987 Edition

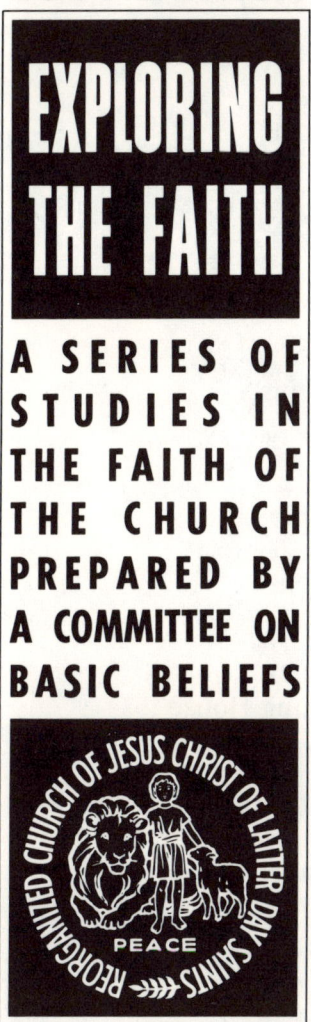

EXPLORING THE FAITH

A SERIES OF STUDIES IN THE FAITH OF THE CHURCH PREPARED BY A COMMITTEE ON BASIC BELIEFS

Edited by Alan D. Tyree

Reorganized Church of Jesus Christ of Latter Day Saints
Independence, Missouri

Copyright © 1987
Herald Publishing House
Independence, Missouri

All rights in this book are reserved. No part of the text may be reproduced in any form without written permission of the publishers, except brief quotations used in connection with reviews in magazines or newspapers.

Printed in the United States of America

Reorganized Church of Jesus Christ of Latter Day Saints
Independence, Missouri

93 92 91 90 89 88 87   1 2 3 4 5 6 7

FOREWORD

For many years the most widely circulated statement of the beliefs of our church was the Epitome of Faith. The Epitome was originally written by Joseph Smith, Jr., in answer to a request by a Chicago newspaper editor. There have been some modifications of the original statement through the years.

In more recent times it has been recognized that a more adequate statement of the beliefs of the church should be developed. Historical and traditional points of view needed to be expanded in view of the contemporary religious experience and scholarship. Recognizing that the understanding of religious experience is always qualified by the human nature of those involved, the church has traditionally avoided creedal statements and has sought to preserve the openness and humility of the admonition to "seek learning by study, and also by faith."

Over a period of nearly a decade a dedicated group of ministers has worked carefully and consistently to bring insights to this task. The committee originally was chaired by President F. Henry Edwards. In 1966 Apostle Clifford A. Cole, serving with the committee from the beginning, was appointed to this responsibility. Those who have served on the committee were carefully selected in order to accommodate the range of viewpoints present within the church and to bring to the task adequate ministerial experience and theological insights.

It is fully intended that the work of the committee in developing the concise statements and interpretative articles will provide members of the priesthood, laity of the church, and inquiring friends with the basis for intense personal and corporate study in the years to come.

Such a work is never finished because each generation brings its own unique insights and experience to the task. Of necessity there is a continuity in the history of religious experience so that any generation cannot regard itself as standing alone without meaningful relationship to the past and to the future. Although we stand on the shoulders of giants, we also hold in our lives potentially a contribution to the enrichment of the succeeding generations. It is in the tension between what has been and what can be that lives are lived, beliefs tested, and the meaningfulness of contributions is determined.

Our grateful appreciation is extended to the members of the committee who have made this notable contribution to the church. In addition to F. Henry Edwards and Clifford A. Cole, the committee has included Percy E. Farrow, Reed M. Holmes, Cecil R. Ettinger, Russell F. Ralston, William E. Timms, Earl T. Higdon, Harry L. Doty, Charles A. Davies, Clifford P. Buck, Alfred H. Yale, Merle P. Guthrie, Geoffrey F. Spencer, and Jacques V. Pement. We believe that they have aided us all by identifying that center-ground where most of the members of the church would stand doctrinally and theologically. We commend their work to the church with our full support and approval.

THE FIRST PRESIDENCY
August 1987

INTRODUCTION

Since the first edition of this work in 1970, the church has found *Exploring the Faith* to be useful in its study and witness. It has informed leaders, teachers, writers, students, and enquirers about the beliefs of the Reorganized Church of Jesus Christ of Latter Day Saints.

Because of its continuing contribution to the Saints, it was regarded as a work which needed to be republished in a second edition. From the beginning, when it first appeared as a series of articles by the Basic Beliefs Committee members in the *Saints' Herald*, it was apparent that it would be a valuable addition to the body of resources in our basic literature. However, some persons offered constructive ciriticism that suggested a rewriting of the work would be of value to the average reader.

This present edition is an attempt to meet that need. Whereas the former articles showed the inevitable traces of the individuality of the authors, it is hoped this edition will offer a more even style in the rewriting. It was also our intention to choose a style that would be generally accessible to most of the adults and mature youth of the church. To help in this process, additional illustrations have been added occasionally.

All the while, our foremost objective was to attempt to retain the content and theology of the work of the committee, so that none of the quality efforts would be lost or diminished. Consequently it would not be inappropriate to refer to this edition as a "translation" of the original work into a simpler literary style.

In the preface to the first edition, Apostle Clifford A. Cole stated,

> The essential part of this book is the Statement of Belief. The articles which have been written to accompany the various paragraphs are but windows through which the reader may catch some glimpse into their meaning. It is our conviction that many books could be written about any one paragraph, and even then the depths would not be plumbed.

We do not present this statement as a final work. Most of all, we do not want people to ever think of it as a creed. It is intended as a resource to assist interested persons in enriching their understanding of the meaning of the gospel of Jesus Christ.

To the Saints, who have already adopted this work as illustrative of their fundamental and basic beliefs, this book is dedicated. May it for some time yet be useful, while the church moves forward in its search for "all truth." We pray that the day will not be long coming when spiritual maturity, faithful pursuit, and scholarly inquiry will result in a new statement of our faith explorations by another generation.

Alan D. Tyree
July 1987

CHAPTER 1
GOD THE FATHER

We believe in God the Eternal Father, source and center of all love and life and truth, who is almighty, infinite, and unchanging, in whom and through whom all things exist and have their being.

Our faith statements grow out of our deepest experiences in life. To talk about God in general ways using our intellect alone will not help us very much in our quest to know God. Nevertheless, it is because of our gift of reasoning and a sense of how things "ought" to be that we, as God's created beings, have sought to find answers down through the ages to questions about the meaning of life. This quest is a very practical one, for it touches on every aspect of our human existence. It provides us with the framework out of which we make our moral choices, as well as the feelings of joy or sadness which result from the choices we have made.

Religious experience of one kind or another is common to all cultures. The marvelous world in which we live is filled with such greatness and majesty that we can see on every hand things that astound, that inspire, that attract, that motivate. The beauties of nature contain their own magic and mystery, so that human beings from the earliest of times have been surrounded with the religious dimension of life. The poet William Wordsworth in *Ode on Intimations of Immortality,* speaks of

>...truths that wake, to perish never:
>Which neither listlessness, nor mad endeavor
>Nor man nor boy, nor all that is at enmity with joy,
>Can utterly abolish or destroy.

The Apostle Paul was making the same point when he said that humans "are without excuse...for God hath revealed unto them the invisible things of Him, from the creation of the world, which are clearly seen; things which are not seen being understood by the things that are made" (Romans 1:20). The Creator is so well seen through the world of creation that virtually every experience of life testifies of the existence and reality of God. The only reasonable answer that human beings have been able to discover, down through the ages, to the question, "Why?" is the religious answer that "God the Creator is."

We believe in God...

Job's friend, Zophar, raised a question which is really the question of every person: "Canst thou by searching find out God? Canst thou find out the Almighty unto perfection?" (Job 11:7). Surrounded as we are by "so great a cloud of witnesses" who from the realm of nature proclaim the divine hand which made it, we ask ourselves if such an awesome and majestic creator can in fact be known by humble creatures like us?

The Hebrew tradition teaches us that God is not some remote object to be searched for, but rather the Holy One who encounters us in the very circumstances of everyday life. The ancient Greeks imagined God in terms of pure thought. Aristotle's God was a perfect thinker, thinking only pure thoughts, and therefore not involved in contemplating this imperfect world, but only himself. However, the Old Testament reveals a God who *acts*, who enters into the limitations of space and time—which are human dimensions—by acting and interacting with creation.

It is easy to see Isaiah's contempt for the pagan gods, for "they bear him upon the shoulder, they carry him, and set him in his place, and he standeth; from his place shall he not remove; yea, one shall cry unto him, yet can he not answer, nor save him out of his trouble" (Isaiah 46:7). In contrast, the God of Hebrew scripture is a "living God." For the Hebrews, Deity is not an inference or an idea, but *He who is.* For them, God is the source of all life in the world, and as a self-revealing Person, is personally involved in the life of the people. God is; God does; God directs; thus God is seen.

As with the ancient Hebrews, by divine grace and goodness, simply and openly, God comes to us as we are. The degree of our openness and receptivity to God's presence will limit how complete that revelation of God to us can be. There is no limitation on God's ability to reveal, but we are very limited in our ability to comprehend. Consequently God comes to us as we are, and where we are in our spiritual development. When revelation occurs, though God would be completely open and withhold nothing of the divine glory from us, still God must approach us according to our limitations, *according to our ability to see God as God is.*

Our only adequate response to this revelation is a confession of faith. Because we have seen God, or seen something of the divine will for us, we confess our belief in God's reality and love for us. The scriptural witness is true: "But without faith it is impossible to please Him; for he that cometh to God must believe that He is, and that He is a rewarder of them that diligently seek Him" (Hebrews 11:6).

Although some scientists have, from time to time, attempted to use the scientific method to establish evidences for the existence of God, the Christian faith affirms, nonetheless, that neither science nor any other human source can provide the grounds for either belief or disbelief in God. The prophet Joseph Smith, Jr., best stated it when he wrote: "All truth is independent in that sphere in which God has placed it, to act for itself..." (Doctrine and Covenants 90:5b). Although some scientists through scientific research have attempted to provide support for an atheistic faith position, still others have tried equally to prove their religious faith by a scientific justification. Similarly in error are those religionists who attempt to prove a particular view of the scientific world, nature, and creation by means of a particular faith stance. It is just as incorrect for creationists to deny the theories of evolution because of their scripture-based faith position as it is for atheists to use scientific arguments to disprove the scriptures or any other item of faith. The one is apples, the other oranges. By adding and subtracting apples, one can never hope to have a total in oranges. The realms of faith and science do not intermix, and neither one can offer any kind of proof about the other. They are as parallel lines which never meet or touch but which move forward in the same direction.

We may infer some things from science that are helpful to our faith, or we may with a faith stance proceed in research that would seek to enlarge the range of scientific knowledge. But they still remain separate entities. For example, it may be helpful to the person who believes in a continuity of life beyond death to find strength for that belief by taking note of the conservation of matter and energy which operate in the physical world. However, when the scientist tells us that nothing can be permanently lost from the created order of things, that does not justify us in assuming that such a "law" of science "proves" that the spirit of a human being lives on after death. Indeed, most scientists would affirm that there is no such thing as absolute scientific *knowledge*, but rather scientific *faith* based on available data.

All our ways of knowing anything are tainted by our very humanity. There is no such thing as pure knowledge, uncontaminated by human minds. No matter what the source of information or truth may be, it is always perceived or understood by a human being. And inasmuch as none of us are free from our own humanity, the gathering of information is itself marked by our own frailty.

But because this is so, it suggests to us how very important our personal experience with God is. Somehow, Deity lives and moves in our very midst. We are able to perceive God in the events of history, in the lives of our loved ones, in intense worship experiences, and in the surrounding environment of natural beauty. In these places of revelation, we are sometimes deeply impressed with the fact that God has been very close to us indeed. Our lives and hearts have been touched by God's Spirit, and we have seen and understood things that we had not previously known. There is no other area of human knowledge or experience that can come to us with any greater force or objective clarity. We have stood in God's presence, and *we know that we have.* By faith, we have communed with God.

For those of us who have been raised and schooled in the Judeo-Christian culture, our personal experiences with God have focused in the revelation of the person Jesus Christ. We do not need to ask, as did Saul of Tarsus, "Who art thou, Lord?" (Acts 9:5). We know that it is the Lord Jesus Christ who has touched our lives. And similarly, we do not need to ask as did Philip, "Show us the Father, and it sufficeth us." We already know the answer, "He that hath seen me, hath seen the Father" (John 14:8, 9).

the Eternal Father...

It is one thing to have had some spiritual experience with God. It is quite something else to be able to describe it to someone else. As soon as we attempt to put into words the totality of our experience, including that which we have known, felt, yearned for, received, and given, we do not find words enough or even the right words to help us describe what has happened. We try to borrow words from everyday life, but find that they are nearly useless. So we use analogies and parables and metaphors, but realize that in each case they always break down and fail to describe what really happened. We finally describe God by using terms that lie at the extremes of our experiences: If we find joy in someone repenting, then we suppose that God's rejoicing must be even greater than ours. If we are saddened by someone's sinning, then we presume that God is deeply offended by the human trespass. If God is not bound by time as are we, then we use words such as "infinite" and "alpha and omega," although these are words which have very little real meaning for us in spite of their frequent use. Not having experienced infinity, we do not really know what it is. We thus use language that is not very precise simply because we lack a better way of talking about the

One whom we have experienced in deep and moving ways. We lack the terminology for a clear and precise discussion.

When we acknowledge God as "Our Father," we imply several things about God. First of all, we imply that God is a very personal being toward us. As a father is a person, so is God in his relationships to us. When we stand in God's presence, we experience love. Only *persons* can love like that. God is not a *thing* before which we should bow and pay obeisance or offer particular gifts and sacrifices. Rather God is personal, a loving person.

Secondly, the term "Father" implies a personal relationship that is very close indeed. It is not as if we are simply speaking to some stranger or receiving love from some unknown individual. On the contrary, the most intimate of relationships seem to develop between ourselves and God when we are in God's presence. In trying to describe it, we say it is like the love we experience from a loving father. Such a love is benevolent, it is kind, it is forgiving, it is wise, and somehow knows all about us. Indeed, most of the attributes that we ascribe to parenthood at its best are also to be experienced with Godhood.

Although we use this sort of analogy to compare our experience with God to the human child's experience of fatherhood, on the other hand, we go too far if we attempt to limit God to a description of what fathers are like, even the very best of fathers. While referring to "God the Father," we need to take care that we do not mean that "God is like a human father." If we were to do that, we would be creating God in our own human image. It is God who has created us in his image, and if there is any similarity, it is because we have been made in his image rather than the other way around. To describe God as our heavenly Father may be one of the most useful descriptive terms that we employ, but it, too, falls short of the true reality of what God is like.

source and center...

In speaking of God as the source of our world and being, we are interested in more than a scientific account of the origins of things. Once again, our language falls short. When we talk about someone being a creator of a work of art, a building, an institution, a set of laws, or whatever, we are only talking about how someone reforms and re-shapes elements and concepts of matter which already exist. But when we speak of God as creator, we mean something much more comprehensive, which includes both matter and form. As creator, God's relationship to the world and to us is quite different from our relationship to anything which we may happen to create. We may be completely serious when we talk about our utter dependence upon God who sustains us, but we are at a loss for words to explain how we are dependent upon God. It is still quite a mystery to us how we were created and how we relate to our creator through that process. The distinguished biologist, L. Charles Birch, wrote:

Creation then has not to do primarily with *origins*. It has primarily to do with *dependence*, man's dependence upon God's activity. It is not a story which begins 'Once upon a time.' It has not to do with how things began, but how they are—what they are in their inner nature. And their nature is interpreted in terms of their dependence upon God.—*Nature and God*, page 84

There are several meanings caught up in this profound symbol. First of all, God as our source is also our ultimate sovereign. We are created within a proper framework where we may function—genuinely and with authority. Therefore, our lives, though limited to approximately "three score and ten" years, have meaning which far exceeds the futility of time limitations. Furthermore, because everything within the world is time-bound and therefore is temporary and contingent, even the whole of creation cannot be the source for an explanation or cause for its own existence. It, too, is ultimately dependent upon God, and our lives are claimed by a power and will beyond anything that we can experience in this life, including our own will.

The Christian doctrine of creation boldly places God outside the created world as creator. Another way of saying this is to state that God is *transcendent* to the world. We who are finite are made out of the same stuff as all other finite creation. The molecules comprising our bodies are no different than those found elsewhere. Although God identifies with the created world, the world is not God and God is not it. Our salvation then is not to be found in terms of shedding our creaturehood so as to be absorbed into a natural world which, though created by God, is God (pantheism). Rather it is as Carl Barth has succinctly stated it: "God who alone is real and essential and free is one; and heaven and earth, man and the universe are something else; and this something else is not God, though it exists through God" (*Dogmatics in Outline*, page 55).

At the same time, the doctrine of creation also affirms that the world is basically good because God the creator is good. Although deism may have acknowledged God as the prime mover or "First Cause," our understanding of God goes beyond that rather distant or cold image of an unmoved or uncaring God. Persons who have had any experience at all with the Spirit of God in their lifetimes will understand that God is not distant but immanent, at hand. God did not simply take the universe as a very fine watch, wind it up and set it into motion, flinging it out into the vast expanse of space, there to run down under its own power. On the contrary we find God very much involved in creation, in the unfinished work, encouraging and motivating us toward divine purposes and ends.

Thus, in spite of God's separation from the world in terms of transcendence due to the difference between creator and creation, God is also immanent within that world, seeking to bring forth the divine cause and purpose. God is with and through all of creation. The principle of the Incarnation catches up this abiding paradox. God's *being*, though transcendent, is off-set by godly activity, divine presence, immanence.

of all love...

If we are at all serious when we ask "What is God like?" we are immediately brought face to face with the limitations of our inadequate language. As F. Henry Edwards has pointed out in "The Latter Day Saint Concept of God" (*Priesthood Study Outlines*), "Something of ourselves goes into all of our understanding of God, even our understanding of His moral attributes. Full comprehension must await a growth which we do not fully attain in this life." Our knowledge may be incomplete, our language may lack in sophistication to cope with the realities of what God is like, our intellect may need the quickening of the Holy Spirit for us to see with spiritual eyes. Yet essentially what we most need lies not so much in areas of scholarship as in the continuing attitude of worship, the yielding of a contrite heart and a broken spirit, to worship "in spirit and in truth." Although we may need to know more about God, the truth is we need more to know God.

We understand some things almost intuitively. When we ask, "What is God like?" we can readily respond, "God is like Christ." Jesus, who was in all respects human, was at the same time Eternal God (Philippians 2:5-8). Because God has entered into the structures and realities of human experience, because Jesus is Emmanuel (God with us), then we have the answer, not only to Philip's request, but to the question posed by the world: "Show us the Father."

When asked, "What is God like?" we may confidently answer, "God is someone who can be loved." As John expressed it: "We love him because he first loved us" (I John 4:19). As modern psychologists have pointed out, the truth is we only know how to love someone else because we have first been loved ourselves. This is what John brings to our attention. Divine love is possible even to us—even *for us to express to others.* We know that this is so because we too have received the divine love of God in Christ.

God always takes the initiative in loving us. Although unwilling to coerce us, God will not leave us unaware of the continuing, attracting influence of divine love. In the life and death of Jesus, we see God at a particular moment in history, drawing back the veil to expose the depth of Godly eternal love for the world. There literally is nothing that God will not do because of such immensely gracious love for us.

When we are exposed to that kind of love, hope springs forth miraculously, intuitively. If we are only willing to receive God's love, it provides such assurance, for love never fails. How like a fire is the love of God! The person who has experienced God's love can never again know the satisfaction of worshiping at the shrine of his or her own self-centeredness. It is not an exaggeration for the writer of the Hebrews' letter to have said, "It is a fearful thing to fall into the hands of the living God" (10:31).

and life...

Because God is love, God's life is shared with us. "I am come that they might have life, and that they might have it more abundantly" (John 10:10). But what kind of life is it that God intends to share?

First of all, it is purposive, it is *being,* it is *becoming.* Whereas the Greek view of human history was cyclical like the endless round of the seasons, the Hebrews saw life as moving in a certain direction in fulfillment of divine purpose. The God who was setting in motion the forces that would liberate the Israelites from Egypt was called "I AM THAT I AM." Some translators have suggested the appropriateness of rendering this phrase, "I cause to be what I cause to be." Thus, when John reports Jesus' having said, "My Father is working still...," he partly suggests that the One who gave light and life to the Israelites is still providing light and life to the world. In harmony with that understanding, the scripture reports Jesus continued by saying, "...and I am working" (John 5:17). Our God is dynamic, purposive, active, involved in bringing to pass the divine will upon the earth.

The life which God shares with us is eternal: "For this is my work and my glory, to bring to pass the immortality and eternal life of man" (John 17:3). Throughout human history, most peoples have held tenaciously to life with all of their resources. We grieve especially when a life is cut short, but Christian faith moves beyond the area of bare immortality. Eternal life is interpreted not in terms of duration but in terms of relationships. It is only the life of significant relationships which is worth experiencing as long as possible. The life that is most worth living is the life that is lived for the sake of others—and consequently the life that is worth living eternally is the life that has established its loving relationships with others throughout a lifetime. Length of life has extremely little value unless it is enriched by ties of love and friendship. It is therefore not surprising that Jesus should define eternal life in terms of relationships: "And this is life eternal, *that they might know thee* the only true God, and Jesus Christ, whom thou hast sent" (John 17:3).

The life which God shares is good. The ancient scripture says that God, on the eve of each day of creation, pronounced the accomplished work as "good." For us, a thing is good if it fulfills the purpose of its creation, of its intention. We measure everything against this criterion, whether it be a knife, a chair, an apple, or a book. But when it comes to humankind, our "good"-ness can only be determined in terms of relationships. A "good" husband is observed in how he relates with his wife. In the final analysis, a good person is determined in how he or she relates to God. It is as Augustine exclaimed, "O God, thou hast made us for thyself." If the life that God shares with us is good, it means that his creation is capable of fulfilling the will of the Creator.

But, someone asks, what about the problem of evil which exists in this world where God exercises sovereignty? In Jesus we find two attitudes existing at the same time. While he speaks of the destructive powers of evil, he also speaks of his complete confidence in God's present rule over the world, and the triumph of the coming kingdom. We are not to deny evil or to retreat from it, but to meet it directly and creatively, with as much insight as the grace of God will permit. F. Henry Edwards has stated in an article in the *Saints' Herald* entitled, "We Believe in God":

> To have faith in God is to have the assurance of things hoped for—the conviction that because God is the kind of person he is, that which truly ought to be sometime shall be.... To have faith in God, to truly *believe in* him, is to work in the confident assurance that "a loftier race than e'er the world has known shall rise." And it is to know that the grandeur of that coming day will be in the godlike quality of its people.—*Saints' Herald*, October 15, 1964

and truth...

God is both true and truth. By "true" we mean that God is faithful. By "truth" we mean that God is the embodiment of all that really is. Therefore, whenever we encounter truth in the world, we actually encounter a description of what *is*. Because "the Spirit of truth is of God" (D. and C. 90:4c), God's universe may be thoroughly investigated and found to be consistent. The scientific method of investigation has demonstrated to our satisfaction that the universe is a stable and trustworthy unity rather than a multiverse. It is one system which works well together, rather than many which seem to be at war with one another. It has been noted historically that the Christian belief in a God-created universe provided the climate in which modern science could develop, built on the assumption that nature contains a real order that the mind could investigate.

It is impossible for us to perceive something of truth about the world, about the universe, about ourselves, without learning something of the truth about God. To know the truth, any truth, is to know something more about God. For God is truth. The insatiable curiosity with which God has endowed humankind is another evidence of the way in which God has tilted us forward, ever stretching outward to know, to perceive, to reach out and touch God.

The insight that God is light and truth brings with it the conviction that God is also trustworthy. The Lord is everywhere and always the same, so we have come to have complete trust in all of our relationships with God. There is no separation between divine love and divine judgment. God's judgment is always a loving judgment, and godly love is always discriminating.

Because we have experienced the magnificent love of God for us, we instinctively know that we can trust God. We know that we will not be led astray, and we know that the Holy Spirit will only prompt us to do good. When we stand in the presence of God, we see things more clearly than ever we have seen them before. We see ourselves as we really are, and no longer can deceive ourselves by the little games which we play. To stand in the presence of God is to stand in the light of truth. It is in such experiences of worship that we frequently come face to face with the truth which we most seriously need to encounter. Such a truth, if it were not offered in love, could be devastating. As it is we are overwhelmed even while we are enveloped in God's love. But because the truth comes into our life with the love of God, we are made free, even as we are forgiven.

who is almighty, infinite and unchanging...

Sheer power or force have very little religious value. When people raise questions about what God can or cannot do, they simply fail to grasp the nature of God's power. Contrary to what many Christians believe, omnipotence (which means "all powerful") is not concerned with sheer power. The important thing to remember is that God is sovereign, the Creator, who transcends the natural order. Whatever limitations we may think apply to God actually exist only because of those manifestations of God's love and grace which override all else. If God wanted to exercise sheer brute force, God could do absolutely anything; but because God is love, divine power is seen in divine love (which some of us might take to be a sign of weakness).

The only power worth talking about is the power of salvation which is, no matter how you describe it, the power of God's love. That God is "almighty" simply means that God is free and able to deal with creation in terms of the divine purpose for it. There is no difference between what God wills to do and what God can do. God's power is best seen in the crucifixion of the Son, which was foolishness to the Greeks, and remains a profound mystery to most of humanity. In a similar way, we talk about the *infinite* qualities of God without really having any awareness of what infinity means. In mathematics and science as well as religion, we may talk about infinity, but none of us have ever experienced it. It is one of those abstractions about which we theorize.

When we talk about God and infinity and time and eternity all together, we are simply affirming that God is not limited by time as we are. Although God transcends time, God has chosen to participate in it as one who is not limited by it. If our reference is to space rather than to time, we simply mean that God may be everywhere in the universe at once, and is not limited to being in one place at one time as we are. While we may sometimes refer to God as being "here" or "there," or "everywhere," the truth is we acknowledge that God is not at all limited by the same spatial limitations which we have. Thus could the Psalmist David ask, "Whither shall I flee from thy presence?" (Psalm 139:7).

In early latter-day revelation, the prophet Joseph Smith said, "The works, and the designs, and the purposes of God, cannot be frustrated, neither can they come to naught, for God doth not walk in crooked paths;... therefore his paths are straight and his course is one eternal round" (D. and C. 2:1). Throughout all ages of time, the testimony of those who have known God best is always the same: God is utterly dependable, reliable, trustworthy. God is faithful to all promises made, to the covenants made with us. It is God's hope that in such relationships with us, godly consistency shall become our consistency, divine faithfulness will become our faithfulness. Even as Paul wrote to his friend Timothy, "If we are unfaithful, yet he remains faithful, for he will not deny himself" (II Timothy 2:13). As the Book of Mormon reminds us, "He changes not; if so, he would cease to be God..." (Mormon 4:82).

At the same time that God is ultimately faithful and dependable, God is also completely free to bring the divine will to pass, to do that which is "expedient" in order that the work will not fail. It would indeed be arrogant and presumptuous on our part to assume that we know all that God knows, and therefore can predict in advance what God will or will not do under any given circumstance. The Lord's quality of changelessness is best perceived as we are able to understand God's faithfulness and persistence to bring to fruition "the works, and the designs, and the purposes of God [which] cannot be frustrated...."

in whom, and through whom, and by whom all things exist and have their being.

God truly is the source of all that makes life rich and noble—indeed of all that constitutes life. By divine grace and love, all things exist. Through God all things have their being and find their meaning. Our own meaning is found in relationship to God, to the divine purposes in us, to each other, and to the boundless universe God has created.

F. Henry Edwards has written:

We believe that Divinity is the one stable and undeniable and unchangeable fact in the world of change. The power and love of God combined to guarantee that someday he will realize his purpose in us, and that some men shall become fit companions for God and for each other, walking in all holiness before him. The marvel of this conception is not that God is able to bring this to pass by his own fiat, but that he is powerful through sacrifice, bringing it to pass through his patient persistence in well-doing; for us, and in us, and through us.—"The Latter Day Saint Concept of God," *Priesthood Study Outlines*

CHAPTER 2
Jesus Christ

We believe in Jesus Christ, the Only Begotten Son of God, who is from everlasting to everlasting; through whom all things were made; who is God in the flesh, being incarnate by the Holy Spirit for the salvation of all humankind; who was crucified, died, and rose again; who is mediator between God and humanity, and the judge of both the living and the dead; whose dominion has no end.

We believe in Jesus Christ...

The Christian faith is historical. It does not grow out of philosophy or general principles of religion. Instead, it results from the revelation of the living God in specific events in history. It is true that many people search for meaning in life by asking the question, "How is God found?" But the distinctive Hebrew and Christian questions have been, *"How, where,* and *as whom* has God chosen to be revealed?"

The reason for this difference is simple: Jews and Christians have never thought of God as being a fact, a law, a force, or anything else to be discovered. Rather, God is the One who is self-revealing, whose personhood is shown in God's own acts. John Baillie in *The Idea of Revelation in Recent Thought* asserts: "God reveals himself *in action*—in the gracious activity by which He invades the field of human experience in human history which is otherwise but a vain show, empty and drained of meaning" (pages 49-50).

For us to seek to know something of God then is more than a human quest on our part. It is a divine undertaking requiring God's participation as well. That is why the Bible is far from being a simple and systematic listing of religious themes and doctrines. It is instead the accounting of a story, the record of what God has done, written by people who saw through eyes of faith. From this perspective, human history becomes a very great drama, alive with meaning for those with eyes to see, for they see the hand of God moving in and through history with majestic power and all-encompassing love. And somehow, the whole of the story, from beginning to end, is permeated by the one event which occurred in the meridian of time, the life and ministry and death of the Lord Jesus.

This understanding is clearly affirmed in the opening verses of the Hebrew letter: "God, who at sundry times and in divers manners spake in time past unto the fathers by the prophets, hath in these last days spoken unto us by his Son." Greek philosophy could not conceive of a transcendent God willing to be subject to the limitations of a genuine human experience. Yet that same Greek philosophy did not wish to so circumscribe Deity as to eliminate the possibility that God might be more than they could understand. This latter point of view led them to consecrate one altar to "the unknown God" which the Apostle Paul discovered on Mars Hill. It is obvious that if the eternal God is forever isolated from temporal humanity, the infinite separated from the finite, then there is no means for communication between them. They have nothing in common, they do not speak the same language. Lacking some means of piercing the veil of separation, humanity would be forever shut off from the deep things of God.

This does not, however, detract from the fact that the heavens declare the glory of God and the earth demonstrates divine handiwork. We may well be deeply moved by the magnificence and beauty of the natural order of God's creativity in its infinite variety. As Wadsworth stated it,

> I have felt
> A presence that disturbs me with the joy
> Of elevated thoughts, a sense sublime
> Of something far more deeply interfused,
> Whose dwelling is the light of setting suns....

The biblical writers were certainly not lacking in such appreciation for God's handiwork. Yet this was only supportive to the main revelation of God's nature and purpose in particular moments in their history. The word of God was more than what could be seen in God's handiwork in nature. It was more than what could be heard by way of specific command to specific people at specific times. Instead, the word of God was a continuing dialogue of relationship between God and humanity through the events of their common history.

The earliest Christian witnesses were absolutely convinced that God indeed had entered into their experience in such a way that the word was made flesh. What had previously been declared by prophets of earlier generations was now embodied in the life of Jesus Christ. Jesus was not now simply sharing additional prophetic words to be added to the store of prophetic words of previous generations. He was himself the "last" word, the ultimate word that God would have to say to humankind, the word that would endure throughout all generations. We do not hesitate to echo the testimony of John, "And the same word was made flesh, and dwelt among us, and we beheld his glory, the glory as of the Only Begotten of the Father, full of grace and truth" (John 1:14).

the Only Begotten Son of God...

The early disciples walked and talked with Jesus. In their associations with him, they became aware of the fact that he had a unique relationship with the God of Israel. Later reflection only further confirmed this early impression. We cannot be certain how long it took them to become persuaded that Jesus was indeed the divine Son of God, because the scriptural records which we have were written some years after the events occurred. But very soon after the resurrection, Peter was preaching, "God hath made this same Jesus whom ye crucified both Lord and Christ" (Acts 2:36). There seems to be little doubt that this was an early held common conviction among the disciples. By comparing their own relationships to God the Father with the way that Jesus related to his heavenly Father, they did not hesitate to acknowledge that Jesus was God's Son in a way that was radically different from how they themselves related to the Father.

Some theologians have attempted to make of Jesus a "super man" who was no more Son of God than any of the rest of us may be. Although they would agree that he is the supreme example of the image of God in humankind, yet they would affirm that Jesus remains but one son from among the many. However, the testimony of the scriptures does not leave us with this alternative. The Apostle Paul declares that in this one human's life, "dwelleth all the fullness of the Godhead bodily," that Jesus was "the image of the invisible God" (see Collosians 2:9 and 1:15). The testimony from the Book of Mormon is similar: " 'I would that you should understand that God himself shall come down among the children of men and shall redeem his people. And because he dwells in flesh, he shall be called the Son of God....' " (Mosiah 8:28-29). God was in Christ in a way not found in other human life.

The Apostle Paul clarifies the distinction between our "son-hood" and Jesus'. "For as many as are led by the Spirit of God, they are the sons of God...but ye have received the Spirit of adoption..." (Romans 8:14-15). Although we become children of God through adoption, Jesus is identified as being the "Only Begotten." Perhaps the most frequently quoted verse from the New Testament is that which is attributed to John on this subject: "For God so loved the world that he gave his Only Begotten Son, that whosoever believeth on him should not perish; but have everlasting life" (John 3:16). The distinctions between Jesus' relationship to God and ours are quite clear: we are creatures of God, Jesus is born of God. We are adopted into the family of God, Jesus is rightful heir of all that God is and has. As the Book of Mormon clearly states, it is God himself who has come down to share with us in our human estate. As such, we cannot separate the Son from all of the attributes which are the Father's.

who is from everlasting to everlasting....

The longer the disciples lived with Jesus and the more they became aware of his divinity, the more they came to realize the eternal nature of his life—which really existed prior to his birth into human life. Just think for a moment what they must have experienced! Here was the Master with whom they had lived and walked and eaten and slept for many months. He had suddenly been taken from them through death on a cross. Just as suddenly, he was once again with them, in their midst, speaking with them, eating with them—but with a difference, for they recognized that he was the resurrected Lord, possessing qualities relating to an eternal realm. For them, it was not possible to believe that the events ending in eternity could have had a beginning in time. Consequently they believed in Jesus' preexistence with the Father in the beginning. The Gospel of John affirms this in its opening verses. As John Knox stated,

It is the answer stated most fully and unqualifiedly in the Fourth Gospel. This answer begins with the affirmation of the preexistence of Jesus: When Jesus ascended to the Father after his resurrection, he merely resumed the place which he had never really relinquished. For he was the eternal Wisdom or Logos of God.—*Jesus, Lord and Christ*, page 143

Paul referred to Jesus' preexistence when he said, "When the fullness of time was come, God sent forth his Son, made of a woman, made under the law" (Galatians 4:4). Paul also held the conviction that when Jesus entered human flesh, he voluntarily accepted its limitations, emptying himself and taking upon himself the nature of a servant.

It is difficult for us to think of eternity without thinking in terms of time. We may even suppose that eternity is simply the adding together of more and more time without end. To be more accurate, the two exist in different spheres altogether. To say that the Son is co-existent with the Father in the beginning, and that it was in and through Jesus that all things were made at the time of the creation, identifies him with the same eternal qualities as the Father. He is thus "from all eternity to all eternity, the Alpha and the Omega."

But it is not possible to separate God from God. God remains God still. For God to have left the realm of eternity and to have taken the form of human flesh does not mean that God was somehow absent from eternity during any time at all. If eternity were simply sections or sequences of time, then we could say that for a certain period of time, God the Son was absent from the eternal realm. But it is this projection of the divine into the human realm that defines the very sonhood of God. As Joseph Smith stated it in Section 90:1b-c of the Doctrine and Covenants: "I am in the Father and the Father in me, and the Father and I are one; the Father because he gave me of his fullness; the Son *because I was in the world and made flesh my tabernacle,* and dwelt among the sons of men. I was in the world and received of my Father...." Donald Baillie echoed this sentiment in *God Was in Christ:* "It is impossible to do justice to the truth of the Incarnation without speaking of it as the coming into history of the eternally pre-existent Son of God" (page 150).

The very attributes which we note in the life of Jesus are indeed the attributes of God. If Jesus is self-sacrificing, then we know God to be self-sacrificing. For the timeless ministry of the Christ, this means that not only was God willing to give his Son in the meridian of time, but that gift is the same as if it were given in every time and in every place for every person. It is the eternal Son of the Living God who is offered for our salvation, offered in the meridian of time for the benefit of all time and all eternity. The ultimate gift is an eternal gift, and not simply the chronologically last gift in a series of gifts.

This is the meaning of Hebrews 9:26: "...but now once in the meridian of time hath he appeared to put away sin by the sacrifice of himself." A similar reference is found in Doctrine and Covenants 39:1b, announcing Jesus as "the same which came in the meridian of time." It is further declared that his redeeming ministry extends to those who were born both before and after "he came in the meridian of time in the flesh" (17:5e).

We should avoid being overly concerned with the

meaning of the term "meridian." This language is figuratively used to indicate that the Lord Jesus came in the very midst of human history. With our imprecise methods of measurement, it would be fruitless to attempt to count the years from Christ's birth back into ancient history and human prehistory, in order to determine how many years would be required for the Second Coming of Christ, or as a means of predicting the end of times. So fruitless would such an effort be that Jesus plainly said not even the angels of heaven would know the time of his second coming. What *is* important is the fact that Jesus came in the meridian of human time. He was not in any way to be identified with the periphery of human experience. He was in the very midst from any way you might choose to look at it. He is the central event of the history of humankind. He came not alone to color that which would occur thereafter, but to have an equal impact upon all which had preceded. He came as a reinterpretation of human history. He came as a re-evaluation of all that had previously been thought lost. His life and ministry becomes an appreciation of all human life and ministry. In the very deepest sense and meaning, Jesus is from everlasting to everlasting, and this eternal One came into the midst of our time.

through whom all things were made...

In Doctrine and Covenants 22:21b, c, the prophet Joseph Smith sensed something about the creative role of the Son of God. "And by the Word of my power have I created them, which is mine Only Begotten... and worlds without number have I created, and I also created them for mine own purposes; and by the Son I created them."

According to a strict reading of the scriptures, it is the Son of God who is the agent of creation. By the time the fourth Gospel was written, this understanding was apparently well extant within the church, so that it was generally believed, and memorized by the early Christians, that "All things were made by him; and without him was not anything made which was made" (John 1:3). The New English Bible translation of this passage has it read: "All that came to be was alive with his life, and that life was the light of men." For the early New Testament saints, all of God's creation, including humankind, were created by God through the agent of His creation, the Lord Jesus Christ.

In the process of establishing Jesus Christ as creator, Paul also establishes Christ's sovereignty over all.

[God's dear Son] is the image of the invisible God, the firstborn of every creature. For by him were all things created, that are in heaven, and that are in earth, visible and invisible, whether they be thrones, or dominions, or principalities, or powers; all things were created by him, and for him; and he is before all things, and by him all things consist.—Colossians 1:15-17

who is God in the flesh being incarnate by the Holy Spirit for the salvation of all humankind...

To seriously study the Incarnation is to admit that we are inquiring into a phenomenon, a mystery, which defies our adequate description. Even the Apostle Paul had to admit this when he wrote to Timothy, "...without controversy, great is the mystery of Godliness...." But in the same sentence, he proceeded to affirm that "The pillar and ground of the truth is,...God was manifest in the flesh" (I Timothy 3:16). As difficult as it may be to understand, and as shrouded as it may be in mystery, nevertheless, the firm testimony of the scriptures is that God entered into our human life. The word incarnation literally means "in-flesh-ment." Growing out of personal experiences that affirmed Jesus to be God in the flesh, Christians down through the ages have attempted to bear their testimony about that, offering various explanations as to how it might be possible. The theological term "Christology" is used to identify this search for meaning. But all of our attempts to describe what God has done in Jesus Christ fall short of the true reality. It would be idolatrous on our part to attempt to take any one definition and lift it to status as a dogmatic statement which everyone should believe. At best, all we can do is to confess what we understand of how God is in Christ, reconciling us to himself.

We need not apologize for our inability to be more precise. As any research scientist will tell you, those who stand on the frontiers of human experience and understanding, and reach out into the unknown seeking further insight, find both greater confidence and greater security in confessing both that which they do and do not yet know.

The doctrine of Incarnation affirms that no less than God came down into the grass roots of creation, to rise up again bringing humankind with him. Without being told, we know that humankind's critical needs cannot be met by mere ideas—we need some real facts in our own areas of reality, some experiences within our own history. The Christian gospel finds us where we are, in the midst of life being lived, both at its best and at its worst. We come face to face with the Lord Jesus Christ at every turn in life, because he has not only been there before us, he is also there with us.

The word incarnation itself says something to us about the nature of God and divine activity. We do not try to explain God's action or motives, but simply try to understand what God is doing in relation to our own being and our own future. The first disciples had to squarely face up to two facts: In the first place, they knew Jesus as a man in the fullest sense, sharing truly and completely in the conditions of their humanity. "In all things it behooved him to be made like unto his brethren" (Hebrews 2:17). But secondly, there was another fact which was equally compelling and undeniable by them: they knew that somehow in this human life, they had actually met the living God. This was confusing, and frequently they did not know how to deal with it. It sometimes prompted them to ask for personal favors; it sometimes prompted them to expect Jesus to do the supernatural and the miraculous. It sometimes caused them to lean on him and expect him to see that everything worked out all right, without any effort on their part. Although these unmet expectations brought consternation and confusion, nevertheless, they could not help but affirm their testimony that God was indeed present in Jesus. In time, they came to see this assurance as central to every other affirmation they might have.

In the Book of Mormon, when the question is raised, "Is the Son of God the very eternal Father?" Amulek says, "He is the very eternal Father of heaven and of earth, and of all things which in them are. He is the beginning and the end, the first and the last. And he shall come into the world to redeem his people" (Alma 8:93-96).

It is difficult for us to imagine the rage and the shock which the Jews must have had when they heard Jesus say: "Before Abraham was, I am" (John 8:58). Jesus was not alone identifying the quality of his life as being eternal, but he was also identifying himself as deity, for the pronounced words "I Am" was the name by which Jehovah was known among the Jews. While this must have been blasphemous to his enemies, it certainly must also have produced some concern on the part of his disciples who likely would not yet have perfectly understood what he meant.

Human reason has always proved unable to explain exactly what happened when Jesus came on earth. What usually occurs is something like this: We have experiences in life, some of which may be described as "spiritual," which lead us to understand some things about God and his will for us. We understand these things by faith. They are very meaningful to us, but frequently cannot be described by us for benefit of others. As soon as we attempt to tell someone else about our experience, we find it necessary to use words and terms that we hope will communicate with them. This is extremely difficult to do unless they have had similar experiences. How can you describe snow to a South Sea islander? Where do you find words to describe the color red to a person born blind? Of course, we want our explanations to make as much sense as possible. Consequently we try to be as reasonable as possible in our explanations. This is what testimony and theology are all about—to explain the meaning of our experiences with God.

In the first few centuries of the Christian Church, church leaders were anxious to preserve the account of the actual events of the life and ministry of Jesus and of early church history. As time went on and the church had a growing experience with God and with the Holy Spirit, it was able to offer better explanations for what had occurred in the earliest events. Their growing experience gave them better perspectives and better understanding with which to interpret earlier events. Thus the New Testament writings not only offer us historical detail, but also interpretation as to what it all meant. The early creeds developed by the church in the early centuries should be seen as their attempt to further clarify the nature of the Father and the Son so that people would not be misled about their true relationship.

One of the early questions the church had to deal with was whether or not Jesus was fully man. The Apostles' Creed affirms, "born of the Virgin Mary," in order to establish once and for all that Jesus was actually born of a woman. The early church was anxious to preserve the testimony of the first disciples, that Jesus was fully human. The scriptural accounts of the birth of Jesus represent one of the ways the church testified that Jesus came *into* history, and not out of it.

A series of councils occurred, among them being one held in A.D. 451 which produced the Creed of Chalcedon. It declared that Jesus Christ was

at once complete in Godhead and complete in manhood, truly God and truly man... of one essence with the Father as regards his Godhead, and at the same time of one essence with us as regards his manhood, in all respects like us, apart from sin.

Some of the positions taken in the creeds are difficult for us to interpret meaningfully today, partly due to the difficulty of the Greek and Latin terms used in the descriptions. We must nevertheless recognize the integrity behind the endeavor of those early church disciples to find a logical way of explaining the experience which the Christian Church had had through the years to that point. What is most surprising to us today is that, taken as a whole, all scriptures contained in the Bible, the Book of Mormon, and the Doctrine and Covenants, lend support to these positions taken by the early church fathers in the fifth century.

There have been attempts from time to time to find other ways of explaining the Incarnation. Some would have Jesus be a super human. Others would make of him a demigod. Others with humanistic views would have him be fully human while denying his divinity. During the nineteenth century there was a strong emphasis to see Jesus as an outstanding teacher or moral example. The Docetic theory would deny his true humanity, and suggest that he was God playing the role of a suffering human being. The theory of Adoptionism would consider Jesus as simply another man who gradually grew into divinity and eventually was qualified to be made a Son of God.

It must be said however that any theory which tends to minimize either the manhood or the divinity of Jesus falls short of preserving the unique character of the "good news" which came with him, and which he was. Such attempts fly in the face of the scriptures to be found in all three standard books. We must always remember that the Incarnation is focused both in Jesus' likeness to us and his radical difference from us, at one and the same time. He is not less than the same God who confronts us in our own real experience. He confronts us in ways which redeem us from ourselves.

Arthur Oakman bore his testimony in this way:

> So our heavenly Father came and dwelt in the tabernacle of clay. The identity was total and not partial. It was complete. The word did not appear in flesh; it wasn't a theophany. It wasn't a drama which was worked simply for our benefit. The nature of the incarnation of our Lord was of such character that it required his complete and total identification with us. He became man.... In the soul of this one perfect man the whole of creation was penetrated and lifted by the love and the power of God and raised to divine heights.—*He Who Is*, page 68-70

being incarnate by the Holy Spirit for the salvation of all humankind...

The way God entered into creation is astounding enough, but it is equally astounding when we know why our Lord did it. Paul's testimony was quite clear: "God is in Christ, *reconciling* the world unto himself" (II Corinthians 5:19). To Timothy he said, "Christ Jesus came into the world to save sinners" (I Timothy 1:15). The word "atonement" is used to describe the means by which the life, death, and resurrection of Jesus make this reconciliation possible. The word itself offers its own definition: at-one-ment. This is the way in which Jesus becomes "at one" with us in order that we may become "at one" with God. He is the mediating, unifying means of our being reconciled to God.

It is in the context of our life lived on this earth that the reconciliation occurs. It is not some other life that Jesus lives but our own. In this startling and decisive way, we see how far God is willing to go to reclaim rebellious people, such as are we, from the horrible alienation that divides us from God.

Probably the majority of humankind are not even aware that they have rebelled against God. It is said that Henry Thoreau was asked upon his deathbed, "Henry, have you made your peace with God?" He replied, "I wasn't aware that we have ever quarreled." Most of us can probably say like him that we really have no quarrel with God. We cannot be so insensitive as to be unaware that we have everyone walked in our own way, and after the image of our own god, "whose image is in the likeness of the world, and whose substance is that of an idol, which waxeth old and shall perish in Babylon, even Babylon the Great, which shall fall" (D. and C. 1:3e).

But, someone may ask, "If God is ready to forgive us, why isn't this enough? Why all the suffering and sacrifice that seem to be required in Jesus' atonement?" The answer to this question lies in the difference between good-natured indulgence and costly reconciliation. God does not take sin lightly. It is a very weak analogy to liken God's suffering for our sinfulness to the way that one of us may suffer when a good friend offends us deeply. Because our love and forgiveness for the friend are both real, it will be impossible for the friend to suffer as much as we have suffered, even if the friend repents the hurt caused us. The one who forgives still carries the heavier burden. The self-giving compassion and passion of God are a part of God's very nature. In Doctrine and Covenants 36:6–7, we have a dramatic, almost allegorical, illustration of God's character: "And Enoch said unto the Lord, How is it that you can weep, seeing you are holy, and from all eternity to all eternity?...The Lord said unto Enoch, Behold these your brethren; they are the workmanship of my own hands...but, behold, they are without affection."

Parents almost naturally learn how to bear the burdens of the sins of their children, experiencing the tribulation and pain as if in their own beings. They also vicariously share in their joys and achievements. They can no more escape these burdens and effects than they could deny their parenthood, for the bonds of love lay upon them this gift and obligation. It is in similar though deeper bonds of love that Jesus in "his own self bare our sins in his own body on the tree" (I Peter 2:24).

Some religionists have attempted to explain the atonement in a "bookkeeping" kind of manner, using such terms as debts and indebtedness, redemption and payment. Some would make it appear that God was "satisfied" by Jesus' "substitution" for us, or by Jesus having utilized his "moral influence" to persuade God to accept us once again. Any of these attempts to explain the Atonement fall short. Some of them imply that somehow God and Christ are separate and opposed factors in the equation, with Jesus functioning as our lawyer and advocate, pleading our cause. If we but think for a moment, we know that we cannot separate God from God. The Father and the Son are one, and are not in any way to be seen as opposing elements in our salvation. Nor was Jesus offered as a sacrifice to placate an angry God, or to substitute for us in our rightful punishment. All of these are attempts on our part to explain how God could have done such a great thing: to give of God's own self in the form of the Son in order that we might be saved.

It is God and God alone who offers sacrifice, and the sacrifice which God offers is the sacrifice of self. God's mercy and love are not purchased by anything Jesus or anyone else may have done. It is God who is merciful, it is God who is love. Our only appropriate response, then, is to recognize what God has done for us, and to respond in love to such a generous love already shown toward us.

The Apostle Paul stated it most clearly:

Christ died for the ungodly. For scarcely for a righteous man will one die; yet peradventure for a good man some would even dare to die. But God commendeth his love toward us, in that, while we were yet sinners, Christ died for us....For if, when we were enemies, we were reconciled to God by the death of his Son; much more, being reconciled, we shall be saved by his life.—Romans 5:6-10

It is likely true that the Atonement will always be difficult for humans to understand. To start with, it is not something that is common to our experience. We do not know how, nor do we know of any others who are willing, to bear the burdens of sin for others that Jesus has borne. We are not good enough to be such bearers of others' burdens of sin. And when, through religious experience, we become aware of the fact that Jesus *has* so borne our own sin, we are overwhelmed with that reality. We hardly know how to understand it. Our mind cannot cope with this. We have no rational explanation for it. The only thing we can do is to receive God's forgiveness in this way. And that is precisely God's intention. He gave his only begotten Son that we might learn how very much he loves us, and be willing to accept that love and forgiveness.

For some modern-day Christians, it is rather confusing to note the symbolic language in both the Old and New Testaments which refers to the offering of animals upon the altar of sacrifice. References to "the lamb" and "spilt blood" are sometimes puzzling and even repulsive to some. We need to keep in mind that Old Testament customs were not pagan rights offered to appease a God of wrath. The implications of such early sacrifices were that those who offered gifts to God should themselves be without spot or blemish. To choose from among their flocks the first fruits, and those which were without spot or blemish, was acknowledgment of their intention to present the best that they themselves could be as human living sacrifices upon the altar of service to God. That God was willing to accept such sacrifice offerings in lieu of themselves was an indication that God was indeed willing to forgive their sins. God accepted them as they came in offering themselves. Both they and God expected that God would continue to be the Lord of their life and of their flocks and possessions. And it would be to God that the first and best of all their fruits should be offered.

When Jesus himself replaces the sacrificial lamb, he demonstrates in the clearest possible way what it means to be without spot or blemish in one's life. Jesus shows what it means to offer the first and best that one has to God. He demonstrates what it is to be wholly pleasing and acceptable to God. He reveals what the love of God will work in our lives if we permit God's salvation to reside there.

As F. Henry Edwards has pointed out in his book, *The Divine Purpose in Us* (pp. 164-165), the Crucifixion was not a tragic miscalculation. Jesus was not a helpless victim at his crucifixion; he presided over it. As Augustine said, Jesus is both victor and victim; he is victor precisely because he was victim.

It is our testimony that it is indeed God who has come to redeem us through Jesus Christ our Lord. Truly God bridges all barriers of alienation and opens the avenues for peace between us through our having been received into God's new creation.

who was crucified, died, and rose again...

The Apostles' Creed seems almost to be too brief and too blunt: "Jesus Christ...suffered under Pontius Pilate, was crucified, dead and buried." However this brevity only accentuates the facts of what happened. Christians simply do not accept the notion that Jesus somehow escaped the death which is recorded in the New Testament.

In fact, if we remove this theme of the crucified and risen Lord, the New Testament has very little substance. The disciples were positive about two important events: they knew that Jesus had been put to death, and they also knew that he had risen from the dead. All else in their experience took its meaning from these two events. The Cross became their earliest and most pronounced symbol for it seemed necessary to an understanding of all their beliefs. They saw it as a fulfillment of scripture. Paul said, "For I delivered unto you first of all that which I also received, how that Christ died for our sins according to the scriptures" (I Corinthians 15:3). Peter's testimony on the day of Pentecost was that Jesus' death was in keeping with the will of God, for Jesus was "delivered by the determinate counsel and foreknowledge of God..." (Acts 2:23). Although the disciples were surprised at its actual happening, in hindsight they saw the necessity for the Crucifixion and Resurrection. They saw it as being inseparably connected with God's plan of salvation for humankind.

J. B. Phillips, a modern translator of the New Testament, adds his testimony:

> No one could honestly read the letters of the New Testament without becoming aware that not only the writers themselves but scores of other people were looking at life and death in a way in which they had never been looked at before, and were experiencing a contact with the living God unprecedented in human history. No one could fairly deny that in the first century A.D. something unique and remarkable had happened and that the letters spontaneously record its repercussions of human personality.—*God Our Contemporary,* page 86

Perhaps the greatest proof of the Resurrection is to be seen in the lives of those who have actually believed in it. There is no power on earth which offers greater assurance, greater hope, greater motivation to achievement, greater comfort in the face of adversity than the knowledge of Christ's resurrection and its implications for us. The Cross takes on meaning only in the light of the One who hangs upon it. No talk of Resurrection has meaning which does not focus upon the Person who was resurrected. This is no general principle about human survival after death that one can speculate about, argue about, reason about, or otherwise handle rationally. Unlike some other fables or myths, the resurrection story has meaning to those who understand it because they know Jesus and his power of life. No other stories of resurrection in other cultures have had much impact. Even the parable of the prodigal son has great power only for those who know the Lord Jesus and the truth he embodied. For those who have faith in the resurrected Lord, resurrection is the very power of God unto salvation.

Jesus' rising from the dead brought the assurance that no work of sin or bond of death could restrain the power of life which his disciples had found in him. In fact, the

Gospels do not explain the Resurrection—it is the Resurrection which explains the Gospels. Each was written from the perspective of one who already knew about and believed in the Resurrection. Therefore, the very recounting of the life of Jesus breathes resurrection from every syllable.

It is really useless to try to argue whether or not Jesus' resurrection was a "spiritual" or "physical" event. Either term, or both terms together, may well be inadequate to describe how he arose from the dead. The only words which the gospel writers had available to them to attempt to describe what happened are words which are used only in this earthly, physical realm, and are inadequate to describe spiritual things. We do use our language to try to describe the events, but we must always reserve in our minds the knowledge that these words are truly inadequate. Consequently we cannot define with any real accuracy what resurrection in Christ Jesus means.

But there are two ways by which we may understand the Resurrection. We may see Jesus' rising from the dead as an illustration or example of human immortality. In surviving death, Jesus demonstrated that all good persons shall also survive death. Secondly, by means of the Resurrection, we realize that Jesus has been able to do something for us that we could never do for ourselves, something that is beyond the laws of human nature. Jesus becomes for us the first of a new order of creation. It is as Paul stated to the Romans,

And if the Spirit of him that raised up Jesus from the dead, dwell in you, he that raised up Christ from the dead shall also quicken your mortal bodies by his Spirit that dwelleth in you.... For as many as are led by the Spirit of God, they are the sons of God.... The Spirit itself beareth witness with our spirit, that we are the children of God; and if children, then heirs; heirs of God, and joint heirs with Christ;... for the earnest expectation of the creature waiteth for the manifestation of the sons of God.—Romans 8:11-19

For the early disciples, the victory was already won, and they were participating in the life of that victory even then. The Resurrection placed the divine stamp of approval on Jesus' Sonship and sovereignty.

J. B. Phillips tells of a schoolboy who asked: "If the events of the crucifixion are so terrible, why do we call it Good Friday?" Arthur Oakman suggests an answer when he reminds us that "the struggle of humanity against sin was won in principle and in fact at Calvary." And he adds that Easter was the means of revealing that victory decisively (*He Who Is,* page 105).

who is mediator between God and humanity...

The common testimony of the early creeds and all three standard books of scripture is that Jesus ascended into heaven following his resurrection. The ascension graphically emphasizes the importance of the historical event of the Resurrection. It not only implies the reality of the Resurrection from the dead, but also God's sovereignty over all creation.

In the letter to the Hebrews, the "new covenant" of which Jeremiah spoke (31:31-34) is seen as being fulfilled through Jesus as the mediator of the new covenant. According to John 14:6, it was Jesus himself who told the disciples, "No man cometh unto the Father, but by me." Paul's personal experience was that this was true for all those who followed after Christ as well as those who were his contemporaries. Paul's testimony was, "I live; yet not I, but Christ liveth in me; and the life which I now live in the flesh I live by the faith of the Son of God, who loved me, and gave himself for me" (Galatians 2:20). For Paul and those of succeeding ages, the ministry of reconciliation was not a phenomenon of past history, but would continue to break down the walls of separation and bring people into confrontation with the living God.

As our mediator with the Father, we know Jesus as our abiding resource for moral victory and servanthood. He opens God to us in new ways, and provides the basis for how we may respond to that revelation. Because we may see the Lord Jesus as a man from among men, we are finally permitted to see him as "very God of very God," and therefore can realize God's intention and purpose in us. He not only reveals God to us, he reveals to us God's will for us.

and the judge of both the living and the dead....

It is in the nature of the worship experience that when we stand in the presence of the Lord Jesus, we see ourselves as we really are, fully judged, weighed in the balance, and found wanting. It is always true that when Jesus comes into our world, he represents the judgment of God. He is the yardstick by which we all measure ourselves, and see how far short we come.

John Whale, in *Christian Doctrine*, says,

Those who argue (with the best of intentions, of course) that Jesus Christ is "like us" are silenced as soon as they are asked, "like which of us?" The truth is that his likeness to us—"the likeness of sinful flesh" only accentuates his qualitative and fundamental unlikeness to us, in that his relationship to God is unlike anything that our race has seen.—page 66

In Christ's reflection, we become aware of our own tragic incompleteness, and sense the judgment of God upon sin. To the degree that we ourselves are sinful, we experience that as personal judgment. Consider how the sinful woman in the house of Simon the Pharisee discovered the reality of judgment (See Luke 7:36-50). When she learned that Jesus was going to be in Simon's house, she came prepared to anoint his feet with oil. In his presence and convicted of sin, the scripture says that she "stood at his feet weeping, and began to wash his feet with tears, and did wipe them with the hairs of her head, and kissed his feet, and anointed them with ointment." Simon, Pharisee that he was, could not understand how such a great spiritual teacher could have anything at all to do with such a sinful woman. We note the gracious restraint and delicacy of the Lord's manner. He glosses over nothing regarding her, yet he expresses no recriminations either. He simply said, "Her sins which are many, are forgiven." The judgment of the Pharisee and the judgment of Jesus are sharply contrasted here. Jesus' judgment reaches us at the same moment as the power of his forgiveness and redemption. We carry no illusion about the gravity of our sin, for standing in the presence of Christ this is unmistakable. But at the same time, we are overwhelmed with his gracious love which seeks us out to save.

We see Jesus as judge in this very personal way, of course. But we also recognize that he is judge of the dead as well as the living. The whole stream of history comes under his judgment, from beginning to end. He is interpreter and judge and redeemer of history, so that all social endeavor, all personal achievement, all human aspiration will fall under the illuminating light of the Cross and be seen for what it is.

whose dominion has no end.

For centuries, artists have depicted the Lord Jesus seated at the right hand of God. These are simply artists' renditions of the verbal descriptions given in New Testament literature. Their intention is not to depict an unmoving, inactive Deity who simply sits in sovereign judgment. Instead, they hope to convey to us the message that Christ, having overcome evil and death, is alive forevermore. With this picture should go the subtitle: "All power is given unto me in heaven and in earth. Go ye therefore,...and lo, I am with you always, unto the end of the world" (Matthew 28:17-19). While Christ is King and sharing the divine throne, he nevertheless exercises his dominion to further his kingdom in the lives of his people. Jesus already reigns in glory, although this truth is largely unrecognized by much of the world. The full realization of his kingship will occur when all things shall be gathered up into him.

In light of this, Paul wrote,

For I reckon that the sufferings of this present time are not worthy to be named with the glory which shall be revealed in us. For the earnest expectation of the creature waiteth for the manifestation of the sons of God.—Romans 8:18-19

To the Ephesians he added,

Having made known unto us the mystery of his will, according to his good pleasure which he hath purposed in himself; that in the dispensation of the fullness of times he might gather together in one all things in Christ, both which are in heaven, and which are on earth; even in him.—Ephesians 1:9-10

Christ rules. His dominion extends over all creation. For those who have "put on Christ," who have been "raised together with him," they share in his reign, and even now are made fit subjects of his kingdom.

It was of this living Christ that Joseph Smith and Sidney Rigdon bore testimony:

And, now after the many testimonies which have been given of him, this is the testimony, last of all, which we give of him, that he lives; for we saw him, even on the right hand of God; and we heard the voice bearing record that he is the Only Begotten of the Father; that by him, and through him, and of him, the worlds are and were created; and the inhabitants thereof are begotten sons and daughters unto God.—D. and C. 76:3g, h

CHAPTER 3
THE HOLY SPIRIT

We believe in the Holy Spirit, the living presence of the Father and the Son, who, in power, intelligence, and love, works in the minds and hearts of persons to free them from sin, uniting them with God as God's children, and with each other as brothers and sisters. The Spirit bears record of the Father and of the Son, which Father, Son and Holy Ghost are one God.

We believe in the Holy Spirit...

From the dawn of human history, people have felt external forces and powers acting upon themselves for either good or evil. Usually these forces or powers are called spirits or Spirit. Members of the Reorganized Church of Jesus Christ of Latter Day Saints testify with the broad stream of Christianity that the Holy Spirit is the divine life active in the world. The work of the Holy Spirit is to comfort, guide, teach, glorify, witness, sustain, reprove, renew, and reclaim humankind. Although we sometimes refer to the Holy Spirit as an influence, and therefore as "it," it is more appropriate for us to refer to the Spirit as "He." The scriptures set this example for us. John records Jesus' words "But when the Comforter is come, whom I will send unto you from the Father, even the Spirit of truth, which proceedeth from the Father, *he* shall testify of me" (John 15:26). It was not easy for the early church to arrive at the decision that the Holy Spirit does represent the personality of God. In this instance, as in all cases where our experience is limited to this one expression of the personhood of God, and where there are no parallels in human history, we have had to move forward in faith, going beyond our ability to reason. This does not imply that God is unintelligible, or unintelligent. It simply says that God is divine and we are not. All our knowledge of God and all our attempts at describing how God lives and works will always be inadequate. Nevertheless, so complete has been the work and power of the Holy Spirit within the church that we have no difficulty affirming the reality of God's Spirit at work within our world.

In the early Christian Church, the testimony was that the God of the Hebrews, known to be present in all creation, was now newly experienced as life-giving energy. After Christ's ascension, and especially at Pentecost, the disciples recognized that God had entered into them in the person of the Holy Ghost. God, in their experience, had become a generating, sustaining, redeeming, and sanctifying force within the church.

During the following centuries, church leaders and followers have had difficulty putting into words what the precise nature of their experience with that Spirit was. Jesus himself had promised the Holy Ghost would come after he left. Jesus assured them that through his presence and power, they would be led into a new and deeper and abiding communion with Jesus himself.

It was not easy for Christians to understand the Holy Spirit in this way. Human experience with the Holy Spirit is always charged with emotion. Therefore, it has been difficult for us down through the ages to deal intelligently with how the Holy Spirit functions in our midst. Among the many virtues we attribute to God are intelligence and rationality. But because God is divine and greatly more than we can comprehend, all of our attempts to describe how God lives and works will always be inadequate.

In spite of the church's difficulty in comprehending how God as Holy Spirit functions in our midst, belief in the work and power of the Holy Spirit has always been understood by the church. Such a belief came more out of experience than through thought. The earliest disciples could say from their previous experience as Jews that the God of the Hebrews, known to be present in all of creation, was now experienced by them in a new way as life-giving energy. Because they had seen Jesus as the "in-fleshment" of God, and due to their experience on the day of Pentecost, the disciples realized that God was somehow able to enter into humans in the person of the Holy Spirit. They experienced him as the generating, sustaining, redeeming and sanctifying force of the church.

In the centuries that have followed, we have had great difficulty putting into words what the precise nature of our experience with the Spirit has been. Jesus had pointed beyond his own life and work on earth to the coming of another, the Comforter or Holy Ghost.

Through his ministry they would be led into a new and deeper and abiding communion with Jesus. In fact, he said, referring to the Holy Spirit, "I will not leave you comfortless; I will come to you" (John 14:18).

The doubt of the early disciples was totally extinguished by their witness of the risen Lord. In the one great event, the Resurrection, God flooded their reason and inundated all of the church with the loving and gracious revelation of God's own self in Christ Jesus. From the day of Pentecost to the present day, it has always been the testimony of the church that Jesus has been with us in the person of his Promise, the Holy Comforter, who has lived and worked in our lives.

Yet it has always been easier for us to know his presence than to describe it. After 300 years of living and working under the influence of the Holy Spirit, the early disciples tried to write a definition of their faith at Nicaea in A.D. 325. They could say only, "We believe...in the Holy Spirit." It had been much easier for them to speak of their belief in God, and even with eloquence to describe their faith in Christ and his church. But words were inadequate to describe God's loving action in their daily lives. This has always been true, and is true for us today. After twenty centuries of experience, we still try to define the Holy Spirit. However, there are not many subjects which occupy less space on library shelves or receive less treatment by the church's teachers. We can speak in great detail about the mechanics of our faith and of the necessity to believe. We can bear articulate witness of the endless ways in which the Spirit has sought to bring God's purpose for our lives. But of the precise nature and inner character and functioning of that gracious ministry, we can only say with our earlier brethren, "We believe in the Holy Spirit."

the living Presence of the Father and the Son...

When Jesus entered the world of the early disciples, he

spoke to them about his Father's kingdom. Through their experience of his life and ministry, his crucifixion and resurrection, the early Christians formed their belief in the message of Jesus. In those early days when the experience of the church was so newly fresh with Jesus himself and with the Holy Spirit, they were not overly concerned about the language they used to describe God. Their experiences with Jesus and with the Holy Spirit were so recent, so unquestionable. But with the passing of time and the passing of those who were eyewitnesses to Jesus' ministry, the church was confronted with the task of trying to understand the relationship between the Father and the Son and the Holy Ghost.

The early witnesses did leave their testimony: "There are three that bear record in heaven...and these three are one" (I John 5:7). Jesus had also spoken of his personal unity in God when (as recorded in John 17) he prayed for the disciples' unity. But these and other testimonies still left room for many questions. Was Jesus God, or the Son of God? Were they one, or two? Was the Holy Ghost yet another deity?

Working with the information contained in the New Testament, the early church leaders came to understand what they described as a "tri-unity" in the Godhead. This was not the notion that there were three gods. Such a view would have been an offense to the prophetic legacy left them by the Hebrew prophets who had cried: "Hear, O Israel; The Lord our God is one Lord" (Deuteronomy 6:4). What they meant was that when speaking about God or Christ or the Holy Ghost, they were simply talking about different aspects of the same God.

When we speak about God, of course, all analogies break down. For God is not really like anything else that we can ever experience. But to think of the three functions or aspects or persons in the Godhead as being one God is something like recognizing that the substance which is chemically described as H_2O may be experienced as a solid (ice), a liquid (water), or a gas (steam or water vapor). These are not three different substances, but rather three aspects of the same substance.

In a somewhat similar way we use the analogy of Father and Son to describe the relationships between those two persons of the Godhead. But there are many ways in which Jesus and his heavenly Father are not at all like the relationships we have with our earthly fathers. To begin with, for us, the father/son relationship implies that one existed before the other. In the scriptures, however, we understand that "in the beginning...the Son was with God, and the Son was of God. The same was in the beginning with God" (John 1:1-2). Additionally, we become an earthly child of an earthly parent by means of procreation through the union of our father and our mother. In the instance of Jesus, however, the Son was the Son in the beginning, and did not need to wait until he would be born of the Virgin Mary on earth. So when we talk about the Father/Son relationships in the Godhead, we are not talking about priority or about procreation. We are not talking about the inheritance of genes and traits that subsequently follow. Instead, we are speaking about something that is infinitely more significant.

Jesus Christ is the projection into our world of the divine God in heaven. Jesus is the incarnation of God, who, while fully divine, willingly accepted humanity and became fully human. This he did in love for us, that we might see God revealed in the only way we could understand. To see God revealed in the living out of human life was to fully describe God in terms that we could experience and comprehend. In that sense, God was speaking our language. This God did in order that we might believe and trust and be reconciled to God.

This is what Paul means when he says "God...hath reconciled us to himself by Jesus Christ, and hath given to us the ministry of reconciliation: to wit, that God is in Christ, reconciling the world unto himself" (II Corinthians 5:18-19). The Holy Spirit is sent by Jesus from the

Father (John 15:26). Paul refers to the Holy Spirit as being the Spirit of God's Son (Galatians 4:6). He also refers to the Holy Spirit as being the Spirit of God (Romans 8:14). There are many such references throughout our scriptures. All this suggests to us the unity within the Godhead. The function of the Holy Spirit in our lives is to serve as a living presence of God, enlightening our minds and filling our souls with joy (D. and C. 10:7a). He guides us into all truth (John 16:13), and unfolds to our minds the mysteries of God (I Nephi 3:30).

All of these functions of God in our lives does not mean that God is trying to control our destinies or take from us freedom of will. But it does mean that God knows what is for our best good. Through the Holy Spirit God continually strives to bring that good to pass. As it is stated in Moroni 7:11: "Behold, that which is of God invites and entices to do good continually; wherefore, everything which invites and entices to do good and to love God, and to serve him is inspired of God."

The function of the Holy Spirit is to make real in our lives the person and witness of Jesus. The same things Jesus would do if he were here, the Holy Spirit does. If Jesus were here, he would testify of the authenticity of life in the kingdom of God. He would love and minister to the bruised and brokenhearted and distressed people. He would proclaim the need for righteousness to be expressed in the structures of society. Jesus would stand in opposition to inequity and injustice. He would champion the cause of the weak and the poor, and would heal their suffering. All of these things the ministry of the Holy Spirit does in our day. By the Holy Spirit, God is still at work in the world.

who, in power, intelligence, and love, works in the minds and hearts of persons...

No one has been able to unravel the mystery of human existence. Scientists are learning more and more about cellular life and genes and heredity, but we still know nothing whatsoever about the nature of the glue that holds our existence together. We have discovered some things about matter: we can probe the form of atoms and their substructures in electrical particles. But when we have finally said all that we can say about the nucleus of an atom, we still cannot explain human existence. The foremost scientists readily admit that they are dealing in terms of scientific "faith" rather than scientific "knowledge." We who are people of faith do not hesitate to say that by the power and the intelligence and the love of God, we are.

We confess that our very being depends upon these three elements: God's power and intelligence and love. That confession brings us face to face with a shocking revelation of our own nature. *By the grace of God, we, too, have power and intelligence and the capacity to manifest love.* When God created us in his own image and after his own likeness (Genesis 1:27), he was not suggesting anything at all about our physical construction. Rather, as God is the source of power, we also are creatures of power. When, in the parable of creation (Genesis 3:28) God says, "And I, the Lord God, said unto mine Only Begotten, Behold, the man is become as one of us, to know good and evil," the implication was that we may live and function like God. We may "be anxiously engaged in a good cause, and do many things of [our] own free will..." (D. and C. 58:6d). And we do so by manifesting our inborn, God-given intelligence. With the gift of divine intelligence comes moral obligation as well. While it may rightly be said that we have the *freedom* to do according to our own will, whether good or evil (Mosiah 1:126), it is also true that we never have the *right* to do wrong. We have the right, as a moral obligation, to exercise the gift of God's intelligence in the manner God would use it. What we call "our" intelligence is really God's intelligence within us. When we recognize this we become sensitive to the way in which God's

Spirit leads us to choose the right because it is right. In this way God's Spirit works to give us

> conscience strong
> enough to tell them right from wrong
> and will enough to heed.—from a poem by Naomi Schwensen

It is interesting to note how the scriptures record the work of the Holy Spirit in the creation process. It was the Spirit of God which "moved upon the face of the waters" (Genesis 1:5). The psalmist said, "Thou sendest forth thy Spirit, they are created; and thou renewest the face of the earth" (Psalm 104:30). And Job added, "By his Spirit he hath garnished the heavens" (Job 26:13). In the creation of human life, Job 33:4 also records Elihu saying, "The Spirit of God hath made me, and the breath of the Almighty hath given me life."

The witness of the scriptures is clear: By means of the Holy Spirit, we are more than animals possessing an animalistic principle of life. We are finite, spiritual beings, with personality, even as God is infinite Spirit and personality. God's purpose in working his miracle of creation in us is to bring us onward to eternal life. In power, intelligence, in love, the Holy Spirit continues that work of creativity.

to free them from sin...

How remarkable is human history! The thinkers and philosophers and writers of every age have wrestled with the human predicament, trying to find answers to the questions of why we are, and what we are to do in the presence of good and evil. The astounding thing is that when we permit the Holy Spirit to do his work in our lives, our predicament seems to find resolution—even though we cannot fully comprehend nor explain how the Spirit performs his holy and redeeming work. All we know is that somehow we are free from sin, and that we are led to do good.

The news media daily reveal the sad stories of humanity enmeshed in evil and sin. Time and again we are reminded that sin has not served the best interests of society. But how can humankind avoid sin's constant betrayal?

The answer lies in the revelation of the amazing love and grace of God. For our sakes, while we were yet in our sins, God sent Jesus Christ to save us. Paul said it so beautifully:

> The love of God is shed abroad in our hearts by the Holy Ghost.... For when we were yet without strength...Christ died for the ungodly....God commendeth his love toward us, in that, while we were yet sinners, Christ died for us....If, when we were enemies, we were reconciled to God by the death of his Son; much more, being reconciled, we shall be saved by his life...by whom we have now received the atonement.—Romans 5:5-11

We were powerless sinners and enemies to God. Yet God loved us so much that the Son was sent to die for us, that we might be reconciled to God and receive the atonement. The word *atonement* is a word coined in English. It literally means "at-one-ment." That's how the word was designed in our language. The function of making us one with Jesus Christ, one with God, one with the Holy Spirit, is the function of reconciliation, atonement. This the Holy Spirit constantly strives to do.

We cannot begin to fathom the extent of what the Holy Spirit does to offer ministry for us in this regard. Time and again the Lord's servants have testified of how they have been led, unknown to themselves, through a series of coincidental occurrences whose mathematical probability would be in the order of one chance in millions. The net result of these chance encounters is the offering of a precise ministry at a precise moment of need that brought a sense of unity with God and an awareness of his all-encompassing love. It is as Brother Elbert A. Smith, the presiding patriarch, once said in an inspired communication to the church, "The Lord hath many forces at work in the world that ye know not of."

Truly, sin binds. On occasion it binds us so tightly that

we are deprived of our personal and social freedom and our ability to be productive. But the Holy Spirit frees us from rebellion against God, and at the same time opens our hearts to God's reconcilng power. Jesus certainly spoke the truth when he said, "I am come that they might have life, and that they might have it more abundantly" (John 10:10). Those who have seen the effects of both good and evil know that this is so. They can testify of how abundant life is when one follows the leadings of the Holy Spirit. Unfortunately, many can also testify of great sorrow and unhappiness when such leadings are ignored. This is not to say that those who respond to the Spirit's invitation will never have to face trial or affliction. But it does mean that they will not also have to carry with them the added weight of guilt that sin brings as a burden. Furthermore, those who obey the voice of the Spirit will have resources provided at those times when they most need them.

uniting them with God as God's children, and with each other as brothers and sisters.

Whenever we push ourselves to try to state what we know about God, perhaps the most significant thing we can say is that we know God really exists. One of the testimonies which the world most urgently needs to hear is that God is real. The insight given to Moses as to how God should be named among the Hebrew children was simply, "I AM THAT I AM." Jesus took that same definition and name upon himself when was he asked by the Jews for some explanation of himself. He simply said, "Before Abraham was, I am" (John 8:58).

One of the things we can say with full conviction is that God is not divisive. Nothing in our experiences with God would suggest that the divine purposes have ever crossed. On the contrary, people are continually saying, "God is the unifying principle of our lives," or, "with God I find peace and unity." Even our human scientific mind calls the created order a *uni*verse rather than a *multi*verse, because we sense the way in which God has brought about unity in all creation.

But most of what we know of God, we know because Jesus Christ has revealed it to us. He is the revelation of God in our lives. The work of the Holy Spirit is to reveal Christ to us, and through Christ to make God's life operate in our lives. One of the basic functions of the Holy Spirit in our lives is to unite us with God as God's children, by drawing us resolutely toward God and, consequently, toward one another. John records that Jesus said, "If I be lifted up . . . [I] will draw all men unto me" (John 12:32). We are drawn and united to God through Jesus Christ. Jesus performs that divine work through the Holy Spirit which now functions as the active revelation of God in Christ *in our lives.*

By bringing us together to themselves, the Holy Spirit and Jesus Christ also bring us together with ourselves. This is the fundamental unifying principle which operates in the ministry of the Holy Spirit. It makes us members of a new kind of family. Under the influence of the Holy Spirit, people who come from various races and nations and tongues find that they have a common family origin. By the gift of the Holy Spirit, if we will permit it, we may even experience the grace of God to accept every other human being, not only as a child of God, but as kin to ourselves.

The Spirit bears record of the Father and of the Son, which Father, Son, and Holy Ghost are one God.

We believe in the Holy Spirit who is the living presence of the Father and the Son. The testimony contained in III Nephi 13:22-23 is true: the Father gives us the Holy Spirit to bear witness of Jesus. Because we know that it is not possible to separate God from God, we know that when we have the Holy Spirit with us, the Spirit will bear witness of the truth about God to us. We also know that when we have been in the Spirit's presence, we feel ourselves in the very presence of God, and not some other. It was John who expressed the testimony of the early church in I John 5:7: "There are three that bear record in heaven, the Father, the Word, and the Holy Ghost; and these three are one." In our own era, Joseph Smith bears the testimony of the latter-day church in Doctrine and Covenants 17:5h, saying the Holy Ghost "beareth record of the Father, and of the Son, which Father, Son, and Holy Ghost are one God, infinite and eternal, without end. Amen." For those of us who have heard the Spirit bearing record in our minds and hearts, we can only simply add our own "Amen."

CHAPTER 4
THE GIFTS OF THE SPIRIT

We believe that the Holy Spirit empowers those who are committed to Christ with gifts of worship and ministry. Such gifts, in their richness and diversity, are divided severally as God wills, edifying the body of Christ, empowering persons to encounter victoriously the circumstances of their discipleship, and confirming the new creation into which they are called as children of God.

The work of the Reorganized Church of Jesus Christ of Latter Day Saints is sometimes referred to as the Restoration movement. This is essentially a "spiritual movement." The church is an institution through which the Spirit of God, the Holy Spirit, works to bring to pass God's purposes on earth.

We believe that the Holy Spirit empowers those who are committed to Christ...

When you read the scriptural account of what happened among the disciples after Jesus' departure, the most impressive thing is the moving power of the Holy Spirit in their lives. Although Jesus had physically left them, they believed that he continued to be with them through the Holy Spirit. Jesus had told them, "He that believeth on me, the works that I do shall he do also; and greater works than these shall he do" (John 14:12). He had promised to send the Comforter to abide with them forever. These "greater works" would be done through the Comforter. He further promised that the Comforter would teach them all things. The word "Comforter" literally means "with strength," thus meaning one who greatly strengthens another. Jesus was speaking of the ministry of the Holy Spirit, which would strengthen his disciples in many ways, including the spiritual direction which they would need.

Already Jesus had warned them of persecutions that would come to them. Nevertheless, their hearts were not to be troubled, neither should they be afraid. Paul reflected this attitude when he said, "For God hath not given us the spirit of fear; but of power and of love, and of a sound mind" (II Timothy 1:7).

with gifts of worship and ministry.

Jesus was certainly well aware of his disciples' spiritual condition. While he was with them, their immaturity made them unfit to comprehend all of the truth about the Father, and his love for them and their earthly brethren. But Jesus promised them that they would be led by the Holy Spirit into all truth (John 16:13). Those who are committed to Christ and are seeking the truth about God have the promise that their lives will be nourished by the Holy Spirit. As they share in the love of the Father, they will be enabled to express more and more the nature of God's love in their own lives. It is by means of this process that their personalities are transformed. It is a spiritually rewarding cycle. As a personality matures spiritually, it develops a communion with God. The gift of communion with God permits a person to partake of the love, understanding, and nature of God. This increases the person's powers of ministry for God. It is by this means that the personality matures and grows, developing more and more through the ministry of the Holy Spirit.

As we experience the Holy Spirit in our lives, leading, guiding, teaching, and nourishing our personalities, we try to describe what our experience has been. But from the moment we begin to share our testimony with a friend, we discover how inadequate our words are to convey the thoughts and feelings which were a part of the experience. The Apostle Paul was commenting about the merits of the words of testimony as compared with the witness of the Spirit when he said, "For our gospel came not unto you in word only, but also in power, and in the Holy Ghost, and in much assurance" (I Thessalonians 1:5). Paul acknowledged time and again his dependence upon the Holy Spirit for his understanding of the gospel of Jesus Christ. This was because he received the gospel after Jesus' earthly ministry had ended, and he had had only limited association with the disciples who were nearest to Jesus.

Such gifts, in their richness and diversity....

We are dependent as individuals and as a society on the

ministry of the Holy Spirit for the development of personality. We hope that our growth may reflect more nearly the Spirit and intelligence of God. Such development can occur as we respond to the teaching and nurturing of the Holy Spirit.

God blesses us with many gifts. These gifts help us to achieve within our lives something of the likeness of Deity, the source of our gifts. Although some biblical literalists might assume that there are only nine spiritual gifts—the nine enumerated by Paul in the twelfth chapter of I Corinthians—most of us would recognize that there are many gifts. As the prophet Joseph Smith stated, "There are many gifts, and to every man is given a gift by the Spirit of God" (D. and C. 46:5b). John F. Garver listed some which are usually considered normal human characteristics: intelligence, integrity, graciousness, poise, adaptability, fellowship, accord, music, prayer, teaching, and visiting (*Priesthood Study Outlines*, 1946). We have reason to believe that there are still other gifts, as diverse as the imagination of God and the personality of humans can be. All life is a gift from God, and we possess no gifts apart from God.

When Paul wrote to the Corinthian saints about spiritual gifts, he was trying to say something more than to simply list the spiritual gifts. He was trying tactfully to meet a problem. These disciples had become possessed with an emotional enthusiasm for their new religion. New concepts of God and new relationship to God through the Holy Spirit gave them an extraordinary sense of freedom. Paul did not want to dampen their enthusiasm and dedication to the Lord Jesus Christ, but neither did he want them to become victims of confusion because of their unwise use of the gifts of tongues and prophecy.

He was careful not to tell them that these gifts should not be used, but he tried to suggest an order of value to the gifts (I Corinthians 12:31). He pointed out that impulsive persons are often tempted to seek after the sensational. He tried to help the Greeks to understand that

God is concerned with character and personality growth, not a meaningless display of awesome phenomena (I Corinthians 14:1-33). Paul was concerned that they see the diversity of gifts, and at the same time recognize their source—the Holy Spirit. He did not want them to put the greatest value on the wrong things.

He pointed out that the purpose of the manifestation of the Spirit in the various gifts is for the common good (I Corinthians 12:7). He seems to be asking these questions: Does the manifestation of the Spirit through this particular gift enrich the life of the person and the community? Does it help the disciple and the community to witness more effectively?

The enumeration of gifts in this letter from Paul reminds us that the many gifts of the Holy Spirit differ in scope and circumstances of their expression. Some are *primary* in their function and have an undergirding impact on our lives. Others are *secondary* to these basic gifts, and are governed by them. Still others result from the physical, mental, or moral limitations of our experience, and therefore relate to the *circumstances* of life. Paul's list of the gifts in I Corinthians illustrates these three different kinds of gifts of the Holy Spirit.

Faith, Knowledge, Discernment, Wisdom

Faith, knowledge, discernment, and wisdom represent those *primary* gifts which have a basic influence on our growth and maturity. These have an enduring quality and partake of the nature of eternity. As primary gifts, they govern the development and expression of all other gifts.

Faith is the essence of the God/human relationship. God has placed in us a quality for trust which is the power by which we can achieve what the Lord intends for us. The degree of faith varies from individual to individual. At its best it is wholehearted and unfaltering trust in God. It sustains us in our darkest hour. It is the quality of complete confidence that Jesus demonstrated when, as he hung on the cross and his life's energies were ebbing away, he said, "Father, into thy hands I commend my spirit" (Luke 23:47). Faith is our fitting response to God, and keeps us open and receptive to the divine will.

Knowledge is a God-given understanding of the truth experienced in life. Some persons may become enlightened in understanding certain things and are able to represent a large quantity of information. But there is another dimension of knowledge that comes to us when our personality has been touched by the Spirit witnessing the love of God. Knowing God and God's love for humanity gives particular meaning and perspective to all other truth. This knowledge is available only through experience with the Holy Spirit.

Discernment is closely related to knowledge and wisdom. It is the power to see what can be seen only by yielding to the Spirit of God. It is accuracy of judgment, especially in appraising meaning, character, and motives. Paul referred to the "discerning of spirits" as a means of discrimination among the expression of the gifts in order to recognize the authentic from the manipulated. Paul also used the word in another way. He said, "It is my prayer that your love may abound more and more, with knowledge and all discernment, so that you may approve what is excellent, and may be . . . filled with the fruits of righteousness" (Philippians 1:9-11, RSV). This gift makes it possible for some to disentangle their thoughts from their emotions and prejudices, and to see clearly the issues of a given time and place.

Wisdom as a gift blesses us with the ability to judge soundly. It provides a keen sense of perception. Wisdom is a deeper insight and capacity to organize facts, motives, and means for making a right decision. People with knowledge may be able to state the facts of a situation, but people with wisdom are able to see the bearing which those facts have upon the work of God as it is expressed for the common good.

Wisdom was valued highly by the ancient Hebrews. The writers of such works as Job and Proverbs gave considerable emphasis to the theme of wisdom. A good example is to be found in the Book of Job:

> Whence then cometh wisdom?
> And where is the placing of understanding?...
> God understandeth the way thereof,
> And he knoweth the place thereof....
> Behold, the fear of the Lord, that is wisdom;
> And to depart from evil is understanding.
>
> —Job 28:20-23, 28

Prophecy, Tongues, Interpretation of Tongues

Subordinate to the primary gifts, and to be exercised in conjunction with them, are the *secondary* gifts of prophecy, tongues, and interpretation of tongues. If sought for themselves and exercised without wisdom and discernment, these gifts fall short of the work set for them. They can bring confusion rather than enlightenment.

Prophecy is the capacity for insight into spiritual truths. Persons who are blessed with an understanding of the mysteries of God do not stand aloof from life. They walk in the midst of humankind, grappling with the issues of the day. With their special insights, they become keenly aware of the struggle of forces in the world. Their intelligence is touched by the Holy Spirit in such a way that it enables them to express the love and truth of God as revealed in Jesus Christ (Revelation 19:10). Prophetic disciples are studious, prayerful, understanding, and concerned for humanity. Because of their insights into the forces at work from out of the past and in the present, they may be empowered to foretell events to come. Genuine prophets do not act for self-display or personal aggrandizement, but as God's messengers—to bring enlightenment, edification, and development to humankind. Typical of that prophetic spirit is the message proclaimed at the opening of the Restoration movement: "A great and marvelous work is about to come forth unto the children of men: behold, I am God, and give heed unto my word" (D. and C. 6:1a, b).

Tongues and the interpretation of tongues should be understood in the light of God's desire to bring to humanity revelation and the power to express feelings beyond the normal experience of worship. Revelation is the disclosure of God. Prophecy is the impelling testimony of that disclosure claiming person's lives and giving them direction. Tongues and their interpretation are (and must be) related to this process of communication between God and humanity. The way these three gifts relate in the process of communication was illustrated at Pentecost. The Holy Spirit came with the sound of a "rushing mighty wind" and they "began to speak with other tongues, as the Spirit gave them utterance" (Acts 2:2, 4).

Language is the means of communication among people of common heritage. It can also be a barrier between persons of diverse heritage, no matter how they may yearn to communicate. At the very moment when their hearts burned with testimony, the Galileans at Pentecost were faced with a language barrier. But people from other nations marveled when they could speak and be understood in the various languages represented. "We do hear them speak in our tongues the wonderful works of God" (Acts 2:11). The joint action of comprehension and astonishment convinced many who heard that Jesus was truly the Christ. Mysteriously the Holy Spirit had bridged the gap, and testimony was given wings. Brought together in this one experience of revelation were testimony, communication through intelligible words, and the ministry of the Holy Spirit.

Some persons are found to possess more than an ordinary facility in language. This too is a gift although it seems to be more developmental than spontaneous. Although it may not seem to be so dramatic, it is in fact a very real assistance in carrying the revelation of God to other cultures. Sometimes one who is speaking forth the truths of God comments about possessing great liberty of speech, as in the instance of the disciples who testified that Christ had "loosed their tongues that they could utter" (III Nephi 12:7).

Another aspect of the gift of tongues, also very much a part of the process of communication, is when supreme insight and worship take us to the very edge of language where poetry is born. When words will no longer suffice, the soul sings a new song and superb music is heard.

There may be moments when the exultation and excitement are so intense that no customary expression can be used as a means of sharing. This may be due to an inadequacy of the worshiper, or of those to whom the Spirit would speak. Even if by discernment words were to be found, they might not be understood by the hearer. Paul gave instruction to the Saints of Corinth which relates to this: "Let all things be done unto edifying. If any speak in another tongue, let it be by two, or at the most by three... and let one interpret. But if there be no interpreter, let him keep silence in the church; and let him speak to himself, and to God" (I Corinthians 14:26-28). To edify is the key. If the expression of any gift brings confusion instead of edification, it is suspect.

To guarantee edification, the gift of tongues has its natural and necessary counterpart in the interpretation of tongues. The scripture is explicit: If there is no interpretation to be offered by an interpreter, then the one with the gift should keep silent in the church. But what tremendous responsibility rests on the interpreter! In a sense, more is required of the interpreter who is responsible for both insight and communication. The real burden of this function is to convey the disclosure of the Divine in terms which are understandable by the average hearer. Obviously, these awesome gifts are not to be trifled with.

Healing and Miracles

The gifts of healing and miracles are examples of the

category of gifts which function due to incidental *circumstances,* such as physical or mental distress. That is, the incidents of life create a need for the ministry of the Holy Spirit in these particular ways.

The power of the Holy Spirit to heal and to perform miracles is an extension of the power of God the Creator, full of love and compassion. In miraculous happenings, it seems to us that God sets aside or rises above the ordinary laws of nature. But wasn't the creation of the world itself a miracle? Isn't the creation of a human being also a product of God's miraculous power? Doesn't God continue to create, bringing new things into being and restoring order out of disorder? When God acts with power in ways which seem to be beyond nature, such action comes out of a desire to reveal God's own nature. Included in the revelation are God's power, the nature of creation (the cosmos), and God's purpose. By such revelation, we are enabled to see that nature, though dependable, is not a self-enclosed system which locks God out. It is rather a system in which God continues to create out of love for creation.

It is God's purpose that we should become whole. Jesus and his apostles went about healing body, mind, and spirit. In nearly every instance, the person being healed or the person who was the instrument of healing acted in faith. Happenings which grow out of an exercise of faith are of greater significance than simply taking note of God's love and compassion. This greater significance has to do with our response to God. It is illustrated in the story of the woman who "said within herself, If I may but touch his [Jesus'] garment, I shall be whole" (Matthew 9:27). She merely touched the hem of his robe and was healed. Immediately Jesus sought her out in the crowd, and said to her, "Daughter, take heart, it is the power of faith that has made you well" (adapted from Luke 8:49). Jesus' message, both in what he said and did, is this: Believe in God's love and power; believe great things of God and expect the miraculous. Individuals and society are robbed of much richness in life because of their pride, doubt, and lack of faith in God.

There is another element associated with the healing of the sick. Forgiveness of sin occurs in the experience of healing. In fact, it may be a necessary part of the therapy of healing. It seems in some instances that Jesus was more concerned about making the sick aware that their sins were forgiven than he was in pronouncing them healed. An instance of this is the occasion when he healed the man with palsy (see Matthew 9:2-5). James wrote, "Is any sick among you? Let him call for the elders of the church; and let them pray over him, anointing him with oil in the name of the Lord; and the prayer of faith shall save the sick, and the Lord shall raise him up; and if he have committed sins, they shall be forgiven him" (James 5:14). The same idea is implied in latter-day revelation in Doctrine and Covenants 42:12c, 13. According to God's graciousness, healing is granted through the gift of the Holy Spirit, but in conjunction with the gift of faith.

Miracles are usually thought of as events which arouse feelings of awe, amazement, terror, or wonder. They are shrouded in mystery. Sometimes we simply explain them by calling them "God-events." Prophets of the Old Testament and disciples of the New Testament saw the manifestation of God in such events. The creation of the physical universe, the wonder of the creation of humankind with intelligence and freedom of will, and the incarnation of God in the person of Jesus, are the basic miracles upon which all other miracles depend. A miracle is an event in which God is revealed. But in order for us to discover God in any event, we must have faith in God. Faith is our response toward God. It enables us to acknowledge and become involved in God's mysterious and creative nature.

Love

In his discussion of gifts of the Spirit, Paul leads us

through a discussion of the other gifts to the one which he considered the ultimate gift. He said, "I will show you a...more excellent way" (I Corinthians 12:31, RSV) and then described the superiority of the gift of love. All the other gifts have their roots and purpose in this one. Unless our other gifts are nourished by this dynamic force they have no value. Love is shared by all and should be cultivated by all.

What is this gift of love? It is like other great forces in the universe: it is difficult to define. Paul did not define it, but he did tell us how it works. Love is patient and kind and rejoices in the right. The words of James describing the qualities of wisdom are similar: "But the wisdom from above is first pure, then peaceable, gentle, open to reason, full of mercy and good fruits, without uncertainty or insincerity" (James 3:17, RSV). It is the undeserved grace of God to humanity. In Jesus Christ we see and feel its presence. Our most fitting response to God for this gift is to love our earthly brothers and sisters as God loves them. As Jesus said, "A new commandment I give unto you, That ye love one another; as I have loved you, that ye also love one another" (John 13:34). In the Book of Mormon narrative, King Benjamin stated the same concept: "When you are in the service of your fellow beings you are only in the service of your God" (Mosiah 1:49).

are divided severally as God wills....

Through the Holy Spirit God has given us a variety of gifts. Every normal person possesses a number of gifts and talents in varying degrees. No one of us is endowed with all the gifts, but as a community we may possess all the gifts collectively, "differing according to the grace that is given to us" (Romans 12:6; see also I Corinthians 12:11).

Paul admonished the disciples not to neglect their gifts in I Timothy 4:14, and added, "Having gifts that differ...let us use them" (Romans 12:6, RSV). In this passage he included such gifts as prophecy, service, teaching, and exhortation, along with others. His advice to the disciples was to seek and cultivate the best gifts (see I Corinthians 12:31). Gifts are to be cultivated for the common good, not for the selfish enjoyment of the individual. The individual must remember that the gifts which he or she possesses are a trust to be used responsibly and constructively in God's service.

edifying the body of Christ...

In the scriptures the church is often referred to as the body of Christ. Paul was concerned that the members of the church in his new missions understand the ministry of the Holy Spirit in their midst. When he described the group of believers as the body of Christ, he was not suggesting that it had attained an equal state of perfection with Christ. The church is limited in vision, understanding, and ability to minister for Christ, simply because it is composed of persons who are not spiritually mature. Because of this imperfection, both the individuals and the entire body must surrender to the ministry of the Holy Spirit if the church is to grow toward perfection. The Holy Spirit then can edify the body of Christ, and build it up as an instrument of ministry for the Lord.

No one is capable of understanding all the powers which God uses in the salvation of humankind. But when joined together in bonds of fellowship with Christ, if we are guided and growing in maturity through the gifts of the Holy Spirit, we may become a functioning body—a body with powers of intelligence, influence, and righteous achievement that cannot be attained in any other way. Unfortunately, even the very diversity of gifts among our members can pose a threat to our unity. However, through allegiance to Christ and by the constant renewal of the Spirit, this diversity will bring a symphonic richness in unity that produces strength and beauty.

Because the church is to be a symphonic instrument of ministry for Christ, it must be constantly under the direction of his Spirit which brings purpose, life, and unity. Regarding the early church, the scriptures say that the "churches...throughout all Judea and Galilee and Samaria...were edified; and walking in the fear of the Lord, and in the comfort of the Holy Ghost, were multiplied" (Acts 9:31). For those disciples who had witnessed the power and awesomeness of the resurrection of Christ, and the experience of Pentecost, it was easy to believe that any righteous thing was possible through the ministry of the Holy Spirit. However unpredictable life might be, they were sure that nothing could thwart the victory of righteousness. The establishment of God's kingdom on earth was assured under the leadership of this Holy Spirit of power.

empowering persons to encounter victoriously the circumstances of their discipleship...

More is expected of Christ's disciples than from the pupils of some great philosopher. Jesus' disciples saw a new vision, a new way of life in him. God was with them in the flesh, and they were to continue that incarnation, making the vision actual in their own lives. This was more than the mastery of a set of ideas about Christ. It was being new creatures in him.

Jesus said in effect to his disciples, "I am the way. What you have seen me do, you should do." They were to bear testimony of him. And they did, as at Pentecost and before Agrippa. But their words were authenticated by what they *were* and what they were *doing*. Jesus said to them, "If any man will come after me, let him deny himself, and take up his cross and follow me. And now for a man to take up his cross, is to deny himself all ungodliness, and every worldly lust, and keep my commandments" (Matthew 16:25-26).

Jesus knew that the conditions and requirements of

discipleship would be difficult. Even so, his purpose was to draw them from their sin and immaturity and lead them toward perfection. He was aware of the opposition they would have to face from without, and their human weaknesses from within. He knew they would be accused before governors and kings. He knew they would be divided from members of their families and suffer persecution. He knew that living the gospel would bring them into conflict with custom, tradition, and political power interests. However, he spoke words of courage and counsel to them. He told them not to fear those who could kill the body, but rather those who could destroy the soul. He cautioned them to beware of hatred, greed, self-love, and lust of the body. His invitation to all, however, was: "Come unto me, all ye that labor and are heavy laden, and I will give you rest. Take my yoke upon you, and learn of me; for I am meek and lowly in heart; and ye shall find rest unto your souls; for my yoke is easy and my burden is light" (Matthew 11:29-30).

The disciple's promise of victory is sure for those who trust God and walk in steadfast faith. The Apostle Paul asked if tribulation, distress, persecution, famine, and war could separate the disciple from the Lord. He concluded that those who are led by the Spirit of God are the children of God, and there is nothing that can separate them from the love of their heavenly Father (see Romans 8:14-39).

and confirming the new creation into which they are called as children of God.

The grace of God was manifest in the life and ministry of Christ. The life, death, and resurrection of the Son of God both announced and portrayed the new creation. God was moving mightily in that life of thirty-three years to work reconciliation with humankind. During his ministry, Jesus said to those around him, "He who heareth my word, and believeth on him who sent me, hath everlasting life, and... is passed from death into life" (John 5:24). Those who surrender to the call of God through the Spirit of Christ become new creatures. They possess the spirit of Sonship in their hearts. They are new persons living in a new world which is centered in Christ. Life takes on a new perspective. They now have new and different values. They see everything in a different light.

Before being touched and united with the Holy Spirit, they live in the passions of flesh and follow the desires of body and mind (see Ephesians 2:3). Through the Spirit of Christ, a transformation takes place in them; they become aware of their relationship to God. They are spiritually reborn by their response to the grace of God. In a real sense they become citizens of heaven with a perspective of eternity. Now they are involved with the concerns of eternal values. They are new creatures, "created in Christ Jesus for good works" (Ephesians 2:10 RSV). As members of the family of God, they bear within their being the likeness of God. Because of this, they give themselves without reservation in ministry to their neighbors.

As the Holy Spirit ministers through these new creatures in Christ, a new world and a new universe are being created (see Romans 8:19-23). Entering into a new relationship with God makes possible a new relationship with all whom they meet. The old separation of person from person by hostility and fear disappears through the reconciling act of God. A whole new society comes into being: the kingdom of God becomes a reality on earth. The disciple blessed with the spirit of prophetic insight can see it coming. The span of God's creation from beginning to end is moving toward the purpose of the Creator and the Redeemer.

CHAPTER 5
THE GIFT OF SAINTLY GRACES

We believe that the Holy Spirit creates, quickens, and renews in persons such graces as love, joy, peace, mercy, gentleness, meekness, forbearance, temperance, purity of heart, saintly kindness, patience in tribulation, and faithfulness before God in seeking to build up the kingdom of God.

By the power of the Holy Spirit, we may be able to partially grasp the beauty, majesty, and holiness of the divine in life. Job was speaking about this when he "answered the Lord, and said, I know that thou canst do everything, and that no thought can be withholden from thee.... Therefore have I uttered that [which] I understood not; things too wonderful for me, which I knew not" (Job 42:1-3). Because we are human, we simply fall short of the mark whenever we discuss the nature and work of the Holy Spirit. Latter-day revelation, in Doctrine and Covenants 22:7b, c refers to the "nothingness" of humanity in comparison with the reality of God. We can never fully understand that which is greater than we are. With this keen awareness of human limitations, yet with faith in the perfection toward which God lifts us, Paul wrote, "For we know in part, and we prophecy in part. But when that which is perfect is come, then that which is in part shall be done away.... For now we see through a glass, darkly; but then face to face; now I know in part; but then shall I know even as also I am known" (I Corinthians 13:9-10, 12). Someone suggested our relationship to the Holy Spirit as being like our relationship to electricity. Though we do not fully understand what it is, we can use it and effectively channel it to good purposes. This illustration calls our attention to the fact that we do not need to reject or deny what we do not fully understand. It has been said prophetically, "For as the heavens are higher than the earth, so are my ways higher than your ways, and my thoughts than your thoughts" (Isaiah 55:9). But, like all analogies, the electricity illustration can be misleading if we attempt to apply it in every sense. The Holy Spirit is not simply power: the Holy Spirit is person, and therefore is also intelligence and personality. The Holy Spirit is not less than we are, and therefore is not subject to our direction. On the contrary, we know that the Holy Spirit is the personality, the power, and the intelligence of God at work. So for many centuries now, people have foud that they cannot adequately speak of the Holy Spirit as "it." They tend instead to use a personal pronoun such as "He," or to simply keep in mind that it is God in our midst which we experience when we experience the Holy Spirit. In the Holy Spirit, we feel the presence, love, and energy of God. Samuel M. Shoemaker, writing about experience with the Holy Spirit, said:

> But I think there is often a *nearness* about the presence of the Holy Spirit, as if He were taking the initiative with us Himself. At rare times this will be so numinous, so charged with a sense of the supernatural, that it will almost frighten us; we shall know beyond all questioning that this is no subjective imagining, but a living presence. It is as if He had not just come; He had come for something.... I think He is with us many times when it is not made known to us in such startlingly vivid ways; but let us not push from us the thought that at times He makes Himself unmistakably known by His very presence.—*With Holy Spirit and with Fire,* page 27

We believe that the Holy Spirit creates, quickens, and renews in persons...

We believe that humans are spiritual beings. The writer of the Book of Job declared: "There is a spirit in man; and the inspiration of the Almighty giveth them understanding" (Job 32:8). Our experiences as well as the scriptures support our belief in the spiritual nature of persons. There is clearly a distinction between humankind and the animals which separates their worlds. However, we readily admit that this division separating the two is not always so clearly drawn as we sometimes would like to think. There is clear evidence of almost human understanding and behavior from mammals such as whales, dolphins, and porpoises; and regrettably we note persons whose weakened minds or spiritual perversity incline them to animalistic acts.

The creator of all things places in each order of creation the anticipation of higher forms. It is good for us to be reminded that our roots go deep down into the earth from which we spring. We need to be aware of our earthy relations, for this helps us to understand that the earth from which we come has been made forever holy by God himself. He not only created it, but sent his Son to share our origins with us, that we may see them as sacred and sacramental.

Consequently we confess that we are rooted in nature. We are attached both to the inanimate order of creation and to the flesh of the animal life which we also share. We carry in our bodies the passions, drives, and even some of the instincts of other forms of animal life. Yet we human beings can soar to nobler heights of affection, self-sacrifice, and group loyalties. But we also find that lower forms of animal life in some measure challenge our superiority with attributes of their own. We should expect this, of course, for the God who created us created all else, and did not fashion us without regard to the rest of creation. There is a continuum in God's creations through which the higher orders rest upon the foundations of earlier forms. To survey God's handiwork causes us to stand in awe of the marvelous things God has done. We can but simply acknowledge the magnificent processes by which God has chosen to create us and all else that exists. The beauty of the system is itself testimony of the intelligence of the Creator.

In the lower forms of animal life we find the elementary expression of reasoning, affection, fidelity, and respect for the welfare of the group. However, humankind is capable of transcendence in these realms which sets humans apart from the beasts of the field. Indeed, humanity rises above all the other creations of God. Human beings are capable of living in the world of symbols, values, and moral law. Understandings of communication, of what is honest and good, lift people above and give them a sphere of life beyond material things. We have the marvelous capacity to participate in a world of language. This is of major significance, for the ability of the soul to express itself in language goes far beyond immediate communication. It not only ties us to living contemporaries, but links us as well with the past. We are figuratively standing on the shoulders of former generations. Although we have their material culture which has been passed on to us, of greater value are the immaterial knowledge, attitudes, values, and loyalties which have become a part of our way of life. We do not, like the other animals, have to start from the same beginning point in each generation. We have the ability through language to retain the experience of our ancestors. Our greatest joys and deepest griefs are found in this realm above the material and the animalistic.

There is, however, no antagonism between the physical and the spiritual aspects of life. Indeed, both are a part of God's gifts. The nonmaterial aspects of life are dependent upon the foundation of the physical and animalistic. But we have been created to go beyond this. Our greatest tragedy occurs when we turn away from the sphere of the Spirit to preoccupy ourselves with the material and the satisfaction of the physical desires. When we do that, we refuse to become what God has created us to be.

We are most truly separated from the rest of the animal world by our awareness of God and our awareness of our self. No other animal appears to be able to recognize any power higher than nature and humankind. Dr. Emil Brunner has rightly pointed out that it is at this point where one begins to see the significance of human life being created in the "image of God." Dr. Brunner states:

The Bible expresses the distinctive quality of a man by saying that he stands in a special relation to God, that the relation between God and man is that of "over-against-ness," that it consists of being face-to-face with each other.—*The Christian Understanding of Man,* page 158

This gift sets us apart from the rest of God's creation. It gives us the power of being, which is sometimes spoken of as the self. Our awareness of ourself, separate from all other selves, is a gift from God. It even transcends the physical body which is the self's abode. Being aware of our selves as being separate and apart from all other selves makes it possible for us to be aware of God as separate from ourself. Without this awareness, we could not know God at all. It is this "over-againstness" which makes it possible for us to have and to exercise agency. It is this power that enables us to rebel against others, and even against God.

But on the other hand, it is this same gift that makes it possible for a person to have fellowship with other persons and with God. Humankind has been given the power to live within the realm of symbols and immaterial values, and yet stand apart from them. Because of this, it is possible for us to live by faith and rejoice in the promises which we have not yet received—but which we know will surely be, because God is. This unique element in humankind, whether we call it "self," "psyche," or "being," is known to us as the spirit within us. It is the gift of God who created us in his own image. In simple yet beautiful language, the scriptures have recorded this mystery: "And I, the Lord God, formed man from the dust of the ground, and breathed into his nostrils the breath of life; and man became a living soul" (Genesis 2:8). Without attempting to make any scientific explanation, our testimony is that God has done a wonderful thing which lifts us above all other creatures. We are equipped for fellowship with God, for he has created in us a spirit.

This state of being has truly enough granted us the powers of choice. Such a gift permits us to choose to become a child of God; but it also provides the possibility for rebellion against God. Left to our own resources with the appetites of the flesh and the ambitions of the self-seeking spirit, we would surely become monsters. The rest of God's creation has no spirit such as we have, no power of "over-againstness," and no will to rebel against God. The rest of creation simply fulfills the intention of the Creator. This is the meaning of Doctrine and Covenants 85:6a which states, "The earth...filleth the measure of its creation, and transgresseth not the law."

But humankind has the inevitable will to sin. We rebel against God. Left to our own devices, we will surely pervert to selfish ends the gifts that God implants in us. This in the long run will destroy and debase rather than ennoble.

However, God has invested so much in us that he does not leave us to our own devices. The universe is set to lift, refine, and redeem, for all of God's creation is in harmony with his will to perform that miracle in us. The entire course of human history, and particularly God's entry into the world in the person of Jesus Christ, demonstrates God's involvement with us to bring about our redemption. The Apostle Paul put it this way: "God is in Christ, reconciling the world unto himself" (II Corinthians 5:19). But the end of Jesus' life and ministry was not the end of God's action for our good. Christ promised his followers the Comforter, the Holy Spirit, "even the Spirit of truth," which he said would teach us all things and bring all things to our remembrance (see John 14:16-18, 26).

The Holy Spirit will not wrest from us our agency. But when we voluntarily surrender our prideful sovereignty to the will of God, then the Holy Spirit can enter into our life to help us do what we could never do apart from God. This surrender requires repentance and commitment. It is represented tangibly in baptism, and the response of God is symbolized in the laying on of hands. It is intended that by these acts we enter into a quality of life that can only be described as "eternal life."

In reality, the power to yield our life to God is in itself a gift of the Holy Spirit. No one really has a testimony that Jesus is the Christ unless the Spirit bears witness of this truth. This is what Paul meant when he said, "No man can say that Jesus is the Lord, but by the Holy Ghost" (I Corinthians 12:3). Because the Holy Spirit is intelligence and personality, we feel the love of God that goes beyond our understanding. And when we are in the Spirit's presence, the Holy Spirit lightens our hearts in such a way that with all our being we want to become a part of what God is. Or some would say it is becoming a part of the kingdom of God. Our loving response is possible only when we are in the presence of a loving person—in this case, the Holy Spirit of God. Thus, we too can say, without ever having known Jesus in the flesh, that "We love him, because he first loved us" (I John 4:19).

The Holy Spirit, the abiding Comforter, is not merely a force, but a presence. The early Christians spoke of this as the "mind of Christ" which dwelt within them. They found that the Holy Spirit quickened their own spirits with powers of ministry and service. These new-found powers within their beings were not entirely new: they had been latently present, but never before developed. The early saints found their own bodies and personalities renewed and refreshed by qualities which they recognized as gifts through the Holy Spirit. As the psalmist of old had said, they knew God had created a clean heart and renewed a right spirit within them (see Psalm 51:10). Consequently they said they were reborn.

This power of the Holy Spirit to quicken and renew was mentioned by Samuel M. Shoemaker:

This is not like the physical power of a dynamo—it is power of a different sort. Something comes into our own energies and capacities and spans them. We are laid hold of by Something greater than ourselves. We can face things, create things, accomplish things, that in our own strength would have been impossible. Artists sometimes feel this in a verse or phrase of music or some direction that comes to them, and say that it was "given" to them. The Holy Spirit seems to mix and mingle His power with our own, so that what happens is both a heightening of our own power and a gift to us from outside.—*With Holy Spirit and with Fire,* page 27

such graces as...

Whenever we are cleansed, and renewed in spirit, it takes place under the power of the Holy Spirit. It must be recognized not only as a gift from God, but an unmerited gift at that. The amazing wonder of the whole process regenerating the human spirit is that God moved in human hearts when they were still unlovely and blinded by sin. The Apostle Paul had this to say to the Romans:

The love of God is shed abroad in our hearts by the Holy Ghost which is given unto us. For when we were yet without strength, in due time Christ died for the ungodly.... For if, when we were enemies, we were reconciled to God by the death of his Son; much more, being reconciled, we shall be saved by his life.—Romans 5:5-6, 10

To the Corinthians, he said,

For God, who commanded the light to shine out of darkness, hath shined in our hearts, to give the light of the knowledge of the glory of God in the face of Jesus Christ. But we have this treasure in earthen vessels, that the excellency of the power may be of God, and not of us.—II Corinthians 4:6-7

When we say that our lives are transformed by the grace of God, we are admitting that we are enabled to do what would otherwise be beyond our power. When Christian graces radiate from our lives, they reflect the nature of God. These graces are given without restraint as the fruit of godly lives. As Jesus said, it is by such fruit that his disciples are recognized (see Matthew 7:25-29). On another occasion, while talking with his disciples, Jesus said,

Now ye are clean through the word which I have spoken unto you. Abide in me, and I in you. As the branch cannot bear fruit of itself, except it abide in the vine; no more can ye, except ye abide in me. I am the vine, ye are the branches. He that abideth in me, and I in him, the same bringeth forth much fruit; for without me ye can do nothing.—John 15:3-5

As we look briefly at some of these graces, we need to keep in mind that the quality of these characteristics as expressed by Christian disciples is somewhat different than the usual definitions.

love...

Love when expressed as a Christian grace is the love referred to by the Greek word *agape*. It is the love which is characteristic of the nature of God. It does not come as a result of some favor done, or friendliness shown by another. The love of God is not affected by the nature or action of the one who is loved. God's love arises from the nature of Divinity and not out of our own nature. This is the kind of love to which Jesus referred when he said:

> Ye have heard that it hath been said, Thou shalt love thy neighbor, and hate thine enemy. But I say unto you, Love your enemies; bless them that curse you; do good to them that hate you; and pray for them which despitefully use you and persecute you; that ye may be the children of your Father who is in heaven; for he maketh his sun to rise on the evil and on the good, and sendeth rain on the just and on the unjust. For if ye love only them which love you, what reward have you? Do not even the publicans the same?—Matthew 5:45-48

Such love is described by the Apostle Paul in the thirteenth chapter of I Corinthians. It is the affirmative love that keeps the soul free from the poison of resentment, and overflowing with the ministry which blesses others. It is the love that qualifies us for service in the kingdom of God.

joy...

We have the abiding assurance that God is all powerful, including the power to keep that which is good. Therefore we can experience an inner joy, the joy of faith. We find joy in the security of God, but we also have assurance of the ultimate victory of all righteousness. It is the affirmation of worth which comes to those who sense that God loves them and trusts even the precious things of the kingdom to their stewardship. As a Christian grace, joy is the overflow which comes from the abiding presence of the Holy Spirit. It results from our confidence in the future which the communion of the Holy Spirit confirms. It is from communion with others that our greatest happiness in life comes to us. Our severest punishment is separation from others or solitary confinement. When those who have been separated in spirit from God are reunited with him, the joy of that communion excels, giving meaning to all true happiness.

peace...

Jesus said, "Peace I leave with you, my peace I give unto you; not as the world giveth, give I unto you. Let not your heart be troubled, neither let it be afraid" (John 14:27). Some people seem to feel that peace can be achieved only by the changing of outward conditions. The follower of Christ knows that "the peace of God, which passeth all understanding" comes not from without but from within (Philippians 4:7). It is the calm assurance that "all things work together for good to them that love God, to them who are the called according to his purpose" (Romans 8:28). It is the peace that enables us to stand with poise and dignity in the midst of danger or confusion, knowing full well that in the long run the purposes of God will prevail. This saintly grace is the ground upon which peaceful relationships among all humanity are based.

mercy...

Jesus said, "Blessed are the merciful; for they shall obtain mercy" (Matthew 5:9). Forgiven disciples must always be aware of the abundant grace that bridged the gap between the holiness of God and their own sinfulness. God lifted them up when they could rightfully claim no mercy. Because God has forgiven so much, surely the forgiven disciples must forgive those who do them injury. Mercy is the reasonable response of one who loves in some measure as God loves. Therefore it is not a bargaining lever, but a freely extended acceptance of the offender. It is the fulfillment of the prayer which Jesus taught his disciples to pray when he said, "Forgive us our trespasses, as we forgive those who trespass against us" (Matthew 6:13).

gentleness...

The quality of gentleness has sometimes been considered a feminine trait. It is often true the hand of a mother or a wife seems to depict the greatest gentleness imaginable. Yet gentleness is quite as possible in the strong hands of a man or the concerned counsel of a minister, regardless of gender. The one who is moved by the Holy Spirit to bring forth fruit for Christ sees all work as a ministry and all service as a labor of love. The disciple will be gentle even as Christ was gentle. In this life such gentleness is expressed in consideration for others. It is the sympathy which emanates from deep love, and is expressed in its finest delicacy.

meekness...

Meekness is expressed by a willingness to consider fairly all the evidence available, to respond to that which is good, and to readily accept that which is true. Meekness is love on the growing edge of life. It makes us teachable. When we yield our life to Christ, we must also recognize the worth of our brothers and sisters. In doing so, we find joy in accepting from them knowledge and instruction which they may be able to share for our welfare. The meek, Jesus said, "shall inherit the earth" (Matthew 5:7).

Such meekness can never exist until we feel secure in Christ. Insecure persons are not meek. They hide their fear even from themselves, or whimper in self-pity. Persons who are meek in the Spirit of God are not afraid; they have a confidence born of faith in God who is all powerful.

Meekness is the source of strength which comes to persons who have disciplined their lives under God rather than expending their energies in self-assertion. They become strong as the instruments of the Divine.

forbearance...

Forbearance is godly restraint. It keeps us from unrighteous judgment and hasty acts that harm. It is the patience with others' weaknesses that characterized Jesus. It grows out of a godly understanding and the deep-seated love which always seeks to help another. It binds up the wounded soul and sets it forth again on life's road with renewed aspiration and faith. Forbearance is a gift of the Spirit, but it needs cultivation in the life of the disciple. The exercise of forbearance is important in developing trust and unity. It builds saintly relationships within the fellowship of the church, as well as in ministry to the world at large.

temperance...

Temperance is the discipline made possible by an awareness of eternity. It is living by a balanced view of life, one that is enlightened by the light of the Holy Spirit. A prerequisite to temperance is an appreciation for all of God's creations as good. Temperance keeps us from allowing the appetites of our physical and social desires to lead us into excesses. Without temperance, our life may become distorted or its ultimate purposes obscured. Temperance requires our willingness to forego some immediate satisfaction in the short run, for the achievement of more valuable and enduring goals in the long run. It implies our willingness to give up cherished possessions and hopes when we realize they are either needed for the work of God, or are stumbling blocks which hinder our stewardship.

purity of heart...

The pure in heart are those whose love for God has so cleansed their thinking that ugly desires, resentful feelings, jealous self-centeredness, and wasteful lusts no longer find lodging there. The well-springs of the heart are cleansed by the Spirit of God through frequent prayer and worship. By an act of will, we can direct our thoughts toward wholesome considerations. But real purity of heart is the fruit of those whose lives have been oriented to the first great commandment: "Thou shalt love the Lord thy God with all thy heart, and with all thy soul, and with all thy mind" (Matthew 22:36).

saintly kindness...

Kindness is the teammate of love. When we love as God loves, kindness is the only reasonable relationship we can extend to others. We cultivate sympathy which helps us to share the feelings of others. We develop powers to heal the tormented soul or broken spirit by the kindness which understands and cares. To be a brother or sister to everyone, especially to the lonely, weak, and broken soul, is a godly service indeed.

patience in tribulation...

It is an easy temptation for us to think that God ought to protect those who serve faithfully. Like Job, we find it hard to understand why apparently good men and women have to endure tribulation. We do not know the answers to these questions. But we do know that God has not promised ease or freedom from suffering to the disciples. God did not spare even the Lord Jesus from the agony of the cross. Furthermore, we know that only men or women of faith can carry this burden with dignity, assurance, and patience. They know that eventually even this burden may be the means of accomplishing God's purposes. Because we believe that the arms of love undergird all of life, we are assured that there is no eternal tragedy to those who love God. Such faith gives the disciples patience and courage to face life unafraid.

and faithfulness before God in seeking to build up the kingdom of God.

Jesus taught His disciples to pray, "Thy kingdom come.

Thy will be done on earth, as it is done in heaven'' (Matthew 6:11). When the mind of Christ truly dwells within us, our greatest joy is to use our lives to assist in the Lord's work. The Apostle Paul pleaded with the Roman saints: ''I beseech you therefore, brethren, by the mercies of God, that ye present your bodies a living sacrifice, holy, acceptable unto God, which is your reasonable service'' (Romans 12:1). Faithfulness in seeking to build up God's kingdom is the only reasonable response of someone who loves God. It is the only decent response from those who sense keenly what God has done so abundantly for them. It is the opportunity given by God to the disciples to devote their lives to those things which are of eternal worth. In this, they not only lay up for themselves treasures of quality, but rejoice to see that what they have lived for continues on into eternity. It is the opportunity for both them and their works to be saved in the kingdom of God. They know that they have not labored in vain when they have served the Lord in his task.

While the work of the Holy Spirit is beyond our understanding, it is not beyond our experience. Perhaps the most amazing work of the Holy Spirit which we have experienced is the change it has brought in our own lives and in the lives of our companions in the gospel. It has turned us from death to life everlasting. That gift of the Spirit with which God has created us has now been quickened and renewed. God's presence is closer than even our own bodies. Indeed, the divine life has become a part of us. By the ministry of the Holy Spirit, God is helping us to develop those godly characteristics which, when fully matured, will make the church truly representative of the Lord Jesus Christ.

CHAPTER 6
HUMANITY

We believe that humanity is endowed with freedom and created to know, to love, and to serve God, and to enjoy communion with God. In following the dictates of pride and in declaring independence from God, humanity loses the power to fulfill the purposes of creation and becomes the servant of sin, whereby persons are divided within themselves and estranged from God and their neighbors. This condition, experienced by our ancestors who first came to a knowledge of good and evil, is shared by all who are granted the gift of accountability.

We have already affirmed our belief in God the Father, Son, and Holy Spirit. While we have done that, we recognize that our words are inadequate to define what is really indefinable. Yet we sense that we belong to some thing or some one beyond our reach, which at the same time seems to be hounding us as if we were pursued. We yearn to understand our feelings.

We believe that humanity is endowed with freedom...

We are peculiar creatures. All else in creation fits into its place, apparently without taking thought about it, untroubled by imagination or conscience. It is given to humanity alone to ponder our part, to smile or fret, to hold past and future simultaneously, and to know good and evil. As Shakespeare said in *Hamlet* (act 2, scene 2),

What a piece of work is a man! How noble in reason! How infinite in faculty! In form and moving how express and admirable! In action how like an angel! In apprehension how like a god! The beauty of the world! The paragon of animals!

Of all God's creation, we humans alone hold the earth in our hands, using, controlling, and diminishing its resources. We are the only creature capable of deliberate control of environment, genetics, and behavior. We seem to be impelled by an insatiable desire to climb the heights, probe the depths, explore space, and even escape the confines of earth. We also are capable of exploding in violence at an unwelcome gesture or the turn of a phrase. Gifted with capacity for wisdom, faith, and love, we are apt to toss it all for momentary excitement of passion, to destroy a loved one in a fit of jealousy, or knife our enemy, and, at least momentarily, feel good about it.

What shall we believe about this ambivalent creature we call ourselves? We seem to represent a joining of flesh and spirit hung halfway between heaven and earth, both liking and hating the honor. Confronted with the life of the spirit, we cling to the flesh like a reluctant pilgrim from Pharoah's Egypt. In the grip of the flesh, we yearn for release like the prodigal son. Perceiving good and evil, we are drawn and repelled by each of them. When we do good, we find evil inviting our attention. When we would find satisfaction in evil, good spoils our fun. No wonder we expect our creator to be patient with us. In creating humanity, God has written a riddle. It is as Alexander Pope has stated it in his *Essay on Man:*

> Created half to rise, and half to fall;
> Great lord of all things, yet prey to all;
> Sole judge of truth, in endless error hurled;
> The glory, jest, and riddle of the world!

We possess a potential for freedom that appears to be different from all other creatures. Our concerns range all the way from physical to psychological and to the philosophical. We are free to create art, and to know ourselves as a part of history. We also sense that we are a part of some remote life as well as the immediate community. We are somehow capable of transcending the normal limitations of animal life. That transcendence is a breakthrough to a freedom that is unique.

We humans are distinguished by the character of our freedom. We are free to imagine, to think, to anticipate consequences, to speak, to envision, to construct, to know beyond the range of our own experiences. We are free to value, to benefit from defeat, to suspend judgments, to choose, and to love. We are free to detach from ourselves, to see ourselves as objects, and to react to what we see. We may be pleased or offended by what we observe. We may evaluate and judge ourselves. We may direct our own lives.

Such freedom is a gift. It is a part of human nature by the grace of God. It is an endowment, granted in order that we may become truly human—after the likeness of God, but not God. We are forever dependent upon the higher power, no matter how much we try to shake loose. We have liberty, but not completely, for Providence has not created us to be entirely independent so as to become gods in our own right. We are compassed about by dependence upon the Creator. We also recognize our interdependence with our neighbors, granting to them an equivalent freedom or else our own liberty is diminished.

We belong to God, but uniquely so. For the privilege is given only to us to be over against God. This enables us to draw away for a look, an appraisal, a judgment, and to say yes or no in anticipation of consequences.

The counterpart of such freedom and agency is, of course, responsibility. We are free because we are responsible—and responsible because we are free. These are inseparable and each depends upon the other. Without responsibility, we revert to the animal level of life. It is in the ability to answer for our conduct and obligations that we become a free moral agent. This is the divine expectation for humanity. However, we are prone to dodge the very accountability that marks our freedom. We deceive ourselves that freedom is escape from responsibility instead of its companion.

Frequently we are foolish enough to covet the freedom of the birds and the beasts. This is freedom from responsibility, a freedom within severely restricted confines. Although the arctic tern is free to fly 11,000 miles, it is severely limited by instinct and pressures of environment that make its flight mandatory. The bird does not will to fly or not to fly. The pattern is fixed. To trade for this, we would have to trade liberty for captivity and restriction. In trading, we would erode our will and make it progressively ineffective.

Instinctive response is unwilling obedience—and the being that acts in that manner is less than human. In a sense, all persons are like Esau, sacrificing birthright to appetite. When we forfeit deliberate control of ourselves, our freedom deteriorates. Therefore, lacking intelligent control of ourselves, we make ourselves liable to coercion from other persons or powers.

We are endowed with freedom to escape the bonds of

forced obedience, to the highest freedom of becoming. We may decide to be or not to be. Any form of suicide is a perverted expression of our freedom. We may will to become or not to become. This is the supreme privilege of our humanity. As a matter of fact, it is our humanity.

and created to know God...

It is given to us to know God. In fact, "this is life eternal, that they might know thee the only true God" (John 17:3). Apparently no other creature on earth is aware of its creator or even the creative process. We have never seen a honeycomb of four sides instead of six, and we do not expect to, unless it is fabricated by someone. Why is this? It is because humankind can observe the processes of creation, and bring forth things that have not been seen before, even creating new elements. From observing the creative process we conclude that there is a creator. And then, by reasoning or by experience, we move into a knowledge of the Being that is the source of all being, and, in awe, we breathlessly exclaim, "Abba, Father."

This power of discernment is an endowment by which we are drawn "God-ward." However dull this gift may be in many persons, it has been heightened in some who have borne testimony of their own experiences with God. Describing such an experience is a difficult task; it must be couched in words arising from our common daily experiences. But Isaiah, Saul of Tarsus, Enos, and Joseph Smith, among a host of other witnesses, have spoken of the awesome intimacy of their experiences with God's revealment.

In such worship, Mind speaks to mind, and spirit answers to Spirit. Our higher powers respond to the grace of God which reaches out to our human condition, seeking to warn and to win us from our persistence toward destruction.

Having the potential of knowing the infinite God, we

can never be completely content with our finite knowledge. Drawn by that power which calls forth a response from deep inside us, we reach beyond what we can grasp, stretching our awareness. Without some knowledge of God and the infusion of God's Spirit and purpose, we find our life a barren place. As T. S. Eliot has phrased it in *Wasteland,*

> A heap of broken images, where the sun beats,
> And the dead tree gives no shelter, the cricket no relief,
> And the dry stones no sound of waters.

This was the concern of Haggai generations ago, when the people declared their independence from God:

Ye have sown much, and bring in little; ye eat, but ye have not enough; ye drink, but ye are not filled with drink; ye clothe you, but there is none warm; and he that earneth wages, earneth wages to put it into a bag with holes.—Haagai 1:6

Bent on knowing much and succeeding remarkably in the expansion of knowledge, we are often drunk with intemperate knowledge. Again, as T. S. Eliot has phrased it, we experience the "weariness of [those] who turn from God to the grandeur of... arts and inventions and daring enterprises, to schemes of human greatness" (*The Rock,* Part 3). These fruits may indeed reveal human greatness. But eventually they will have the "taste of sand," unless they result from laboring together with God. We are created to know God and will always be unfulfilled until filled by the knowledge of God.

to love and to serve God, and to enjoy communion with God...

Some of us may yearn to see the "finger of God," or to observe God in the familiar forms and functions of humans. It would be convenient for us to see a "God" who is like ourselves. But that is not to be our experience. Nor are we left to merely observe the One who is beyond our humanity. We are privileged to have the possibility of a far more significant experience. God has invested in us a restlessness. Few have expressed this better than Edwin Markham in *The Testing:*

> I will leave man to make the fateful guess,
> Will leave him torn between the No and Yes,
> Leave him unresting till he rests in Me,
> Drawn upward by the choice that makes him free—
> Leave him in tragic loneliness to choose,
> With all in life to win, or all to lose.

Others bear testimony of the relationship God has intended for us, and of the haunting nostalgia that persists in us until we surrender to our creator. This story of God's yearning for humankind, and of our frantic, foolish, headlong escape from the self-revealing intimacy of close relation with God, is told by Francis Thompson in his magnificent poem, "Hound of Heaven."

> I fled Him, down the nights and down the days;
>   I fled Him down the arches of the years;
> I fled Him down the labyrinthine ways
>   Of my own mind; and in the mist of tears
> I hid from Him, and under running laughter.
>   Up vistaed hopes I sped;
>   And shot precipitated,
>   Adown titanic glooms of chasmed fears,
> From those strong Feet that followed, followed after.
>   But with unhurrying chase
>   And unperturbed pace,
>   Deliberate speed, majestic instancy,
>   They beat—and a Voice beat
>   More instant than the Feet—
> All things betray thee, who betrayest Me...
>
> That Voice is round me like a bursting sea:
>   "And is thy earth so marred,
>   Shattered in shard on shard?
>   Lo, all things fly thee, for thou flyest Me!
>   Strange, piteous, futile thing,
> Wherefore should any set thee love apart?...
>   Alack, thou knowest not
> How little worthy of any love thou art!
> Whom wilt thou find to love ignoble thee
>   Save Me, save only Me?
> All which I took from thee I did but take,

> Not for thy harms,
> But just that thou might'st seek it in My arms.
> All which thy child's mistake
> Fancies as lost, I have stored for thee at home:
> Rise, clasp My hand, and come."

God woos us but will not storm our gates to take us by force. God may run before us as Jonah discovered, or we may be followed by God, haunting and hounding. But the gift that makes us human will not be destroyed by God. The communion which God seeks is for our sake. We are the beloved although we merit it little. Indeed, we seem to justify the divine love not at all. And yet we are assured in the understanding of Joseph Smith's Inspired Version of the scriptures that the Creator aches for us, and because of us:

> How is it that thou canst weep? The Lord said unto Enoch, Behold, these thy brethren, they are the workmanship of mine own hands, and I gave unto them their intelligence in the day that I created them. And in the garden of Eden gave I unto man his agency; and unto thy brethren have I said, and also gave commandment, that they should love one another; and that they should choose me their Father. But, behold, they are without affection, and they hate their own blood.—Genesis 7:38-41

We can understand something of heaven's heartache. We, too, cry inside at the separation which our own children sometimes cause. Their struggle becomes our own, and yet we cannot spare them the pain, because that would be robbing them of the freedom which God has given to all humanity. We yearn for them because we love them.

The love of God is all this which we experience and more. It is the well from which our own love is drawn. Christ is our example of God's love; and that love was surrender and gift, rather than conquest and gratification. We can never fully know God's love without surrender. Such a love was born when God sent Christ to the world. In Christ, this love was surrender of himself to the needs of others. It was surrender of personal will to the will of God. Such love, such surrender, brings about oneness with God, communion and covenant.

Those who are most comfortable living in this spirit take joy in being the first to forgive another person. They love others as they love themselves. They cherish the bruised and brokenhearted. They are slow to anger and slower still to judge. Their love is unyielding, and therefore they may be trusted. At the very point where they can control it, they shut off the flow of hatred in the world. The commandment of Jesus becomes their own commandment among themselves: "That ye love one another, as I have loved you" (John 15:12).

The love of God in the hearts of people brings about respect, affection, and restraint toward one another. This is the testimony of IV Nephi 1:17-20:

And it came to pass that there was no contention in the land because of the love of God which dwelt in the hearts of the people. And there were no envyings, nor strifes, nor tumults, nor whoredoms, nor lyings, nor murders, nor any manner of lasciviousness. And surely there could not be a happier people among all the people who had been created by the hand of God.... They were in one, the children of Christ, and heirs to the kingdom of God.

Frederick M. Smith was concerned that the church's evangelism be more than simply baptizing people. He said that evangelism is a matter of getting the love of God into the lives of people, and the lives of people into the kingdom of God. Love is the clue to the kingdom of God and to its tangible realization, Zion: "And the Lord called his people, Zion, because they were of one heart and of one mind, and dwelt in righteousness" (Genesis 7:23).

We show that we live in the love of Christ when we live our lives in service to others. It is when we serve others that we serve God. "Inasmuch as ye have done it unto one of the least of these my brethren, ye have done it unto me" (Matthew 25:41). Or, in the insistent words of King Benjamin, "When ye are in the service of your fellow beings your are only in the service of your God" (Mosiah 1:49).

We have been designed for communion with God. But

we must understand that it is a communion of shared concern and commitment. It is a fellowship made meaningful by sacrificial service mutually shared.

In following the dictates of pride and in declaring independence from God, humanity loses the power to fulfill the purposes of creation and becomes the servant of sin . . .

"What a piece of work is man!" declared the poet. "A little lower than the angels," was the tribute of the psalmist. We may be tempted to glory in our distinction and thereby become subject to the tyranny of pride, the source from which all other sins spring. Pride spoils gratitude and adoration, turning them inward upon self. Pride is the opposite of love, and can easily be described by giving the opposites for the definition of love contained in I Corinthians 13:4-7.

Pride is quick to lose patience, unkind, and invariably possessive. Pride is anxious to impress, conceited, and given to rudeness. Pride keeps account of and finds pleasure in the wrong-doings of others, pursues selfish advantage, and is quick to take offense. Pride bears little of the load, is quick to lay down its burdens, and trembles in anticipation of tomorrow.

It is pride which erodes and corrupts one's sense of community with others. It causes us to trust in our own judgment and to be suspicious of others. Pride is the opposite of the idea of the family of God. There is nothing in the world so silly as selfish pride. When Paul recognized this problem among the saints at Rome, he urged them to overcome their worldly pride:

By the grace given to me I bid every one among you not to think of [yourself] more highly than [you] ought to think, but to think with sober judgment, each according to the measure of faith which God has assigned him. For as in one body we have many members, and all the members do not have the same function, so we, though many, are one body in Christ, and individually members one of another.—Romans 12:3-8 RSV

Pride is arrogant. It is divisive, and busies itself in

setting up barriers to understanding. It causes us to misunderstand one another, and therefore to misunderstand God's intention in each of us as well. Our sin is to have the potential for communion with God, and to simply shrug it off. This sin is original with us, and yet continues into every generation, in our deliberate preference for our own will over against the will of God. The trouble began in the Garden of Eden when Adam said, in effect, "My will, not thine, be done." By disagreeing with God, Adam disagreed with his own freedom. He chose a course of action which eventually required external controls to restrict his freedom. He forsook the essential harmony which was his great potential as a partner in covenant with God. What a sharp contrast this is to another statement made in another garden, "Thy will be done" (Matthew 26:39).

The story of Eden is the drama of the freedom of humankind. It is the great example of the dilemma faced by every one of us: To will as God wills, or not. To trust in God, or to trust in ourselves. To be accountable to God, or to no one. From Adam until now, our temptation has been to consider the earth as our own rather than as God's. We often worship creation rather than the Creator. We adore God's gifts rather than God. We prefer not to be answerable to anyone, except perhaps ourselves.

By going the way of Adam, we deny ourselves the communion for which we were created. Declaring our independence from God, we fall into the delusion that we are sufficient unto ourselves. Therefore, intentionally or unwittingly, we begin to play God. Sooner or later, we come to think of our own self-interest as being the same as the good of all, judging by our own pleasure. We become irritable at the signs of self-will in others, and we try to re-create everything and everyone in our own image.

Esteeming our own wisdom to be supreme, we find it difficult to accept counsel from others who are experienced. We want to chart our own course, but then feel cheated when the fences close in upon us. Finding ourselves bound, we no longer are able to free ourselves from the snare of our own making. This is dramatically portrayed in the use of alcohol and other drugs, which hold up the promise of freedom only to turn against the user with limitations on judgment, will, and capacity for living. Thinking we can use sin to our advantage, we become the servant of sin. Though life persists, we experience death because our humanness is forfeited. The right to be, the right to become, and the right to choose, have fallen as victims. "The wages of sin is death" (Romans 6:23).

By our declaration of independence from God, we lose the power to fulfill the purpose of our creation. This divorcement is our sin—that state of being which leads to thoughts and acts which then lead to further separation—from each other and from God.

whereby persons are divided within themselves and estranged from God and their neighbors.

When we look into the heart of a person, what do we find? Sins as open actions? No, these are past and gone. Only their effects remain. Their memory lingers, no longer sweet. But they are gone, and it is better to let them go. To dwell on them, either in pleasure or remorse, is to give them an idolatrous effect that is unwarranted.

What, then, do we find? An inclination towards sin? Yes, but this too is only secondary. Why is there the inclination to sin? There is something deeper still, down where the light hurts, where we hide inside ourselves, preferring darkness to light (see John 3:19). At the core of our being is self-assertion. Under the Spirit of God, our self-assertion is part of being human. But when it becomes rebellion, the will to be separate from God is sin. "Behold, your sins have come up unto me, and are not pardoned, because you seek to counsel in your own ways. And your hearts are not satisfied. And ye obey not the truth, but have pleasure in unrighteousness" (D. and C. 56:4c, d).

It is the age-old story reenacted in each generation: "They...have broken mine everlasting covenant; they seek not the Lord to establish his righteousness, but every man walketh in his own way, and after the image of his own god" (D. and C. 1:3d, e).

Trapped in allegiance to ourself, we discover that this is indeed our punishment. A scathing, self-inflicted punishment prevails for us as well as for the men of Jerusalem in past time: "Your house is left unto you desolate [forsaken by God]...Ye shall not see me henceforth" (Matthew 23:38-39). Left to oneself: What a judgment! As Paul expressed it in Romans 7:26, "O wretched man that I am! who shall deliver me from the body of this death?" Or, as the poet John Milton phrased it in *Paradise Lost,* book 4:

> Me Miserable! Which way shall I fly?
> Infinite wrath, and infinite despair?
> Which way I fly is hell; myself am hell;
> And in the lowest deep a lower deep
> Still threat'ning to devour me, opens wide,
> To which the hell I suffer seems a heaven.

Having declared independence from God, we find it an easy step to deny the spiritual dimension of life. We find it easy to foster division between the spirit and the flesh. Made for each other, spirit and element when fused and in balance bring a fullness of joy (see D. and C. 90:5e). When they are separate and at enmity, or even in imbalance, frustration is inevitable.

When we are in rebellion against God and at odds with ourself, we can hardly be expected to achieve communion with others. Given to self-justification and self-defense, we find ourselves ready to abuse others in order to establish our own priority. We may view others as objects to be manipulated, their worth being determined in much the same way we consider a pet to be our own, a machine to be used, or a forest as something to exploit. With a spirit of estrangement, and with anxiety (which could have been used creatively), we grow hostile even toward those who are close and loving toward us. When one is overly sensitive to any threat to self-will, it is an easy step to misunderstanding and retaliation. We first find a violence of words, and eventually a violation of dignity and the life of others. Wounded pride is quick to lash out.

This condition, experienced by our ancestors who first came to a knowledge of good and evil, is shared by all who are granted the gift of accountability.

We confess that the condition of pride "experienced by our ancestors" is shared by all who have been granted the gift of accountability. At first glance, this appears to be a negative statement, but it is not. In the first place, it recognizes the innocence of those who are retarded or otherwise incapable of discerning evil from good. For those who are accountable, it humbly recognizes that all share in a heritage of pride and separation, and seem bent on enlarging it for coming generations. To recognize this is to take the first giant stride toward a better condition.

The highways of self-striving open large. But the farther one travels, the more breathlessly confining they become. The couple who for years had lavished their generous income on the luxurious furnishings and decorations of their home finally grew bored with the remodeling and redecorating—only to discover that they had little else in common. Their self-serving efforts had not built lasting ties between them, and their marriage ended in divorce. To find the straight and narrow way instead is infinitely wise. Futility then is no longer inevitable. Bondage need not be our fate. There was deliverance from Egypt, and exodus is more than an event—it is eternal hope and process. Separation need not be our condition. Reunion is possible. It was so in Jesus: He was and is undivided being. He is our peace. He is the reconciliation of flesh and spirit, of person to person, and of humanity and God. He is wholeness, health, and the One who takes us beyond death to life. He breaks our most fearsome bonds. He is our freedom.

Who is there to rescue us? "God alone, through Jesus Christ our Lord!" (Romans 7:25 NEB). The church is to be the body of Christ, with members knit together, a holy community re-creating the will of God in the midst of the world. Let Paul's counsel to the Galatian saints (5:1) be our counsel today. "Stand fast therefore in the liberty wherewith Christ hath made us free, and be not entangled again with the yoke of bondage."

CHAPTER 7
THE GIFT OF SALVATION

We believe that humankind cannot be saved in the kingdom of God except by the grace of the Lord Jesus Christ, who loves them while they are yet in their sins, and who gave his life to reconcile them to God. Through this atonement of the Lord Jesus Christ and by the gift of the Holy Spirit, they receive power to choose God and to commit their lives to God's purposes; thus they are turned from rebellion, healed from sin, renewed in spirit, and transformed after the image of God in righteousness and holiness.

"Jesus saves" is a slogan which we read frequently on automobile bumpers, billboards, and even in neon lights on some churches. Easy slogans are seldom adequate as definitions. However, the entire point of this chapter is that *Jesus does save*.

As we examine some of the deepest thoughts concerning our faith, we find that we are asking ourselves questions about things which are almost incomprehensible to us. What does it mean to be "in sin"? What is the atoning work Jesus did for our sake? How are we to understand a loving God who persistently reaches after us, calling us from self-centeredness to a Christlike life? How is it that by responding to this call, we experience a transforming miracle: sin loses its allure and we "walk not after the flesh, but after the Spirit"? (Romans 8:1)

Most of us resolve these questions emotionally by being baptized. However, we probably never have disposed of the intellectual tensions that these unanswered questions create. We usually come to the church while young in years, having been taught that our separation from God is due to our own sin. We are persuaded that Jesus of Nazareth was the incarnation of God who came to take upon himself the sin which is ours. In doing so he had to yield up his own life in death. And we were taught that this death of Jesus atoned for our sin. We were also taught that if we would believe in the value of God's active mercy in Jesus Christ, and if we would show our gratitude for this saving act by uniting with Christ's Church on earth, then we may lay claim on a hope for life with Christ beyond the grave.

Our claim for eternal life is made possible through the sacraments, performed by authoritative representatives. These ordinances require that we continue in a godly walk and conversation, and obedience to the commandments of Christ. Certain prohibitions are usually laid upon us, and the promise of certain graces is offered, if we are faithful. This summarizes all too briefly the traditional Christian faith. Usually this has been enough to resolve our questions about the need for the church, and we consequently are baptized.

However, it is precisely at this point that unresolved tensions caused by the unanswered questions have an enormous effect upon many devout Christian people. Some of the tensions grow out of an arrogant self-centeredness which takes hold of the church. It causes many members to suppose that God's gracious ministry in Jesus Christ is exclusively available to their own particular religious denomination.

In recent years, the word "ecumenism" has been valued among some Christians, but even this inclusive idea carries with it a sense of special privilege and exclusive company. It, too, separates Christians in general from non-Christians. It speaks largely of the grace of God for all Christians, but is quite undecided about the right of non-Christians to receive the same grace.

Parochialism, which excludes the outsider from the fold, leads us finally to the awful conclusion that another person's faith is false in order for our own to be true. But if one person's chances of getting into heaven are dependent upon another person's not getting there, then the first person has a terrifying vested interest in the second person's damnation. If the Christians' chief "claim to fame" is that they are different from and not like others, and that the others have beliefs which are inferior to their own, while their own beliefs are right and the others' beliefs are wrong, then they may assume that those very differences which separate them are needed indicators of who is saved and who is not saved. This kind of spiritual discrimination assumes a role in judgment which is reserved for God alone. Such arrogance is not appropriate for the one who would be like Christ.

We believe that humankind cannot be saved in the kingdom of God except by the grace of the Lord Jesus Christ...

Protestant Christians, particularly the evangelicals,

are thoroughly convinced of two facts: It is Jesus who saves, and saving is through the church. After the Restoration movement began, many converts from the evangelical churches held the point of view that *this* Restoration church is the "true church."

Because of this strong heritage, Latter Day Saints have always believed that it is Jesus who saves. But emphasis was placed on the fact that there was only one true church in which the saving was being done. The evangelicals, on the other hand, believe that fellowship in the church is essential to salvation, but they put their emphasis on the grace of Jesus Christ making salvation possible.

This could have been only a problem in semantics if the Restoration church had not developed a new dimension in its theology. That dimension was clarified the evening when Joseph Smith, Jr., ordained his father presiding patriarch of the church. Following the ordination, he had a vision in which he saw the celestial kingdom. In his vision, he saw his parents and his brother, Alvin, who had died some twelve years previously. Joseph marveled that Alvin should have "obtained an inheritance in that kingdom [since] he had departed this life before the Lord [had] restored the church and had not been baptized for the remission of sins." Joseph heard the Lord say in the vision,

All who have died without a knowledge of this gospel, who would have received it if they had been permitted to tarry, shall be heirs of the celestial kingdom of God; also all that shall die henceforth without a knowledge of it, who would have received it with all their hearts, shall be heirs of that kingdom.... —*Church History*, volume 2, page 16

It was apparently clearly intended to be an eternal principle.

What this has meant to the church and its understanding of ultimate things is of great importance. Because of it, our insight has been opened to the knowledge that education and salvation are not terminated by death. This led the church to a new interpretation of such passages of scripture as I Peter 3:18-19 and 4:6; and John 5:22.

There is no question for Latter Day Saints about whose grace it is that makes this possible, either before or after the grave. It is by the grace of Jesus Christ that humans are redeemed from sin and saved from death to life in the kingdom of God. The scriptures are clear at this point: "Neither is there salvation in any other; for there is none other name under heaven given among men, whereby we must be saved" (Acts 4:12). "And being made perfect, he became the author of eternal salvation unto all them that obey him..." (Hebrews 5:9).

Nor is there any question about whether or not humans are responsible for the things they do in the flesh. They are! II Corinthians 5:10 and Alma 9:22-26 are explicit at this point. At the same time, there is no question about whether or not the church has a role in the saving process. It does! Ephesians 4:12-13, Acts 20:28, and II Nephi 13:21-32 all make this point clear. There is also no question as to whether or not the people of the church participate in the saving experience. They do! This is particularly so because of their role as witnesses, as illustrated in Matthew 28:18-19, and Acts 2:38-39. Nor is there any question that baptized persons are saved—if they believe in the Lord Jesus Christ and are committed to him, they are! (See John 3:3-5.) These issues are not in question.

The question is whether or not mortal death may rob individuals of their opportunity to hear the gospel, to accept Jesus Christ, and to be the recipient of our Lord's saving and redeeming work. It is this note of hope, justice, mercy, and fairness that the Restoration church sounds forth. Every soul has a chance—not a second chance, but a first chance, whether in this life or the life beyond—to hear the gospel without being denied that opportunity due to national or cultural or racial or religious bias.

In exercising their agency, some may still choose to reject their Lord. That remains a matter between them and the one Judge that is capable of righteous judgment. We should resist the temptation to think God's justice is somehow akin to our own. For our own sake as well as for theirs, we are thankful to our Lord Jesus Christ who relieves us of the responsibility of judging others, while he tenderly and graciously exercises redemptive judgment.

who loves them while they are yet in their sins...

When we try to talk about the love of God, we are almost completely at a loss for words. From time to time we have some inkling of what that love must be like when we experience rich moments of loving regard for our loved ones. There are even times when deep introspection or significant insight permits us to see a glimpse of what Jesus was doing for us at Calvary.

But the love of God for humankind and the shared love that Jesus has for every creature is unfathomable. As the Apostle Paul said, "Eye hath not seen, nor ear heard, neither have entered into the heart of man, the things which God hath prepared for them that love him" (I Corinthians 2:9). We cannot describe adequately what God has *done* for us, let alone what God *feels* for us.

One of the most fruitless exercises by religious people is the setting of dimensional limits on the loving outreach of God. Still we continually establish prohibitions and requirements as if we were saying, "If I were God, this is the way I would see this matter." But our chief problem is that often we go a step further to say, "This *is* the way God sees the matter." Of course, we are not always qualified to interpret the mind and will of God. Does this mean that we are also always *unqualifed* to interpret God's will? No! We have a right to interpret to the best of our ability. In fact, all our religious convictions obligate us to do so. It is part of our stewardship in life to interpret the way God works among us, but we must remember that we are *only* interpreters.

Moreover, the prophetic voices who speak to us from out of the past were persons of unusual spiritual insight who interpreted God to humanity. But they, too, were only interpreters. Jesus alone is able to tell us about God. Jesus alone is able to tell us how God feels about us. Even those who were closest to Jesus had only a partial grasp of what he was telling them about God. They were so lost in the wonder of who and what God is that all they could say by way of description was, "God is love," with the added injunction, "Everyone that loveth is born of God" (I John 4:7-8).

It truly is difficult for us to talk about what it means to be loved by God. It is equally difficult for us to talk about what it means to be a sinner. But the greatest difficulty of all is our lack of words to describe what it is like to be loved while we are yet in our sins. There is no question that sin in general, and our sins in particular, are an affront to God. By our sins, we resist his movement toward us and inflict hurt in his heart. Because of our sins, not only are the angels anguished and the heavens pained, but even God also weeps (See Genesis 7:35, 41, 44, 46).

In spite of our disposition to sin, however, we are still God's children. We are completely and totally dependent upon God for our existence. As it is stated in Mosiah 1:52-53, "That God who has created you, and has kept and preserved you . . . is preserving you from day to day by lending you breath, that you may live and move and do according to your own will, and is even supporting you from one moment to another." We were created by God because of God's own righteous purpose. We were placed in this world as we are, bearing the afflictions in our flesh. God fully recognizes the problems with which we struggle, all the while fully loving us in spite of our unloving and unlovable nature.

It is not as if God created the sin in us, and is therefore responsible for us. God knew we might choose to rebel against the way of righteousnes, and was unswerving in a firm determination to love us anyway. Some people become confused at this point. They do not understand what it means to be mortal, or why God chose mortality as a fitting form for our life here. They become victims of poor theology which tells them that mortality is equal to sin.

Orthodox theology tells us that human conception is sinful: that to be born mortal is to be "conceived in sin." Thus "the Fall" is usually equated with our humanity. Those who accept these doctrines say that the separation of humankind from God's "spiritual house" came about when Adam and Eve sinned in the Garden of Eden. Because their sinning led them to an awareness that they were unclothed, and because this lack of dress led them to humiliation, they attempted to hide. Teachers of orthodoxy reasoned that in their original state of innocence, Adam and Eve had been unaware that the exposure of their physical differences would lead to personal embarrassment. Therefore they concluded that the sin of Adam and Eve was directly connected to the physical characteristics they felt a need to hide.

Such notions are the result of a twisted and disordered theology. The human body is made by God. Its properties for the reproduction of the human race were God-given. Moreover, the capacity for reproduction in humankind is in complete harmony with the patterns of reproduction which God expressed in thousands of other life forms. Nowhere in the scriptures are we told that these other life forms are sinful because they also reproduce. Rather, the scriptures teach us that the earth answers the ends of its creation, and animal life is incapable of sin.

It is a human being who sins, and this is because of a conflict of will. Sin is not genetic. It is rooted in human will which stands in opposition to the divine will. To be without affection, to show hate or disrespect for one another is to sin. We were given commandment that we should love one another, and that we should choose God as our Father (see Genesis 7:40-41). When we do not love one another, and when we do not choose God and follow the direction of the Holy Spirit, we are in sin. Still God does not abandon us. While we are yet in our sins, while we continue to be selfish, unloving, and unyielding, God encircles us with divine love.

and who gave his life to reconcile them to God.

The Apostle Paul wrote the Ephesian saints about estrangement of the soul which separates us from one another and from God. A modern English translation by J. B. Phillips (Revised Student Edition, 4th printing, 1980) contains the same understanding as the Inspired Version, and reads as follows:

But now, in Christ Jesus, you who were once far off are brought near through the shedding of Christ's blood. For Christ is our living peace. He has made us both one by breaking down the barrier and enmity which lay between us. By his sacrifice he removed the hostility of the Law, with all its commandments and rules, and made in himself out of the two, Jew and Gentile, one new man, thus producing peace. For he reconciled both to God by the sacrifice of one body on the cross, and by his act killed the enmity between them. Then he came and brought the good news of peace to you who were far from God and to us who were near. And it is through him that both of us now can approach the Father in the one Spirit.—Ephesians 2:13-18

The true followers of Christ have borne testimony to the fact that "God is in Christ, reconciling the world unto himself" (II Corinthians 5:19). The mystery of this reconciling power reaches beyond our comprehension. We do, however, know of his transforming presence in the lives of his disciples. From Mary Magdalene to Paul to us, people who have been at war within themselves, in rebellion against God, and both hating and exploiting their neighbors, have suddenly become new persons. They have sensed the grace of God through the Lord Jesus Christ, and have yielded their lives to him. Then, being renewed by the Holy Spirit, they have been able to do what the Law commanded. They have learned to love God with all their hearts, and their neighbors as themselves. They had never been able to do that previously. Where once they rationalized and justified their own sin and inadequacy, under the reconciling power of God, they found their lives were changed. Now they could say in glad response, "We have been changed from death unto life."

Our own conversion is not all that different from the Ephesians'. The Holy Spirit reached into our life when we are really "afar off" from God, and unconcerned about our neighbors, if not actually estranged from them. We know how willful lust caused us to waste our God-given substance, accepting husks for a wage. Finally, like a prodigal, we come to ourself. At such a time, we come to the foot of the Cross to perceive the grace of God, and we see how much God loves us in spite of our sin, that we may be lifted out of it and be reconciled. Thus the kingdom of God comes to us on earth. In the person of the Son, God came in the flesh that we might be healed and united in peace.

Not only has God broken down the barriers that separate us from each other and from God, but God has moved in Christ to bring all things into harmony. This is a mystery which is represented in the symbol of the millennial reign, so beautifully illustrated in our church seal. Paul was speaking of this harmony when he wrote in Colossians 1:19-20: "For it pleased the Father that in [Christ] should all fullness dwell; and, having made peace through the blood of his cross, by him to reconcile all things unto himself; by him, I say, whether they be things in earth, or things in heaven."

We can never really find peace within ourself or with our neighbors or with the universe until we are reconciled to God. The power for such reconciliation is resident in Jesus Christ who is our mediator, the Word made flesh, who dwelt among us full of grace and truth.

Through this atonement of the Lord Jesus Christ and by the gift of the Holy Spirit, they receive power to

choose God and to commit their lives to God's purposes...

We are the children of God. We were created by divine power and called into existence to fulfill God's loving intention. It may seem that God's work of creation was flawed because we struggle for mastery over ourselves. Instead it is a tribute to his trust that he creates us free to make full and responsible choice. We are also sinners. We are disposed to selfish bigotry, jealous hatred, and political opportunism. We are even content to engage in legalized murder because we are "without affection." Even in this condition, God will not abandon us. Rather God moves forth freely into the same humanity in which we are placed. There our Lord exercises unique moral authority over us, offering a unique ministry of redemption toward us, and demonstrating unique mastery over the powers of evil.

God participates deeply in our own history. Within it, we see God exhibiting bravery, a sense of humor, severity, and also tenderness. The spiteful and ridiculous charge that Jesus was gluttonous and a wine bibber (see Matthew 11:20) is only additional testimony that in all things Jesus was like his brethren. He not only ate and drank but knew hunger and thirst and weariness as well. To use Pilate's words, we cannot "behold the man" without seeing the Jesus whom God sent as poor, born in a stable, working as we work, journeying as we travel, being tempted as we also are tempted, being able to sin and perhaps even wanting to do so, nevertheless resisting sin altogether.

We see God coming into our life and being touched with a feeling for our infirmities. Jesus is able to weep over our woes, but is not ashamed to call us friends. He is able to bear on his heart the burden of our shame and sins, yet able to love us always. He was "a man of sorrows and acquainted with grief" who without a trace of self-pity went deliberately to Jerusalem to die. In so doing, Jesus left a legacy for every one of us. The hope of eternal life, and the realization that we move not only from life to death but from death into life also, are the gifts which he brings to us. This is confirmed by the Resurrection and by the continuing presence of the Holy Ghost. It is once again God, as Holy Ghost, who speaks to our hearts, telling us that our belief is not some fantastic tune whistled by fanatics who attempt to keep their courage up. By the Holy Spirit we are convinced that our belief is indeed the central fact both of history and of our times. J. S. Whale, in *Christian Doctrine* (p. 104), stated:

Jesus has the decisive place in man's ageless relationship with God. He is what God means by "man": He is what man means by "God." His sinless perfection is a miracle, in the sense that history is ransacked in vain for another fact like it. Wherever men have been met by him, either in the pages of the New Testament or in the long story of his true followers, penitence, the vision of God and a new spiritual life have been one and the same experience. In the presence of this man, men do not doubt that they are in the presence of [one who is] ultimate and eternal. We do not get away from the heartbreaking and lifegiving certainty that his judgments and his forgiveness are the judgment and mercy of God. To rebel against this prince of human life is the very meaning and measure of sin; the grace of our Lord Jesus Christ is the amazing grace of God; to doubt Christ's promises is to doubt God himself and to be without hope in the world. In him the promises of God are either yea and amen, or there is no everlasting yea, and the long story of human faith and worship is a tragic delusion. Jesus Christ is such that if he is not the destined climax of human faith, he is necessarily the very nadir of human despair.

We have thus been confronted in our human history by the revelation of God in Christ, reconciling the world unto himself. Jesus Christ is nothing less than God's redeeming gift of God's own self, atoning for our sin and declaring us no longer outlaw. By the grace of God, we are both in law and in life. Through the gracious life of God's promised presence, life becomes for us a living reality.

thus are they turned from rebellion, healed from sin, renewed in spirit, and transformed after the image of God in righteousness and holiness.

As promised in John 14:16-17, the loving and redeeming work of God is continued among us by the Holy Spirit. Outside the church, he strives to bring people to God. Inside the church, he strives to bring God's life to them. It is the work of the Holy Spirit to reveal God to us and to draw us to God. Inside the church the Spirit provides additional ministry to lead us to the kingdom of God. In that life in God's kingdom, rebellious persons cease their rebellion. Sin no longer leavens the lives of the children of God. The Spirit renews and transforms them, and they become God-like with righteousness and holiness among them.

Sadly, not all within the church participate in the life of the kingdom of God. Nevertheless, it is the work of the church to bring that heavenly life into existence on earth. This was the burden Jesus prayed that the people of the church would feel: "Thy kingdom come. Thy will be done on earth, as it is done in heaven" (Matthew 6:11). In the Inspired Version of Revelation 12:7, we note the woman who "was the church of God, who [being] delivered of her pains...brought forth the kingdom of our God and his Christ." Not all of the cells in the woman's body made up the child of which she was delivered. Similarly, not all of the souls within the church exhibit the life of the kingdom of God.

Nonetheless, it is from the body of the church that human souls find regeneration and refinement, and are ultimately sent back out of the body into the world, filled with the life of God. The Holy Spirit seeks to confront us with the gospel—the good news of God's gracious act in Jesus Christ. In that confrontation, we are given both the opportunity and the power to choose God and to commit our lives to him. The testimony of the church is that as we do commit our lives to God, the world is never again the same.

The gift of God is a grace that will not let us alone, even in our sin. Indeed, we are made captive by the love of God which, by the power of the Holy Spirit, provides our health-sustaining energy. We are turned from rebellion; we are healed from sin; we are renewed by the Spirit. And we are transformed after the image of God in holiness.

CHAPTER 8
NEW LIFE IN CHRIST

We believe that all are called to have faith in God and to follow Jesus Christ as Lord, worshiping the Father in his name. In this life those who hear the gospel and repent should commit their lives to Christ in baptism by immersion in water and the laying on of hands. Through living by these principles they participate in God's promise of forgiveness, reconciliation and eternal life.

We believe that all are called to have faith in God and to follow Jesus Christ as Lord...

We all tend to focus the direction of our life and all of the resources which we possess around some central conviction. Our activities and our concerns grow out of this conviction about life. We may not even be aware that we are doing this. Nonetheless, this basic conviction is there. It is our primary source of guidance and direction. For some of us, it may be the power of reason. For others, it is a self-centered focus. Still others may concern themselves with a collection of material things. For others, the major focus of life would be human progress. Still others, easily manipulated and pushed around, may only act out of expediency. Whatever that central image of life is, it shapes the nature of our expectations. It directs our loyalties. It dictates how we will use our powers. Very likely the source of our conviction has been a combination of many experiences, but it becomes the overriding influence in our life.

Such an orientation to life, rooted as it is in some conviction about life's meaning, is called faith. Faith may be expressed in a religion, or it may be some system, such as communism. Here is how this faith works. If we were to believe in the active presence of departed ancestors, then we would have to reckon with them daily. Our activities would be determined and our character would be fashioned by such a belief. If you accept the convictions which sustain communism, you will naturally find that the economic and social principles of the communistic system have meaning and value for you. You would consequently yield your life in obedience to that system and your own personality would be shaped by it.

The scriptures tell us that "you are that you might have joy." This is the joy of relationship with the Eternal, not some fickle pleasure of momentary satisfaction. Such a joy is found in the good news about God in Jesus Christ. Christ is God in our midst. It is for this reason that

Jesus was called "Immanuel," meaning "God with us." He is the revelation of ultimate truth. In him we see the nature of God, the nature and purpose of the universe, the nature of humankind, and the end toward which all history moves. Everything that exists is seen as God's sacramental creation. And when everything is directed toward its divinely intended purpose, it is good. By faith in Christ, we are not only made new, but we sense that we are at work with God in a sacred universe, accomplishing God's eternal purposes.

All of us are called to this transformed life. When Jesus walked the shores of Galilee, he called disciples to follow him. However, his call was not limited to a few men who lived at a distant point in history. It was a call to all humanity to commit themselves to a life of faith and discipleship. Consequently, John opened his testimony by affirming that "as many as received him, to them gave he power to become the sons of God; only to them who believe on his name" (John 1:12).

To center our life on anyone or anything else is to pervert God's gift to us. It is a misuse of a great potential. We would be taking a God-given inclination toward divine purposes and relationships, and using our lives in ways that would only bring frustration. The headlines of history recount the stories of persons who have gained fame, fortune, power, and all else they sought after, but who ended their life in frustration and often suicide, because they used their gifted lives in godless and self-centered ways. Through faith in God there is fulfillment. This faith is trust in God revealed through Jesus Christ. The God we meet in Christ is completely trustworthy. Such a Lord is worthy of our deepest confidence. In Jesus, we come to know that God is not only transcendent, but is the personal God of history—who lives, loves, and reveals.

To accept Jesus as the Lord of life, to make Christ the final point of reference for every phase of our life, is faith in action, supporting our discipleship. This faith is more than passive trust. It is "toward God." It is the dynamic that causes us to trust God completely, to dare the unknown in order to achieve God's purposes in ourselves and in society.

worshiping the Father in his name.

To have faith in God is to worship God. We cannot have faith in God without trust, and an awareness of God's greatness and goodness. Such an evaluation of who and what God is constitutes genuine worship, for worship litterally means "worth-ship." To worship is to rejoice in remembrance of God's redemptive efforts on our behalf. The only reason we know God is because of the divine revelation in the mighty saving acts of history: Creation, Exodus, Covenant, Restoration, and finally or ultimately Incarnation. One of the functions of worship is remembering and celebrating these wondrous acts of power and goodness which God has shown toward us.

Worship leads us to communion, and is communion. It is the greatest need in our life. We are so created that we sense a need for relationships beyond ourselves. Yet we find difficulty in sensing the presence of God. This difficulty is resolved in Christ who said to Philip, "He that hath seen me hath seen the Father" (John 14:9). It is possible for us to see God through one who "took upon him the form of a servant, and was made in the likeness of men" (Philippians 2:7). Our celebration and remembering are shaped by the way we have come to know God in Christ.

Communion with God is the only way we can achieve eternal life. The scriptures say that we are "of the earth earthy." This means that we are creatures who are earthbound. We have finite natures making it impossible for us to know the infinite—unless we are transformed by a power from the Infinite. But the infinite is concerned with our rising above our earthiness. For God has said, "This is my work and my glory, to bring to pass the immortality, and eternal life of man" (D. and C. 22:23b). If this is to occur, we must worship God, experience God's presence and God's transforming love. Through worship we partake of God's nature and become more God-like. The more we have in common with God in personality and character, the more satisfying will be our communion with God. This has certainly been true in our relationships with our associates from day to day. We have every reason to believe that this principle applies also to our relationships with God.

In this life those who hear the gospel and repent...

In this life we have ample opportunity to develop a close relationship with God. This means that we also have excellent opportunity for developing a life filled with eternal qualities. Both the relationship and the qualities have been clearly revealed in Jesus Christ. This is good news, the best news we have ever heard! The amazing thing about this good news is that the messenger was also the message. Jesus not only spoke to us about a quality of life which is eternal, but he also demonstrated it. He was the word made flesh who dwelt among us (see John 1:14). He preached the gospel of the kingdom and was the prime revelation of it.

The gospel was proclaimed and enacted by Jesus in all of Galilee. He authenticated his message at Calvary on a certain dark Friday, and he emblazoned its validity across the volumes of human history on the first Easter morning. Jesus' disciples were commissioned to carry the good news far and wide, that the entire world might hear, believe, and be transformed. Of course, many people would not be reached with the gospel. There are always more to be reached than there are reachers, and some who should be reaching fail to exert themselves.

What happens to those who die without hearing the gospel? They are not to be condemned for someone else's lack of bearing testimony. Each is accountable for what each has received. God who sent the Son to save sinners, rescues each of us in God's own way and time. There is no need for prayers and ordinances by the living on behalf of the dead. The testimony of the Book of Mormon is clear at this point, and we need have no fear in their regard (see II Nephi 6:51-56; Mosiah 1:107; Moroni 8:12-27).

We are all without knowledge of the law and the testimony. Even those of us who may know more than some of the rest of us in truth perceive very little of the ways of God. God seeks us all, loving us for our need, even wooing, winning and forgiving us.

We need to hear the gospel. One of the reasons why we were created was that we might hear the gospel. Without the divine in our human lives, we are left restless, unfulfilled, at odds with ourselves and each other.

We need to hear and repent. Repentance is the adjustment of our will to the will of God. This requires forsaking lesser and unworthy values for that which God values. It requires an honest appraisal of ourselves in comparison with the vision of human holiness which we see in Christ. In such a moment of worship, when Isaiah made the comparison, he said, "Woe is me,...I am undone...I am a man of unclean lips, and I dwell in the midst of a people of unclean lips" (Isaiah 6:5). Such an evaluation of himself led him to evaluate his society as well. This awareness, created by worship, led to a changed life. He experienced a purging or cleansing so that he became free from the weight of his sin and disorientation. He became free to respond to the call of God which he then could perceive clearly.

We need to yield ourselves to Jesus Christ. We suffer from frustration and lack of purpose. Aimlessness, insecurity, and feelings of unworthiness drive us to desperation. We need the sense of moving with God in achieving God's purposes. This thrust to life contrasts sharply with the aimless aloneness of self-centered persons apart from God. By the enlightenment of Christ's Spirit, there is new life. This means new insight into the purpose of life, and an alliance with Christ in helping to bring to pass that purpose. It is a sense of being his—of belonging. There is new direction to life and new meaning. Such response to God's gift of forgiveness is repentance, a process which takes a lifetime.

It is with limited vision only that we first see Christ as our Savior, even though it brings repentance to us. Because it is limited, it is essential that we have continued experience with Christ. We need to see the vision in greater depth. We know that our ability to appreciate and enjoy the fine arts rises as our understanding of them grows. So it is also with our ability to enjoy the presence of Christ.

Repentance is not a one-time vision and a one-time response. It is a constant encounter and an enlarging response. At the first meeting with Christ, we may not experience a complete redirection of life. At that point, we may not even have the capacity for a complete response. But repentance is a process. As the light of Christ shines more brightly in our soul, we are enabled to see ourselves more clearly as we are and as we may become. There must be continuous adjustment to this new understanding of ourself and our relationship to the Lord. If we cease to have this revelatory experience and no longer allow repentance to work in our soul, we place ourself in a precarious spiritual state.

should commit their lives to Christ in baptism by immersion in water...

Repentance logically leads to commitment. Repentance is never simply the giving up of bad habits and practices. Instead it is yielding ourselves to the Lord Jesus Christ and becoming immersed in his ways. It is being raised from the old, frustrated way of life into a newness that leads us to sense our opportunity and to dare to grasp it. In order to grow, to find fulfillment, to become, it is necessary for us to be involved in a cause that is greater than we are.

There is an ordinance which symbolizes our commitment to Christ. This sacrament establishes for us a covenant with him. It depicts our surrender to Christ, and leads us to what we call "rebirth." It brings about a newness in our life. We see with new eyes, and we experience a new heartbeat. As Paul said in II Corinthians 5:17, "If any man live in Christ, he is a new creature; old things are passed away; behold, all things are become new." He added, for the benefit of the Roman saints, "We are buried with him by baptism into death; that like as Christ was raised up from the dead by the glory of the Father, even so we also should walk in newness of life" (Romans 6:4). The sacrament of baptism is by immersion in water.

The form of baptism is so dramatic and total as to remain forever in our memory as a new beginning—birth into a new life. In the opening verses of the third chapter of John, the writer of the Gospel describes how Jesus shared this concept with a prominent citizen of the day. It is a physical act symbolizing spiritual involvement, and it prepares us to receive the ministry of the Holy Spirit.

The rite itself is conducted by one who is called of God as a minister. This minister then stands as God's visible representative, so that in our baptism we may surrender ourself to God through this symbolic representative. When God's servant then draws us forth from the waters of baptism, it symbolizes God's drawing the newborn life forth in rebirth. The action of the sacrament is memorable, for we literally give ourselves into the hands of the minister. Being fully aware that the minister is God's servant, we fulfill the symbolism of "being in the hands of God."

Baptism is for the remission of sins (see Mark 1:3, Luke 3:3). Water is a universally known cleansing agent. Baptism in water symbolizes a washing away of sins. In Acts 22:16, Paul tells how Ananias asked him what he was waiting for, commanding him to arise and to be baptized, and thereby wash away his sins. Of course, he did not mean that the water would literally wash away his sins in a physical sense. The important thing is what the washing represents. It is intended to prepare our spirit for the "washing of regeneration" by the Holy Spirit which is described in Titus 3:5. We need to prepare to receive the ministry of the Holy Spirit. God as represented by the Holy Spirit would in no way intrude into our spirit, but has promised to cleanse us when we are receptive. This is an extremely important phase of our encounter with Christ our Savior.

Sociologists, psychologists, and criminologists tell us that guilt is one of the greatest of human problems. Both confirmed criminals and good people suffer from it. The criminal is driven deeper into crime by the overpowering sense of guilt which blocks out any relief. Good people fall far short of the realization of their potential because they are burdened with guilt from which there seems to be no release. Even though we may have no strong consciousness of the problem, yet it weighs heavily upon us like the proverbial millstone. We need to see the vision of the loving Lord who forgives sin and cleanses us from guilt. At critical times in Jesus' ministry, he declared, "Thy sins are forgiven—go, and sin no more" (Matthew 9:2). What blessed freedom! Baptism prepares the human spirit to accept forgiveness.

Surrender and commitment in baptism must be a continuing experience. Baptism therefore is a principle as well as an act. Through it we learn how to surrender ourselves daily in faithful obedience to the direction of the Holy Spirit. The Spirit ministers in the continuing experience of baptism: surrender, cleansing, and commitment. The Spirit does this by reminding us of the love of the crucified and resurrected Christ. It is of vital importance that baptism be a lifetime ministry. In the same way that our understanding grows, so also may our commitment. In this way our original experience of baptism may become ever more meaningful, rather than fading with the passage of time. Our commitment deepens as our transformation becomes more complete.

Giving ourself to God is a long-term process. In momentary enthusiasm we may give in to many different things, but only as a result of maturity do we become completely oriented to a course of action. We also become completely committed to the Lord as we mature in understanding and experience. Peter had to be reminded of this when he rather hastily said, "Yea, Lord, thou knowest that I love thee" (John 21:15-17). As time went on, it is likely that Peter more fully understood the Lord's questioning his depth of commitment at that time. Peter had thought he was stable, but in the Garden of Gethsemane, he slept. Then he was ready to defend the Lord with a sword. And then again, a short time later, he was ready to deny that he knew him. Even after Jesus' resurrection, Peter said, "I go a fishing" (John 21:3). It was at the end of this fishing trip that the Lord asked him, "Simon, son of Jonas, lovest thou me more than these?" (John 21:15). Peter must have remembered often these conversations and pondered the shallowness of his commitment.

Closely related to baptism in continuing ministry is the sacrament of the Lord's Supper. It follows baptism and has a similar purpose—that of remembering the covenant with Christ and expanding our vision of him (see D. and C. 17:18-23). This sacrament is extremely significant as we continue to surrender ourselves to Christ, and to covenant with him.

Beyond this, the sacrament of the Lord's Supper stands on its own in ministry to our soul. We eat the bread and drink the wine "in remembrance" (see I Corinthians 11:23-26). We do not simply have sentimental thoughts about an awesome moment of our history. Rather, we meditate upon the way divine love has worked atonement in us. And by this means we are prepared for the ministry of the Holy Spirit. As we become conscious of

God's love the vision grows brighter, and we know the supreme joy of the divine presence. There is renewal and recommitment—knowledge of forgiveness—and life moves on to a higher level.

Once again the officiating minister stands as God's representative in the stead of Christ, to signify our continuing surrender. The minister leads the people in partaking of the emblems of God's love, going forth to serve the bread and the wine among them even as they are to go forth to serve others in the world.

and the laying on of hands.

Baptism is not complete upon emerging from the water any more than life is complete at the moment of birth. Commitments which are made are not always kept. Even after the great experience of immersion in water and being raised to "walk in newness of life" (Romans 6:4), we still encounter many pitfalls. We need wisdom and strength beyond our own in order to avoid them or to cross safely over them. The ordinance of the laying on of hands comes to us as a remarkable sequel to immersion in water.

It is recorded that Philip went to Samaria and preached to the Samaritans with great success. After many were baptized, the apostles Peter and John came and laid "their hands on them, and they received the Holy Ghost" (Acts 8:17). As in baptism of water, another symbolic action helps to bring about a needful result. Hands may express tenderness and strength, love and power. In the laying on of hands, the hands of a trusted servant of God placed upon the head in prayer bring assurance and trust. We call this confirmation. Our commitment is matched by the gift of the Holy Spirit. Both parties to the covenant have acted. By the laying on of hands, the Holy Spirit is given as an "abiding Comforter" (John 14:16). This Comforter is the living presence of the Savior and ministers the needed strength, wisdom, and love to help us become the person God intends.

In the sacrament of confirmation, there is not only prayer for the gift of the Holy Spirit, but the giving of membership in the church. The church is a body of believers who through their faith in Christ strengthen one another. This body is made alive by the Spirit of the living Christ. The communion of those made more loving and lovable by the Holy Spirit is indeed a thing of beauty. But it is more than joy and beauty. It is a common bond that perpetuates the vision of the Master and the covenant with him.

Since ministers who are recognized as servants of God are the ones that confer the gift, it can be as if the Lord himself makes us a member of his body. By this means we are brought into the fellowship of others who are already confirmed. By the warmth of the human hand and the authority of the minister which we sense, as new members we are helped to feel the presence of God. We are born into the family of God. We are made more available to the promises of God.

Through living by these principles they participate in God's promise of forgiveness, reconciliation and eternal life.

In 1947, in a revelation received by the prophet of the church (D. and C. 140:5d), the Lord said, "My word shall not fail, neither will my promises." In his Son, God has promised forgiveness, reconciliation, and eternal life. This is the most beautiful fact of history. It is beautiful because of the love made known: God recognizes our need and provides for the fulfillment of that need. God provides forgiveness, the means of reconciliation and the capacity to be reconciled. God also supplies the knowledge of eternal life with a potential to appreciate it.

Forgiveness, including the knowledge of it, is essential to life. Further, it is important that *we* be reconciled to God, and *our ways* to God's ways. This can come about only through the initiative taken by God in the Son, and through the ministry of the Holy Spirit in our life.

The Apostle Paul said, "The wages of sin is death" (Romans 6:23). That is what sin does in human life. It is deadly. It destroys because it is a negative force in personality development. It is rebellion against God and separation from God, the source of our life. The hold of sin upon us is such that we cannot free ourself from its grasp. Therefore God has taken the initiative to do for us what we cannot do for ourself. Inasmuch as God has taken this initiative to reconcile us, our need is simply to respond. Even the response is made possible by sensing the love of God in the Atonement. By God's grace, we feel the love of God. This awareness creates the opportunity for the Holy Spirit to illumine our mind. We then can begin to see our own need, and the possibility of a right relationship with God. From this comes our dissatisfaction with ourself, and our desire to be like the Savior. It is a transforming experience—by the power of the Holy Spirit the old self is made new. This process of reconciliation is made possible by the ministry of baptism and the laying on of hands as these principles continue to be experienced in our life.

This is the surrender which is so necessary. We yield ourself to our Lord because we know the love of God for us personally. We thus may claim the marvelous gift of divine forgiveness. While this does not make us sinless nor even free from all of the results of sin, it does free us from the burden of guilt: it allows us to respond wholeheartedly to the direction of the Holy Spirit. The knowledge of sin forgiven can strengthen our spirits. As Paul stated it in Romans 8:28, "We *know* that all things work together for good to them that love God."

Eternal life is, as Jesus said, "that they might know thee the only true God, and Jesus Christ, whom thou hast sent" (John 17:3). Life eternal is partaking of the nature of Jesus Christ, becoming more like him. This transformation of life comes only through the experience of forgiveness made possible by feeling the love of Christ and surrendering to him. The person who is reconciled and committed lives in faithful obedience to the will of God. That obedience develops an eternal quality of life. This is the promise of God in Jesus Christ.

CHAPTER 9
THE CHURCH

We believe that the church was established by Jesus Christ. In its larger sense it encompasses those both living and dead, who, moved by the Spirit of God, acknowledge Jesus as Lord. In its corporate sense, it is the community of those who have covenanted with Christ. As the body of Christ through which the word of God is tangibly expressed on earth, the church seeks to discern the will of God and to surrender itself in worship and service. It is enlightened, sustained, and renewed by the Holy Spirit. It is to bring the good news of God's love to all people, reconciling them to God through faith in Jesus Christ. The church administers the ordinances through which the covenant is established, cares for all within its communion, ministers to the needy, wages war on evil, and strives for the kingdom of God.

We believe that the church was established by Jesus Christ.

This affirmation has often been made by members of the Reorganized Church of Jesus Christ of Latter Day Saints. This is because we believe it so deeply. We believe that the church was established by Jesus Christ. Our church was born in a period of history when intense controversy divided the denominations over the nature of the "true" Church of Christ. This was not a new concern. It was openly debated in the early days of the Reformation. Several groups, quite independent of one another, believed that both Luther and Calvin had really gone only part of the way in reestablishing the "true" church. Many of these united under the umbrella of the Anabaptist movement. In addition to theological differences, they also felt that historical developments had caused the church to apostatize. As John Dillenberger and Claude Welch have noted in their book, *Protestant Christianity Interpreted Through Its Developments* (page 64),

> For many Anabaptists, the adoption of Christianity as the religion of the empire (under Constantine) marked the "fall" of the church. Belonging to the church became no longer a matter of decision but of birth and social destiny. The vitality and very essence of the church as a voluntary association was destroyed. There were others who dated the fall of the church with the Council of Nicaea in 325. This represented the crystalization of trinitarian thought, precipitated by the intrigues of the powerful Roman empire and expressed through the speculation of philosophers. For others, it was the enforcement of infant baptism in 407 (with penalty for failure to comply).
>
> Common to the different theories of the fall of the church was the contention that the true nature of the church as a voluntary disciplined community of saints had been abandoned. To the Anabaptists, Luther and Calvin were not sufficiently clear exactly at this point. The reformers' hopes of community or territorial churches, enforced through the arms of the state, were themselves a part of the pattern which characterized a fallen church.

This concern was not alone the concern of Anabaptists. The Puritans of a later date also insisted that they were returning to the church as it was originally organized by Christ. So it was with the Baptists and the Campbellites. All of these groups used the Bible as a kind of source book of information to guide them to the untainted model of the original primitive Christian church.

It is not surprising then that the boy Joseph Smith, in the midst of this kind of controversy, should be concerned about several questions. According to his own testimony as published in *The History of the Reorganized Church of Jesus Christ of Latter Day Saints* (volume 1, page 8), he asked these questions: "Who of all these parties are right? Or are they all wrong together? If any of them be right, which is it, and how shall I know it?" From this beginning there developed an intense desire on the part of Latter Day Saints to settle for nothing less than the church established by Jesus Christ and recognized by him as authoritative. Consequently, they have affirmed from the beginning that if it is truly the Church of Jesus Christ, it must be established by him. The conviction that God moved in the founding experiences of the Latter Day Saint movement has given to the church a vital and dynamic testimony. This testimony points to (1) the active involvement of God in the world, and (2) the conviction that the church is of divine origin and is important to God as well as to humankind. The persecution which the Restoration church received from other Christian denominations only served to reaffirm their confictions. They believed that the church had been restored by the hand of God, and many of them were willing to sacrifice property, home, and even life itself for the cause of the Restoration.

Because of the nature of the coming forth of the Restoration movement, several vital questions rise to the surface. Among them are the following:
1. In what sense did Christ establish the first-century Christian Church?
2. What is the meaning of apostasy, and in what ways could the church through apostasy lose authority?

3. What is involved in "restoration," and in what sense does restoration make the church the "true" church of Jesus Christ?

Let's look at each of these questions in turn.

1. We do indeed believe that Christ established the first-century Christian Church. This does not mean that Jesus fully organized and structured the church during the three years or so of his ministry here upon earth. Indeed, it is clear that he did not. However, he did draw a band of disciples around him, and did establish a fellowship in which there was both form and organization. He called the twelve apostles and placed them in a position of authority after having spent a night alone in prayer (see Luke 6:12-13). Luke also tells us (10:1) that Jesus appointed "other seventy" and sent them out "into every city and place where he himself would come." He instructed his disciples and commissioned them to "teach all nations, baptizing them in the name of the Father, and of the Son, and of the Holy Ghost; teaching them to observe all things whatsoever I have commanded you" (Matthew 28:18-19). But for the most part, the four Gospels record very little that Jesus said about the church. For this reason there are some who deny that Jesus intended to establish anything like a church. But it has been noted that this would be a strange situation indeed, for it would mean that all Christ's closest followers totally misunderstood his intention. An inevitable fruit of Christ's ministry was the foundation of the church.

Beyond the simple and sketchy organization which Jesus left among his disciples, however, there was a much more important element. That important element was the direction of the Holy Spirit. It was the experience of the early disciples that Christ continued to be with them by the power of the Holy Ghost in their midst. Some students of the scriptures have even gone so far as to believe that the church was really born on the day of Pentecost. In a sense this is true, for had the presence of Christ not continued with the disciples in the person of the Comforter, it would be hard to see how the church could have continued to take form. As Harold Schneebeck, Jr., pointed out in his book, *The Body of Christ* (page 14), the fellowship of the disciples undoubtedly would have died and been dissolved had it not been that they found Jesus' presence continued in the fellowship through the Holy Spirit, even after he had physically been taken out of their midst.

Christ established the church both through his physical presence and later through the Holy Spirit. In this manner he directed and empowered his disciples to continue the work of ordering and organization. As the church grew, its organization and ministries necessarily became more complex to meet the needs of the people. Acts 6:1-6 is an illustration of how this operated. As the church grew in size and became difficult to administer, the Greek churches thought they were being discriminated against in favor of the Hebrew churches: their widows seemed to be neglected in the church's usual charitable care. Apparently the problem was one that had to do with insufficient numbers of qualified ministers, because the Twelve called the church into conference, and said, "It is not reason that we should leave the word of God, and serve tables. Wherefore, brethren, look ye out among you seven men of honest report, full of the Holy Ghost and wisdom, whom we may appoint over this business." Apparently the conference was pleased with this action and chose seven ministers, upon whom the apostles laid their hands to set them apart to their ministry. It is clear that the early church felt the commission given by the Lord Jesus Christ included responsibility for building and expanding the church's organization according to the needs of the time and place. It is also clear that the security of the church was not so much seen in its structure as in its divine leadership. It would be the function of the Holy Spirit that would hold them to the divine purpose in them.

2. The second question is concerned with the meaning

of apostasy, and the ways the church may lose its authority. From the outset we need to recognize that this is not a black-and-white issue. It is not possible for us to say that one person or group is in apostasy and another is not. The basic problem of all of us is that apostasy is ever present with us. In the early days, Paul had to caution against "grievous wolves" that would not spare the flock (see Acts 20:29). He also rebuked the teachers who perverted the gospel of Christ among the Galatian saints (see Galatians 1:6-9). What was true of that first generation in the church has been true of every generation since. Every period of time has its wolves and its perversions. Because of the sin within us, we are constantly in danger of bending the gospel to serve our own purposes rather than God's. We tend to use the power and structure of the church to serve our own selfish ends. We are seldom courageous enough to fully live by the dynamic Spirit and presence of Christ. The very flexibility and adaptability of the early Christian Church is lost to us if we tend to freeze its organization and structure in what we consider to be an ideal, or divine, or "revealed," or traditional form. At that point we may be in danger of what the scriptures call "a form of godliness, but denying the power thereof" (II Timothy 3:5). Authority is lost by a person or an organization representing Christ when they become involved in selfish and ungodly living. Joseph Smith once wrote of priesthood:

Because their hearts are set upon the things of the world and are aspiring to the honors of men; they do not learn the lesson that the rights, of the priesthood, are inseparably connected with the powers of heaven; and that the powers of heaven cannot be controlled nor handled, only upon the principles of righteousness, that they may be confered upon us, it is true, but when we undertake to cover our sins, to gratify our pride, vain ambition, or to exercise dominion or compulsion over the souls of the children of men, in any degree of unrighteousness; behold the heavens withdraw themselves, the Spirit of the Lord is grieved, then amen to the priesthood, or to [their] authority.—*Times and Seasons*, volume 1, pp. 131-132

The call of God and its accompanying authority is given

to everyone, not simply to the priesthood. In an early revelation to the church (D. and C. 4:1c) it is stated in this way: "If ye have desires to serve God, ye are called to the work." Fifty-eight years later, Joseph Smith III phrased it this way (D. and C. 119:8): "All are called according to the gifts of God unto them."

As Roy A. Cheville illustrated in his book, *Did the Light Go Out* (page 195), during the Middle Ages the church drifted into such a degree of apostasy that its teaching and practice oppressed rather than liberated. During such a period, the light of Christianity burned low. Many were led to seek a reformation of the church. It would be wrong to say that the church at any time was totally bad or that it had no authority. In every age honest persons in the church have sought to serve God. Latter Day Saints have always believed that God works in the world in every land and every age, in keeping with human response to God's initiatives. Whenever people respond to God, they are empowered with the authority to do whatever God has called them to do. In this sense we recognize God's hand moving in the Reformation, guiding and empowering various ones in their work. To some degree, the community of believers has continued from the days of Christ to our present time. In fact, we could hardly see how there would be any church on earth at all if at any time after Christ's ascension the life and spirit of the Christian community had been totally blotted out. We recognize our indebtedness to the continuing Christian community through which the knowledge, spirit, and life of the Incarnation have been preserved for us. Whatever the condition of the church during the so-called Dark Ages, its preservation of the memory of Jesus Christ made possible the explorations of the reformers and the searching experience of Joseph Smith.

3. The third question has to do with what we understand the terms of "restoration" and "true church" to be. Just as apostasy is a principle of human life which is

ever with us, so also is restoration a continuing principle. Both the scriptures and history itself are full of examples of those who drifted from God, but were renewed and restored to divine purposes. There has always been present in the world a concern on the part of some, at least, to recapture the vitality and rightness of God's will for humankind. The Anabaptists and others desired to restore the church to its primitive state. This major concern of theirs reached a kind of crest in America in the early part of the nineteenth century. While we Latter Day Saints speak of ourselves as being the "Restoration movement," the fact is we were only a part of a larger, more general movement to restore the church which extended far beyond our own denomination.

The real genius of restoration in Joseph Smith's founding experiences was not so much in recapturing a church of the past as it was in the renewed and vital prophetic contact with God. God is the source of life. It is in God that restoration is found. Because the authority to function as the Church of Jesus Christ rests in divinity, the church which is true must respond to the leadership of the Holy Spirit and to the truth of the Incarnation. Such a truth comes to us by scripture, by the church's history, by the life of the communion of the Saints, and by the endowments of the Holy Spirit in our midst.

Our most serious danger comes from an unwarranted assumption we often make. We assume that because we are the Church of Jesus Christ and have authority growing out of our experience with God, that no other authority to represent God exists outside our own communion. Such a view is not in harmony with our tradition. Very early we were cautioned to leave this matter in the hands of God. In Doctrine and Covenants 16:4d, we were instructed to "contend against no church."

For all its value to us as a source of information about the history of the early Christian Church, the Bible is not comprehensive enough or complete enough to give us an entire picture. It is easy for us to fill in the gaps of the

New Testament story with elements of our own organization and structure which really developed at a much later time. We need only look at the history of the Reorganized Church of Jesus Christ of Latter Day Saints to see that God has continued to work with us in the development of essential offices and ministries over our entire history. By the grace of God, such divine direction continues with us as it was also present with the early Christian church. Adaptation to changing circumstances and needs should always occur under the direction of the Holy Spirit.

We appreciate the significance of the Restoration principle. It is clear that human needs and the basic mission of the church are so similar in every age that the church, guided by the Holy Spirit, develops great similarities of organizational and ministerial pattern in the various eras of time. Because the church must be a witnessing church in every generation, the church will always need to be apostolic. The church's apostolic nature calls for apostolic ministries. The church must always be prophetic and therefore the prophetic office and prophetic ministries will always be required. There must be administration within the church, and thus the offices of administration will universally be found. The temporal and physical needs of people will always be with us. Therefore, the church will always find a need for ministers of temporalities. But the church is not a static organization made up of a certain structural form. It is not so rigid that God cannot inspire and reveal such changes as may be necessary to effectively fulfill the mission of Christ on earth. Human needs are universal, and this universality will always call for certain ministries. But it is essentially our faith in divine guidance, in Christ's willingness to lead and our willingess to follow, which justifies calling ourself the restored Church of Jesus Christ. It is not merely because Christ once founded a church that we affirm our faith that our church is established by Jesus Christ. It is also due to the fact that he continues to work with us in establishing his church among us.

In its larger sense it encompasses those both living and dead, who, moved by the Spirit of God, acknowledge Jesus as Lord.

Arguments sometimes occur when sincere people do not clearly define what they mean when they speak of "the church." In the literature and tradition of the Reorganized Church of Jesus Christ of Latter Day Saints, when we are not talking about a house of worship, we usually mean the corporate organization and function of our particular denomination. In the larger sense, however, Latter Day Saints have always believed in a broader usage of the term *church* to include those, both living and dead, who have responded under the Spirit of God to acknowledge Jesus Christ as their Lord. In fact, in our early history, the church was in opposition to religious practices and teachings which took a narrower view. In chapter 7 of this book, "The Gift of Salvation," mention was made of Joseph Smith's visionary experience. He saw his brother who had "obtained an inheritance in" the celestial kingdom even though he had died prior to the time that the church was organized. Joseph Smith told how he heard a voice which said, "All who have died without a knowledge of this gospel, who would have received it if they had been permitted to tarry, shall be heirs of the celestial kingdom of God; also, all that shall die henceforth without a knowledge of it, who would have received it with all their hearts, shall be heirs of that kingdom" (*The History of the Reorganized Church of Jesus Christ of Latter Day Saints*, volume 2, page 16). Although such persons are not members of our church here on earth, we have been aware that they are accepted and are received as members of the larger communion of the church. Scripturally this is sometimes referred to as the "general assembly of the saints," or the "church of the firstborn." In more recent years, some have used the term "universal church."

The writer of the Hebrew letter spoke of this larger company of the faithful in these glowing terms:

> But ye are come unto mount Sion, and unto the city of the living God, the heavenly Jerusalem, and to an innumerable company of angels, to the general assembly and church of the firstborn, which are written in heaven, and to God the Judge of all, and to the spirits of just men made perfect.—Hebrews 12:22-23

We believe that those who have been faithful to God are accepted by him. They are united with all other Saints in the "general assembly and church of the firstborn." Jesus is the Firstborn and the church of the Firstborn is the church composed of all who have committed their lives to him. They are the ones who have sought to serve him to the very best of their understanding and opportunity. Doctrine and Covenants 90:4a records the words of Christ, saying, "And now, verily I say unto you, I was in the beginning with the Father, and am the Firstborn; and all those who are begotten through me, are partakers of the glory of the same, and are the church of the Firstborn."

There is a unity existing between former generations and those now living. That unity comes from a common purpose and commitment of life. Such a company includes the prophets of old, even though they lived before the birth of Christ. It also includes the many who have sought to serve him in later times even though lack of opportunity may have kept them from becoming a part of the corporate body of the church. It is because of this Restoration understanding that the prophet Joseph Smith declared the word of God to the church:

> Behold, this is my doctrine: Whosoever repenteth and cometh unto me, the same is my church; whosoever declareth more or less than this, the same is not of me, but is against me; therefore, he is not of my church. And now, behold, whosoever is of my church, and endureth of my church to the end, him will I establish upon my Rock, and the gates of hell shall not prevail against him.—D. and C. 3:16-17

Of course, not all those who are members of the corporate church are necessarily included in the larger fellowship of the general assembly of the saints. Matthew records Jesus as having said, "And many will say unto me in that day, Lord, Lord, have we not prophesied in thy name; and in thy name cast out devils; and in thy name done many wonderful works? And then will I say, Ye never knew me; depart from me ye that work iniquity" (Matthew 7:32-33).

The list of those who are enrolled on the books of the church, and the list of those who are truly accepted by Christ as his disciples and saints, may indeed be two different lists. It is nonetheless the mission of the church here on earth to make disciples: it leads its members into that larger company and communion of the saints which reaches to all generations, and stretches to every part of the globe.

In its corporate sense, it is the community of those who have covenanted with Christ.

While the bonds of communion extend to this wide group known as the general assembly of the saints of all ages, we have a compelling need to be part of the tangible church here and now. In this sense, the term "church" describes the corporate body of those living persons who have covenanted with Christ through baptism and membership in the church as an organization.

In Old Testament times, the descendants of Abraham and Sarah were known as the covenant people. That covenant was remembered with the blood of animals sacrificed on the altar. But the new covenant made by Christ and validated by his own life and death is celebrated by Christians in the sacrament of the Lord's Supper. As the author of the Hebrew letter expressed it, "And for this cause he is the mediator of the new covenant, that by means of death, for the redemption of the transgressions that were under the first covenant, they which are called might receive the promise of eternal inheritance" (Hebrews 9:15).

Because the church represents a covenant made through our Lord Jesus Christ, we can never think of the church merely as a human institution. God initiates the covenant. Consequently the church can never consider itself a product of human invention. By entering into a covenant relationship with God and each other, we are bound together through the corporate and authoritative organization of the church. We cannot receive the gifts which God intends us to receive through the ministries of the church unless we truly have faith in God and in the church's authority.

Occasionally someone belittles the church, pointing to the abuses that have sometimes occurred when churches became highly institutionalized. No one would deny that such abuses have existed. But the body of Christ requires organization and physical form just as the spirit of a person requires a physical means of expression. A cause which does not take form and organization will waste its resources with little productive effect and will soon die.

Our heritage of faith was transmitted to us by the corporate church. The authority of the sacraments administered through the church has blessed our lives. The ministries of teaching and preaching have enlightened our minds. The corporate acts of worship have brought us into the presence of the Holy Spirit where lives have been renewed and redirected. The organized church serves as the spearhead to establish God's kingdom on earth. Our own lives are given meaning as they are united with others in the church, and directed to kingdom-building purposes. We believe in the church as a corporate organization of people united in Christ as a covenant people. The testimony of the Book of Mormon (Mosiah 9:49-50), the Doctrine and Covenants (17:7), and the Bible (Acts 2:41-47) all testify that this is true.

As the body of Christ through which the word of God

is tangibly expressed on earth, the church seeks to discern the will of God and to surrender itself in worship and service.

Traditionally the church has been called the "body of Christ." This symbol suggests a unity between Christ and the church in understanding, purpose, and love. Because of this, the church has never been able to distinguish clearly between its purposes and the purposes of Christ. The church is called to exemplify the word of God in the midst of society. Through its life, Christ himself is revealed. Paul Hessert, in his book *Introduction to Christianity*, observes:

> Because of this new intimate relation with Christ, the Church is called not only the people of God but the body of Christ. This means that it is the agent through which Christ can continue to work in this world. But it also means that the relation of the Church to Christ is integral, and the relation of members to each other is absolutely essential. In fact, here is the source of our word "member": It originally referred to a part of the body, as an arm or a leg. Hence when St. Paul writes that in the Church we are members of one body, he means that we cannot function at all independently of our relation to the body (I Corinthians 12:12-31). Yet the church as the body of Christ is no substitute for him: It has no independent life, for he remains its head (Ephesians 5:23).—pp. 284-285

The church is the body of Christ when he calls it into being and gives it life. This does not happen by the will of any human, but by the act of God. Christ invests himself in the corporate community of the church. He is the head of the church. He gives it purpose.

We must clearly understand, however, that Christ is the incarnation of God in the flesh. No other person or group of persons can presume to have such revelatory power or honor. It is true, however, that Christ has called the church into being to reveal his nature tangibly to the world. In that sense, the Word must be made flesh in all of us as well. The revelation of the Incarnation lives on in the church.

A growing misconception in our day is that a person

can serve God separate from the community of the church. Such people prefer not to become entangled in the life and obligations of the church. But the church is not an unrelated aggregate of individuals. It is a body of members fitly joined together, empowered and led by the Spirit of Christ and actively engaged in doing his will (see Ephesians 4:16). As individuals, most of us can do very little. But when our gifts are integrated into the body of the church, they become powerful indeed. None of us is complete as an individual, but all have gifts needed by the body of Christ and its mission.

The idea that a person can be quite as good outside the church as in it often grows out of the mistaken idea that Christian goodness is the same as personal virtue. Such a person would argue that church members are guilty of ethical and moral failure, even hypocrisy. And they would add that a person can achieve the same virtues without the aid of the church.

We have already admitted that the church falls short of its calling. Even the Apostle Paul, as he drew the vivid analogy of the church as the body of Christ, was at the same time writing to the Corinthian saints because of gross error and sin among them. Because the forces of apostasy are ever with us, the church must always be about the business of cleansing and purifying itself. This is both for its own sake and for the salvation of humankind. We need to remember, however, that Christ did not come into the world merely to be a good man. Nor does he call the church into being only to demonstrate high ethical qualities. Instead he commands his disciples to take up their cross daily and follow him (see Luke 9:23). Therefore we cannot presume that ethical goodness alone will suffice. The community of his disciples does the work of Christ in every generation, and is committed to make the word of God a tangible reality in the midst of society. By this means they will leaven society itself until the day will come when "the kingdoms of this world are become the kingdom of our Lord, and of his

Christ'' (Revelation 11:15). This is the end toward which history moves. Through the church as the living body empowered by the Spirit of Christ, the Word is tangibly expressed in the midst of society, so that the kingdom of God may be.

The Church of Jesus Christ is a prophetic church. Its task is to reveal God's word. Therefore it bears witness of Christ, who in himself is the Incarnation. "In him dwelleth all the fullness of the Godhead bodily" (Colossians 2:9). Therefore to witness of Christ is to witness of God. As creator and sustainer of all things, Christ is the revelation of all truth. Caution! That does not mean that you need only to study the life of Christ to learn the laws of physics or to become a physician! It does mean that Christ, as the revelation of God, is the ultimate reality upon which all else rests. He is the revelation of the perfect human, so that we can see the truth about ourselves and all humanity. Christ is the revelation of the nature of the universe, so that we can see the sacramental meaning of all creation. Everything that is has a holy purpose. Christ, as "Alpha and Omega...the beginning and the end," is the revelation of the entirety of human history (D. and C. 18:1). What this means is that Christ, as creator and sustainer from the beginning until the end of human history, is very much involved in and concerned with our daily events. By revealing Christ, the church reveals the purposes of God, and we can know the end of history because the purposes of God are not frustrated, "neither can they come to naught" (D. and C. 2:1).

Jesus is the timeless revelation of truth. The prophetic church by living in this truth reveals the will of God to the world. The prophetic church interprets the meaning of history by revealing the Lord Jesus. To see the Lord is to see God's purpose; and to see God's purpose makes sense out of all our human striving. The church does not need to ask in each specific case what the will of God is for our society, *because the awareness of God's will is a part of the church's very life.* This is what enables the church to speak for God prophetically. To be a part of the church means conversion. And conversion is a thoroughgoing experience. Samuel Shoemaker described it thus:

> Conversion must get through us like humidity gets through a house with the windows open on a muggy day—it is everywhere, in your clothes, in stamps in the desk drawer, even in the rugs! Conversion which only reaches our thoughts, or our outward conduct, is very rudimentary conversion. Conversion is a live, transforming, never-ending process. It is the life of the Holy Spirit in the soul.—*With Holy Spirit and with Fire*, page 90

There is a further responsibility laid upon the church to be under the active guidance and power of the Holy Spirit. We have a right to expect that the Holy Spirit will reveal the will of God prophetically when such direction is needed. The church as a body is designed to receive and respond to such direction. The Spirit comes with the power which causes us to know that God has business with the church and is calling it to a particular mission. It is out of such prophetic experiences that the scriptures are born.

In every time and place, the church is called to be the body of Christ on earth and prophetically express God's will. Therefore it must yield itself to God in worship constantly. Through worship the church is endowed by the Holy Spirit. It is cleansed and strengthened for the service laid upon it by Christ's commission. By surrendering itself to God in worship and in service, the church fulfills its mission. It is prophetic, not when it is gripped by fear or overly concerned about itself, but when it loses its self-interest and expends itself sacrificially in the purposes of God. The church is not called to a life of niceties. In much the same manner as Christ faced Gethsemane and cried out in his agony, "Nevertheless, not as I will, but as thou wilt," so also must the church yield itself to God (Matthew 26:36). In the doing of God's will, the church is born again to live anew.

It is enlightened, sustained, and renewed by the Holy Spirit.

It is possible to have an organization that is lifeless and inert, or moves mechanically as directed by outside forces. The Church of Jesus Christ, however, is more than an organization. It may be helpful to think of the church as an organism, for it is not dead, nor is its course determined by external pressure. The source of its life is the Holy Spirit. Through the Holy Spirit, Christ continues in the church as its head.

It is true that through the church's continuing memory the revelation of the Incarnation is carried on. This memory projects itself into the future as it generates a power which pushes up from the communion of the Saints itself. But we must never forget that this revelatory power has limits, and is subject to distortion unless corrected by the Holy Spirit. We are not God, nor are we the source of God's power. The Holy Spirit is not created by our community. But the Spirit enters into the community to give it life and intelligence and purpose. This does not belittle the essential organization or even the significance of the impact of memory. But it does point out that organization and memory are not enough. Samuel M. Shoemaker described this with an interesting illustration,

> When all this really gets underway, of course, it can and will use organization and forms as a live, growing tree will make a trunk and bark. But one can't take a dead post, nail bark on it, pump sap into it, and expect to get leaves or fruit on it.—*With Holy Spirit and with Fire*, page 89

This gets at the heart of the matter. It was and is essential for Christ to act through the power of the Holy Spirit, to establish and sustain the church. The early Christian church found this active power in its midst, guiding, protecting, and empowering its members in startling and invigorating ways. We can only imagine what it meant to the early saints as they learned of Peter and John's experience with the lame man healed at the temple gate (see Acts 3:1-9). Or consider Peter's amazing experience regarding the household of Cornelius, when it burst into their understanding that God was working with people outside the Jewish race (see Acts 10:1-47). Or consider their joy when they learned of Saul's experience on the road to Damascus and his subsequent conversion (see Acts 9:1-21). Is it any wonder that these disciples had an unconquerable determination to spread the faith? Or that they had an unshakable assurance in the victory of their cause?

But the greatest miracle wrought by the Holy Spirit was the indescribable change that came into their own lives and into the corporate life of the church. By the power of the Holy Spirit, the mind of Christ dwelt within them. Those early saints said, "But we have the mind of Christ" (I Corinthians 2:16), and, "Let this mind be in you, which was also in Christ Jesus" (Philippians 2:5). Through this power they were transformed and spoke of themselves as being new persons (see Ephesians 4:24 and Colossians 3:10).

The church is enlightened, directed, sustained, and empowered by the Holy Spirit. Without this Spirit the whole body ceases to be a living organism. It may become an organization with a lifeless body, lacking real vigor or a clear sense of divine direction. It may even be captured by society to be a tool for the use of the unscrupulous rather than utilized for the purposes of God.

The history of the church through the centuries shows a significant and unfortunate pattern. Periods of renewal when the Holy Spirit was central and potent have been followed by periods of creeping paralysis caused by focusing upon itself. When the church has been captured and imprisoned through ecclesiastical control, there has developed a general hardening of its spiritual arteries. All too frequently the institutional channels for the Spirit's expression have become so rigid that the Spirit has had to burst out of ecclesiastical form.

God, having established the church, will not be captured by the self-interest or the lethargy of the church itself. God does take the initiative again and again to shake the church and even the foundations of institutionalized society. Henry P. Van Dusen points to the problem when he says:

But the Holy Spirit has always been troublesome, disturbing because it has seemed to be unruly, radical, unpredictable. It is always embarrassing to ecclesiasticism and baffling to ethically-grounded, responsible, durable Christian devotion. And so it has been carefully taken in hand by Church authorities, whether Catholic or Protestant, and securely tethered in impotence. But—the Spirit will not long be silenced. When neglected or denied by the prevailing "churchianity," it unfailingly reappears to reassert its power.—*Spirit, Son and Father,* page 126

The principle of restoration and renewal is the expression of God's determination to bring about divine purposes in human history. History bears repeated testimony of how God intervenes in our world to renew and restore the dynamic spiritual life of the church. The church *is* the Church of Jesus Christ when it is enlightened, sustained, and renewed by the Holy Spirit.

It is to bring the good news of God's love to all people, reconciling them to God through faith in Jesus Christ.

No task is of higher importance to the church than proclaiming the good news of God's love to the whole world. The church is called first of all to be a missionary community. It witnesses of Christ and teaches his gospel. This is the meaning of the Great Commission given by Jesus to his disciples:

All power is given unto me in heaven and in earth. Go ye therefore, and teach all nations, baptizing them in the name of the Father, and of the Son, and of the Holy Ghost; teaching them to observe all things whatsoever I have commanded you; and, lo, I am with you always, unto the end of the world.—Matthew 28:17-19

Such a commission was indelibly written on the hearts of those who loved Jesus most. And so we are not surprised that it was expressed by all who wrote about him, or set out to be his servants.

There is no greater message in all the world than the simple affirmation, "For God so loved the world, that he gave his Only Begotten Son, that whosoever believeth on him should not perish; but have everlasting life'' (John 3:16). The church witnesses to that affirmation, and calls the people of all nations to Christ who is the revelation of that love. Only in Jesus do we fully see and experience the love of God.

We can never totally yield our life to God until we are convinced that God is all powerful and can do whatever God wills to do. God loves us so completely that things which are much more abundantly good than mortals can ever understand will be done in us and with us by God. Indeed, it is because we really believe that God has the power to provide for us things that "eye hath not seen, nor ear heard, neither have entered into the heart of man" that we can trust God so completely (I Corinthians 2:9). Because we see the grace of God in Christ, we are assured that God's love is not dependent on us, but it is God's own nature to love us. In spite of our rebellion and sin, God still loves and calls us to repentance so that we may have the blessings intended for us. But we cannot receive them until we trust God and yield ourselves to the divine will.

The church, having experienced the love of God, is called to testify of that love to all people. This is not because God is angry with and punishes those who are in darkness. Instead it is because they who do not know God are imprisoned by both ignorance and evil. They are shut out from hope and are in bondage to their own willful desires to stand in God's place. As Jesus said:

For God sent not his Son into the world to condemn the world; but that the world through him might be saved. He who believeth on him is not condemned; but he who believeth not is condemned already, because he hath not believed on the name of the Only Begotten Son of God, which before was preached by the mouth of the holy prophets; for they testified of me. And this is the condemnation, that light has come into the world, and men love darkness rather than light, because their deeds are evil.—John 3:17-19

The question is, How shall humankind be led out of darkness? How may their warped and distorted souls be healed? As long as they struggle to be their own masters, competing for superiority and position in a hostile world, they cannot. They can turn from darkness and be healed only when convinced of the love of God toward them and of their own worth in God's sight.

Because the church lives in God's love, it also radiates it. The distorted soul unfolds and is healed in the climate of the love of God. This spiritual climate should always characterize the church. Here we find the capacity and power to trust God. It is in the yielding of our willful and hostile selves to God that we may be reconciled. Jesus came into the world to make this possible. The Apostle Paul wrote, "God is in Christ, reconciling the world unto himself" (II Corinthians 5:19). This message is committed to the church, for as the apostle went on to say, "Now then we are ambassadors for Christ, as though God did beseech you by us; we pray you in Christ's stead, be ye reconciled to God" (5:20).

The church is the divinely commissioned ambassador to proclaim the love of God in the stead of Christ. It is to so live in the climate of that love that rebellious and sin-beset people may find in the communion of the church the healing power of that love. The church both proclaims and lives this. It is in itself the demonstration of the meaning of such love.

Paul stated an essential truth, a miracle which has touched the lives of all disciples, when he declared: "But where sin abounded, grace did much more abound; that as sin hath reigned unto death, even so might grace reign through righteousness unto eternal life by Jesus Christ our Lord" (Romans 5:20-21).

The church administers the ordinances through which the covenant is established...

The church is the corporate body of those who have entered into a covenant with Christ. In this sense, its boundaries are defined by the sacraments. By entering into covenant, the sacraments are all available to the disciple. Without some level of commitment, the sacraments are not available. These boundaries have been defined by the church itself as the need has arisen from age to age. Those who choose to become a part of the church do so by entering into the covenant with Christ through the sacraments authoritatively administered by the church. This is not merely a permissive matter. It is imperative for a Christian to become a part of the body of Christ. Similarly it is imperative that we recognize the authority of the church which acts in Christ's stead. This authority makes valid two commitments: the spiritual covenant which we make with God, and the commitment between us and the church community into which we are to be assimilated.

The sacraments by their very nature relate to our needs. They are physical means through which we commit ourselves and receive the promises of others, including God. In our communication with others, we not only use our voice but our entire beings. We shake hands, we embrace, we greet loved ones with a kiss of affection, we raise our right hand to take an oath. Before an altar we stand to pledge our marriage vows, making every effort for that occasion to speak in a memorable way the love which we have, husband and wife. What a drab world it would be if our desires were always and only expressed by the spoken word!

Jesus used the sacraments as a means of full commitment. He was baptized, and commanded baptism. He instituted the sacrament of the Lord's Supper. He gave authority to the Twelve to represent him in administering the sacraments. He gave to the church the authority to seal the covenants of those who commit themselves to God. Those who make such a covenant are also assimilated into that body, the church.

Perhaps at no point in our religious life does our apostasy become more evident than in our attitudes about the ordinances. Whenever people think of the sacraments and the church as a means for escaping punishment for sin and finding a favored place in heaven, then their concern about the ordinances takes on an unhealthy character. The sacraments and the church should be seen as way of committing ourselves fully to God and offering our lives in service to the Christ. If our involvement in the sacraments is self-centered, then our worship is in danger of degenerating into superstition. It takes on the quality of magic, whereby we can use precise formulas, incantations and ritual as a means of getting God to do what we want. This shift in focus creates an unhealthy attitude for us, corrupting us intellectually, morally and religiously. As Harold DeWolf has said, "It gives to the clergy who are thought necessary to such rites an unwholesome power, based on office and not on character and spiritual discernment. This, in turn, tempts the ministers to pride of power and position..." (*A Theology of the Living Church,* page 339).

This self-centered approach to the ordinances leads to undue concern about what authority the church has, and what guarantee the church gives for salvation. Some persons who are caught up in this approach will ask, "Is it possible that any other denomination or priesthood can have the authority which our church and priesthood possess?" We must all recognize that God grants authority to whomever God will, and it is not ours to judge the relationship of others to divine power.

We, however, have the testimony of the authority of priesthood granted to our own movement. No one outside our church has authority to commit our denomination except those who are authorized by the church to function for God and for the people of the church.

It is important that the members of the church uphold and support its priesthood before God, for through them the church itself may receive the power of God through the ordinances by faith. In Doctrine and Covenants 83:3c, we are told: "Therefore, in the ordinances thereof the power of godliness is manifest; and without the ordinances thereof, and the authority of the priesthood, the power of godliness is not manifest.''

We have not only the word of scripture but also the testimony of our own experience that this is true.

cares for all within its communion...

The members of the body serve as "spiritual mirrors" to one another. We are better able to see ourselves when our brothers and sisters of the faith reflect back to us the kind of person that we are. This helps us to understand our strengths and our weaknesses, to find reinforcement of good, and the way to identify areas for repentance. In the loving environment of the communion of the Saints, this occurs without a person feeling threatened or criticized. Our good points are emphasized and encouraged, while we sense the areas where we lack by association with those who are strong in those very same areas.

Not only are we blessed by an identification of the kind of persons that we really are as we look into the "spiritual mirrors" provided by our loved ones and friends of the faith, we also find that these mirrors function prophetically, for by the grace of God, our brothers and sisters are able to discern the kind of person that God will enable us to become! The person that we may become, therefore, is sensed in the communion of the Saints by the Spirit of God, and we are encouraged to fulfill the purpose which God intends for us. This permits our life to take on a meaning and purpose which transcends the immediacy of who we now are, and enables us to aspire to become the child of God and servant which the divine mind intends.

Jesus once said, "By this shall all men know that ye are my disciples, if ye have love one to another" (John 13:35). Such a love demands a total concern for the membership of the body. It can never see ill come to any member without responding. Nor can it remain unappreciative at the success and joys of its members. It is as

Paul said of the body of Christ, "And whether one member suffer, all the members suffer with it; or one member be honored, all the members rejoice with it" (I Corinthians 12:26).

The church cares firstly for the spiritual well-being of its members. When Jesus told the parable of the lost sheep, he was speaking of one who had been within the fold. The church searches after and ministers to any who grow cold in the faith, or who are estranged from the communion.

The church teaches and nurtures the body. Without spiritual interaction between the members, the communion loses its vibrant testimony. Every member has both a need for ministry and a need to share God-given gifts for the welfare of others. Speaking of this interdependent ministry within the body of Christ, Paul said,

We are meant to speak the truth in love, and to grow up in every way into Christ, the head. For it is from the head that the whole body, as a harmonious structure knit together by the joints with which it is provided, grows by the proper functioning of individual parts, and so builds itself up in love.—Ephesians 4:15-16 Phillips

The care which the church has for its own extends to their physical and social needs. Those who belong to the body consider their possessions as gifts over which they have a stewardship. They do not view their possessions as something to be guarded for their own use, but as resources for serving the needs of all. In Mosiah 9:60-64, we read:

And again, Alma commanded that the people of the church should impart of their substance, every one according to that which he had. If he had more abundantly, he should impart more abundantly; and he that had but little, but little should be required; and to him that had not should be given. Thus they should impart of their substance of their own free will and good desires toward God, and to those priests that stood in need, and to every needy, naked soul. And they walked uprightly before God, imparting to one another, both temporally and spiritually, according to their needs and their wants.

In the early days of the church in Palestine, the members found it necessary to develop a method for supplying the needs of the widows. When the saints in Jerusalem suffered, Paul himself gathered an offering from the churches in Greece and Macedonia to help those in Jerusalem.

This concern for the members of the body has led the church to build and maintain schools and hospitals for generations. The church has traditionally been the center of learning, and colleges have frequently been a part of its program. Specific instruction came to us to build a hospital in Independence, as "a place of refuge and help for the sick and afflicted" (see D. and C. 127:1-2). Other institutions for the care of orphans, the aged, the poor, and for the education of the members have been a part of the work of the church.

ministers to the needy...

Jesus was never able to turn away from the needy of his day. He healed the sick and fed the hungry. Similarly, his church cannot disregard such needs. Nor is the church limited to only those who are a part of its own communion. Wherever persons are in need, the church brings the ministry of Christ to alleviate their suffering.

The category of the needy is not limited to those with physical requirements only. Often the greatest need is for faith and knowledge or the warmth of being loved by those who care. When Jesus opened his ministry, he identified himself with ministry to the needy:

The Spirit of the Lord is upon me, because he hath anointed me to preach the gospel to the poor, he hath sent me to heal the brokenhearted, to preach deliverance to the captives, and the recovering of sight to the blind; to set at liberty them that are bruised; to preach the acceptable year of the Lord.—Luke 4:18-19

The church follows the lead of its Lord and carries the needs of humankind on its heart, too.

wages war on evil...

Of the many metaphors and images of the church which we frequently use, perhaps the one which is the least understood is that of the "church militant." Usually we think of the church as loving peace and working for peace in the world. Indeed this is our commission. However, the church must always stand in opposition to evil. It is in this area only that the church may appropriately take on the image of militancy. Christ called the church to take the offensive against the powers of evil wherever they may be found in the world: "The gates of hell shall not prevail against it [the church]." This description in Matthew 16:19 is not of a church besieged by the power of evil, but rather of a militant church which goes to war against evil.

The church's methods and weapons in expressing its militancy are curious indeed! They would be totally foreign to any warmonger. For the church's strength is righteousness. Its weapons are the power of faith and love. When these are diminished, the church then must wage war against evil on two battlefronts: within as well as without. The external enemy is often easier to identify than the besetting sins within. Pride and evasion of responsibility seem to affect each one of us. These enemies infiltrate the ranks to destroy the church's vitality. Such sins sometimes become the basis for further erosion of the spiritual vitality of the Saints. Conflict among the members creates disunity in our warfare against the powers of evil without.

In II Corinthians 10:3-5, the Apostle Paul describes the nature of Christian warfare.

The truth is that, although of course we lead normal human lives, the battle we are fighting is on the spiritual level. The very weapons we use are not those of human warfare but powerful in God's warfare for the destruction of the enemy's strongholds. Our battle is to bring down every deceptive fantasy and every imposing defense that men erect against the true knowledge of God. We even fight to capture every thought until it acknowledges the authority of Christ.—Phillips

and strives for the kingdom of God.

No theme is more constant in Christ's ministry than the kingdom of God. He preached this wherever he went. He taught his disciples to pray, "Thy kingdom come. Thy will be done as in heaven, so in earth" (Luke 11:2). When he spoke of the last days, he said, "And again, this gospel of the kingdom shall be preached in all the world, for a witness unto all nations, and then shall the end come, or the destruction of the wicked" (Matthew 24:32). And when he called them to action, he said, "Wherefore, seek not the things of this world but seek ye first to build up the kingdom of God, and to establish his righteousness, and all these things shall be added unto you" (Matthew 6:38).

It is in the spirit of the coming kingdom that the prophet Joseph Smith brought the divine instruction to the church to "seek to bring forth and establish the cause of Zion" (D. and C. 6:3; 10:3). The followers of Christ seek to establish his kingdom upon the earth. To lose sight of this goal would be to forget the end of all history toward which the church moves.

The church does not always live up to its commission. Because we are weak human beings, the church may falter. Because we are never free from sin, the church may fail the Lord. But as long as the church has a desire to serve, Christ will work within the church to help us overcome. On the night when Christ ate the sacred meal with his disciples, and then faced the agony of Gethsemane, he turned to his disciples in grateful appreciation and said, "Ye are they who have continued with me in my temptations" (Luke 22:28).

At a time when he was himself distressed, he could have reminded them of their failures. There certainly were many: when they tried to keep the little children away from him, or their fear and lack of faith when on the angry sea, or their frequent misunderstanding of his intentions. Instead of chastisements, he expressed love and appreciation. He was not unaware of their continuing weakness, but he was committed to them. To them he had said, "Ye have not chosen me, but I have chosen you, and ordained you, that ye should go and bring forth fruit; and that your fruit should remain; that whatsoever ye shall ask of the Father in my name, he may give it you" (John 15:16).

Christ continues with his church today. Its significance is not so much in its failures as in its successes. It is the body of Christ, and with Christ as its head, it will go forward to victory.

CHAPTER 10
THE PRINCIPLE OF STEWARDSHIP

We believe that all are called to be stewards under God. They are accountable to God in the measure of their perception of the divine purpose in creation and redemption, for managing all gifts and resources given into their care. In the exercise of their stewardship, persons embody the divine will and grow in spiritual maturity through developing native powers and skills, achieving dominion over the physical order and perfecting human relationships in the Spirit of Christ.

Stewardship is rooted in our belief about God and our relationship to God. The concept of stewardship is based on the belief that God is the Creator. God is from everlasting to everlasting. Our Redeemer's love is immeasurable. God is a Father who is personal, but whose personality is not limited by attributes known to fatherhood. Stewardship is a practical expression of our grateful acknowledgment of God's love and sovereignty. It is our response to God's call to give all that we are and all that we have in service to Christ.

We believe that all are called to be stewards under God.

Stewardship brings together the spiritual and the temporal or physical. It affirms that God is the creator of the *universe* (not a multiverse), who looks upon all creation as "good." The scriptures say, "In the beginning I created the heaven, and the earth.... And I, God, saw everything that I had made, and behold, all things which I had made were very good" (Genesis 1:3, 33). The Restoration concept of stewardship affirms that God acted with purpose in creation, even though humankind may not fully understand. Furthermore, the Restoration believes that God's act of creation was not completed in the past, but continues without end. He said, "For my works are without end, and also my words, for they never cease" (D. and C. 22:3).

As physical and spiritual beings, we have been created by God. But we are unique. The scriptures say we were made a little lower than the angels (see Psalm 8:5). We are unique in that God gave us the power of abstract thought, judgment, and freedom of choice. Earthbound though we are, it is the divine intention that we shall be linked with God. We shall be linked with God in communion and in purpose, in spiritual ways but also in the human form. When God became incarnate in Christ Jesus, we became permanently linked with God in our entire being, including the physical. In Christ, God reveals to us what we may become in the flesh. Through Christ, we are called to respond to God's love and compassion with our total human being. We can do this only as we express ourselves within the environment of God's creation—the earth, other person, and all that God has created.

They are accountable to God...

From the beginning, humanity found itself fully surrounded by a physical environment that both sustained and destroyed. It is an environment which presents both challenges and problems. This is the world that God placed in our care, "to dress it, and to keep it," and to have dominion over it (see Genesis 1:30, 2:18). We frequently misunderstand this trust. We imagine that the earth is ours to use as we want, and we fail to see it as a trust for which we are responsible. In the exercise of our freedom of choice, and because of our ignorance, arrogance, and self-centeredness, we misuse, waste and pervert the gifts of God. It is at this point that our response and responsibility become the key to our own development.

Humankind does not suffer because of a lack of resources created by God and made available: "I, the Lord, stretched out the heavens, and builded the earth as a very handy work; and all things therein are mine; and it is my purpose to provide for my saints, for all things are mine;...but it must needs be done in mine own way" (D. and C. 101:2d). Rather, humankind has been the victim of its failure to see the sacredness of God's creation and to manage it for purposes that are unselfish. The opportunities provided by God for us to manage the physical creation are to help us develop the attributes of powers which are eternal. We believe with the psalmist that "the earth is the Lord's, and the fullness thereof; the world, and they that dwell therein" (Psalm 24:1).

God created it. God is the owner, the provider. We are recipients, tenants, trustees.

All that we are and all that we possess belong to God. The great difficulty is that we fail to perceive this truth, and in our failure to understand it, we do not realize that we are accountable to the Owner for what we do with what we have.

in the measure of their perception of the divine purpose in creation and redemption....

Because of God's justice, we are accountable only for that which we have, for that which is within our reach. This includes more than our physical possessions. It includes knowledge, wisdom, and understanding as well as the development of our potential. A small child is not held accountable before God or in the courts of justice for behavior that is not acceptable to society. A child is without understanding of the consequences of its behavior, and therefore is not held accountable before the law. The Restoration has held from the beginning that

little children are redeemed from the foundation of the world,...wherefore they cannot sin...until they begin to become acountable before me;...and he that hath no understanding, it remaineth in me to do according as it is written.—D. and C. 28:13-14 (See also Moroni 8:20-26.)

It is not only little children who are not held accountable because of lack of understanding. This principle also applies to others who, for one reason or another, do not know or perceive the truth. An incompetent person cannot be expected to do the work of one who is competent. Therefore, justice demands that persons are to be held accountable only for as much as they are able to understand and do. Revelation contained in Doctrine and Covenants 45:10 states, "And then shall the heathen nations be redeemed, and they that knew no law shall have part in the first resurrection."

Jesus was mindful of proportionate responsibility. He

described this in the parable of the unfaithful steward when he said,

> That servant who knew his Lord's will, and prepared not for his Lord's coming, neither did according to his will, shall be beaten with many stripes. But he that knew not his Lord's will, and did commit things worthy of stripes, shall be beaten with few. For unto whomsoever much is given, of him shall much be required.—Luke 12:56-57

With increasing knowledge came increasing responsibility. Knowledge and responsibility develop proportionately.

It is not enough, however, to just state this concept. We would certainly not want to run the risk of giving a wrong impression. Some might mistakenly decide that the easy way out for the steward is to avoid knowing what the Lord requires. Of course, this is not a profitable choice. The decision to avoid responsibility and accountability leads to the penalty of an unproductive life. Such a life is less rich with meaning and fulfillment than might have been achieved. Accountability to God brings its own rewards, including sharpened insights into the meaning of life. It points the way to how life should be lived in association with God and the Saints.

for managing all gifts and resources given into their care.

We are accountable to God for that which God entrusts to us. More than this, we are accountable for how we manage those gifts productively in achieving God's purposes. The parable of the talents tells us several things about the relationships of the steward and the Master. In this parable, as found in Matthew 25:13-31,

1. The Lord gave talents to his servants (stewards) unequally, "according to his several ability."
2. The stewards knew that they were free to manage the talents (trusts) and that the Lord would require an accounting of their stewardship.
3. Two of the stewards immediately put the talents to

work in the world of economic life in order to gain other talents, acquire an increase, and develop a surplus.
4. One steward was afraid of losing the one talent given to him and, not wanting to take the risk in the marketplace, buried it in the earth.
5. The stewards with the five talents and two talents each had an increase of 100 percent. They were highly commended by their Lord.
6. The fearful steward returned to the Lord only that which had been given to him. The Lord rebuked him with strong words, calling him slothful and wicked for not producing an increase. The talent he had was taken from him, and he was cast out, losing his relationship with the Lord.

From this account it is clear that God holds us accountable for how we manage his gifts to us. The central theme of this parable is management. The freedom to manage and to take risks was given to the stewards. The management of their stewardships was expected to produce an increase for the Lord. The proof of their faithfulness was that they produced an increase. At the same time, they were developing management skills so that the Lord could assign them even greater trusts.

It is when we achieve an objective that we are tempted to think as the Israelites thought: "My power and the might of mine hand hath gotten me this wealth" (Deuteronomy 8:17). Because of this tendency, we need to be reminded, as Moses exhorted his people: "Remember the Lord thy God; for it is he that giveth thee power to get wealth" (Deuteronomy 8:18). We need to be reminded that we are inseparably bound to the Source of life and power in all we do.

Christ said that he came that we might have life and that we might have it more abundantly (see John 10:10). The stewardship of life is concerned with our whole being. As stewards under God, we are concerned with making life richer in quality and meaning. But because of our human limitations, our vision and understanding about what makes life rich or abundant are limited. We depend upon God for an understanding of what constitutes "the abundant life."

Even though we are limited, at our best we know that stewardship under God has to do with our daily work, our facilities for living, and our leisure activities.

Having heard and accepted the call to discipleship, we have a special kind of stewardship. We are bearers of the testimony of God's love as revealed in Christ. We are committed in our whole being and with all that we have to the mission of Christ. Everything we do—our vocation, our community life, our manner of speaking and doing—is done as an expression of discipleship. This is our stewardship. We bend all our talents and energies to the kingdom way. We minister to the needs of our neighbors. We are actively concerned in bringing hope to the poor and sight to the blind. We are engaged in bringing healing to the bruised and the brokenhearted. We work without ceasing to produce liberty and freedom for those who are enslaved by ignorance, fear, lustful passions, and hatred. We consider the scriptures as our heritage, a trust to be used, enriched, illumined as the testimony of God at work in the world.

The church, as the body of disciples, has a mission. This mission is to awaken in humanity a sense of stewardship. This applies to persons as individuals as well as society as a whole. The church of the Restoration must always sound the clear call of God to promote the kingdom of God and establish the cause of Zion. The commission of Christ to his modern disciples is the same as that to those of olden time: "Go ye therefore, and teach all nations, baptizing them in the name of the Father, and of the Son, and of the Holy Ghost; teaching them to observe all things whatsoever I have commanded you" (Matthew 28:18-19).

In the exercise of their stewardship, persons embody the divine will...

It is in our nature to ask, "What is humanity?" Something within us causes us to want to know. God has planted within us a mind, a soul that reaches out beyond ourself, asking what is the meaning of this existence. What has caused us to be? Is there any purpose for our being? With these kinds of questions the prophets have connected us and related us to the Creator, the cause of our being. We find ourselves caught in a tension between this earthly nature and our heavenly vision. We come to know, even though only partially, that the Creator has set a destiny for us. We have heard the voice of heaven say,

> A new heart also will I give you, and a new spirit will I put within you; and I will take away the stony heart out of your flesh, and I will give you a heart of flesh. And I will put my Spirit within you, and cause you to walk in my statutes, and ye shall keep my judgments and do them.... And ye shall be my people, and I will be your God.—Ezekiel 36:26-28

and grow in spiritual maturity through developing native powers and skills...

Humans have struggled through the ages to improve their earthly existence. History is a story of the ups and downs of humanity. We have had to cope with such problems as hunger and disease, but our greatest problem has been ourselves. When we try to be our own God we engender within ourselves a spirit of pride, arrogance, and selfishness. This spirit destroys the system of values that are productive. Only to the degree that we recognize God as the Creator and Lord of the universe and ourselves as servants will we seek to discover and understand and accommodate ourselves to the laws of God's universe. As we respond to God's call to be productive, we come to know something about self-discipline. We begin to know that our own talents, powers, and skills can be developed only as we spend our own energy. As with all other worthwhile tasks in life, we soon learn that our stewardship under God cannot be realized by wishing for it, or by getting someone else to take it over for us. The student of mathematics or music must undergo the discipline of study in order to become skilled. No one else can do that for us. Latent and native gifts, though God-given, will remain undeveloped unless we respond to God's call to stewardship. Spiritual maturity which encompasses every aspect of our lives is a result of our responding to God's invitation to work with God in shaping the world.

achieving dominion over the physical order...

Usually, whenever we talk about our relationship to God and the physical world, someone is sure to recite the commandment of God as described in the account of creation. In Genesis 1:30, we read God's commandment to "Be fruitful, and multiply, and replenish the earth, and subdue it; and have dominion... over every living thing that moveth on the earth." But this is more than a commandment about physical things. In essence, God is saying to us, "Because you have been created with the powers granted to you, be aware of the fact that my law and my commandment are written into your nature. Be about the business of being fruitful, multiplying, replenishing, subduing, and having dominion *in a responsible way.*" In other words, God is saying to us, "The physical world is in your hands, therefore achieve dominion in such a way that both the process of achieving and the result will contribute to my purpose in you."

Rapid technological development has more than ever reminded us of the fact that we can do things which once seemed impossible. What does this fact say to us about humanity? F. Henry Edwards suggests:

We are creatures of intelligence, exploring the wilderness and making highways across the deserts. Intelligence and self-discipline have pointed the way, and earth and sea and air are gradually yielding their treasures and submitting to our will. We who can read the secrets in the heart of the atom and weigh the stars in their courses surely belong to a higher order of life than either atoms or stars. Mass is not the true measure of what is consequential in the universe, nor is force the final standard. We ourselves hold the key. The stupendously significant fact of the universe is that man is and that we are on the way to greatness, called by a destiny greater than we yet know.—*The Divine Purpose in Us,* page 13

and perfecting human relationships...

That humankind can exercise dominion over the physical order seems to be a certainty. But it is also evident that our continued progress may well be thwarted because we cannot achieve discipline over ourselves. Our ability to destroy and lay waste has developed at an alarming rate. Not many generations ago, our ability to destroy human life was only on an individual and personal basis. With the technology of modern warfare, we have seen that expand to make it possible to kill many with a single blow on a battlefield, to the ability to destroy an entire city, and finally to our present position of being able to bring about total destruction of our world. For some of us, the knowledge alone of this possibility brings paralyzing fear. Such persons give up all hope, and become the prophets of doom and destruction. But God through Jesus Christ holds out the promise that we may yet become sons and daughters of God in the flesh. The promise is that "If ye continue in my word...ye shall know the truth, and the truth shall make you free" (John 8:31-32). God's counsel has always been, "Seek, and ye shall find" (Matthew 7:12, Luke 11:10-11). The meaning seems clear. God promises through the Holy Spirit to assist, to guide and direct those who are seeking to know the truth.

It is a divine calling to which we have been called. The perfecting of human relationships is not merely an option—it is a necessity. God's clear call through the Restoration is to "seek to bring forth and establish the cause of Zion" (Doctrine and Covenants 6:3a). Also, "Zion cannot be built up unless it is by the principles of the law of the celestial kingdom...and my people must needs be chastened until they learn obedience, if it must needs be, by the things which they suffer" (D. and C. 102:2c, d). From these scriptures it is clear that the human relationships which we intend when we speak of Zion are based upon principles of life which we must learn by means of experience. This seeking and learning process must continue. As we see ourselves as persons with personality and character, we may begin to act and react with one another in ways that support this learning process. We cannot avoid the social problems of our day. We must be a part of the solution to them.

in the Spirit of Christ.

We recognize ourselves as stewards who are responsible and accountable. We work together with God to bring about the expression of the godly way of life on earth. We have faith that what we have been called to do we can do. Therefore as stewards we move fearlessly and with power toward the divine objectives, because we are motivated by love and we work with the intelligence of a sound mind.

Stewardship can never be divorced from voluntary commitment to Christ. It is the Spirit of our Lord that leads us to such a responsible and fruitful life. It is indeed as the prophet has revealed: "Stewardship is the response of my people to the ministry of my Son" (D. and C. 147:5a).

CHAPTER 11
THE KINGDOM OF GOD

We believe that the kingdom of God sustains persons as the stable and enduring reality of history, signifying the total lordship of God over all human life and endeavor. The kingdom is always at hand in judgment and promise, confronting men and women with the joyful proclamation of God's rule and laying claim upon them as they acknowledge the new creation in Christ. The full revelation of the kingdom awaits the final victory over evil, when the will of God shall prevail and divine rule shall extend over all human relations to establish the dominion of peace, justice, and truth. To this end the church proclaims the gospel of the kingdom both as present reality and future hope in the midst of a faithless world.

The Christian looks forward to the future. It is there that the consummation of the divine will occurs, both in creation and in the process of redemption. Such hope reflects the fact that we are not content to live with meaninglessness. Instead we are driven by an inner impulse to find some meaning in our total life experience.

Across the pages of scriptural history flows the persistent idea that there is a divine intention for humankind. Integral to this idea is the notion that God also participates with us in the achievement of that intention. This anticipation is caught up in scriptural symbols such as Zion, the New Jerusalem, and the kingdom of God. Each has its own particular variation of the central theme of history, and that is that our history is transformed by the initiative of God and our human response.

In the scriptures, such terms as *Zion* and *kingdom of God* are used with various emphases and sometimes interchangeably. But in the largest sense, when we speak of the kingdom of God we mean the acknowledgment of the total sovereignty of God over all human life and endeavor. Simultaneously, we recognize that God's sovereignty is rooted in the power and reality of redeeming love.

We believe that the kingdom of God sustains persons as the stable and enduring reality of history, signifying the total lordship of God over all human life and endeavor.

Whenever any of us have spoken about the kingdom of God, we are implying that there is a divine purpose for all of human history. To even suggest that there is such a godly kingdom also suggests that God has divine intentions for us. Consequently, it is in yearning for such a kingdom that we have rooted our hopes and expectancies, charted our courses, determined our values, and declared our loyalties. As far as we know, humans alone have the capacity to think about the ultimate meaning of their own existence. Whenever we think seriously and deeply enough about it, we recognize that the ultimate meaning of our life is revealed by its final purpose and outcome. Therefore for us, both the end in terms of the meaning of our life as well as the end in terms of the ultimate outcome of our life, is the kingdom of God.

If we speak of the kingdom as the end toward which we move, we do not, however, mean to imply that it is some predetermined or fixed system blueprinted in heaven. Instead we think of the kingdom as an imperative which draws us constantly into the possibilities of the future. It reminds us of the lack of permanance of all other orders and kingdoms. It is the focal point for the coming together of all that is right, good, and beautiful. And it is God who is constantly striving with us, encouraging us onward toward that ultimate end.

Thus we see the kingdom of God as a real symbol among us today, pointing us to the future where lies the reality of all that we presently hope and yearn for. By the grace of God, we realize that the shaping of the kingdom of God is jointly shared by God with us. It is not so much commanded as experienced. Its laws are not written by legislative fiat but are written instead by the hand of God on the heart of human beings like ourselves. It therefore has to do with all that we do. The Lord intends to share the building of the kingdom of God with us, the loyal subjects. The kingdom of God is the one symbol which stands before us in our future history, calling us to establish divine purposes in our history.

The kingdom is always at hand in judgment and promise, confronting men and women with the joyful proclamation of God's rule...

For the early Hebrews, the kingdom of God meant a condition of peace in Jerusalem for the gathered elect. Through the prophets, occasionally, other views of divine intention for the kingdom of God were seen. For some there developed an awareness of a world mission that would minister peace and plenty to all humanity on the basis of obedience and loyalty to God. Some, such as Isaiah (see 49:6), saw this taking place within the history of the nation. Still later, some adherents of Judaism (such as in Daniel 2:34) saw the ideal of God breaking into human history, destroying the existing order.

Thus when the New Testament account was written, the concept of the kingdom of God already had a very long history behind it. It stretched back into the earliest of primitive times. Rabbinical Judaism saw the rule of God through obedience to law. They looked forward to the full and complete establishment of God's rule at some time in the future when humanity was fully obedient to God's law. On the other hand, New Testament Christians asserted that in a new and peculiar way, the kingdom of God had already come (see Luke 7:20-22; Matthew 12:23). For them, God's rule was a new spiritual principle already working in their lives.

The Pharisees believed that the kingdom of God would "be restored" when the whole law was kept perfectly, even for a single day. This is why they went to such lengths as painting the tombstones white (thus the reference to "whited sepulchres"). They did not want to stumble over them in the darkness of "the last day"! But Jesus affirmed that the kingdom of God was at hand whenever people wholeheartedly responded to him.

The idea of the kingdom was thus taken from Judaism, but radically transformed by Jesus. Early church leaders understood that. Mark's testimony shows that when Jesus took up the ministry of John, he declared: "The time is fulfilled, and the kingdom of God is at hand; repent ye, and believe the gospel" (Mark 1:13). Essentially, Mark was saying that not through obedience to law but by recognizing the revelation in Christ was the kingdom brought to hand. In the New Testament, and specifically in Jesus' teaching, we see the kingdom as

God's presence and sovereignty in the midst of everyday life.

The kingdom was in their midst in a startling new way. God's sovereignty was marvelously manifested in Jesus. There was no single, cataclysmic, world-ending manifestation as the people of that day anticipated. Instead the love of God was seen working in the life of a commoner among other commoners. In the midst of life itself, human life was being transformed so that it could conform to the dynamic will of God.

The kingdom of God was—and always is—"at hand." It was not only at hand for the benefit of those in New Testament times as Mark testified, but it was also "at hand" for the benefit of the early Saints in Fayette, New York, in 1831 (see D. and C. 39:5b). But whenever the reign of God is manifest, the foundations and structures of our lives come under searching scrutiny. Whenever and wherever our own shadow is measured against the shadow of Christ, we see how far short we fall in measuring up. The "measure of the stature of the fullness of Christ" is always before us, as a yardstick by which we are judged (Ephesians 4:13).

The idea that the kingdom is at hand is also a promise to us. We know that God's grace works, for it worked in the life of Jesus. If the kingdom of God can be a reality in him, it can also be so in us. The message of the kingdom is revealed in the Incarnation. We do not see that kingdom in splendid and antiseptic isolation from the harshness of human life. Rather, in the very midst of human frailty, God works to reveal divine grace in achieving the kingdom.

We therefore can see God's action in Christ as a statement of intention: it is the way by which the kingdom of God is at hand. God's intention for us was declared in such a way that that action became the crucial point, the "meridian" of time for all peoples and for all history. As F. Henry Edwards has stated,

Our humanity has forever been dignified by the stupendous fact of the incarnation of the Son of God in the flesh like our own...who...took on himself the limitations of flesh and blood that he might show us the reality of our kinship with Divinity and the boundless possibilities of righteousness and of excellence which life holds before us.—*The Divine Purpose in Us*, page 53

laying claim upon them as they acknowledge the new creation in Christ.

When we come up against the kingdom of God, it is no casual encounter. We are confronted with an imperative. The demanding nature of that imperative is rather well caught up in the J. B. Phillips translation of Matthew 11:12: "From the days of John the Baptist until now the kingdom of Heaven has been taken by storm and eager men are forcing their way into it." This passage, no matter how it is translated, certainly carries the idea that we enter the kingdom at great cost, for it demands a radical change in our perspective on life. We are called into a new life, and become part of a new creation. (See II Corinthians 5:16-17.)

Jesus emphasized the inward qualities of the kingdom. He talked about the quality of personality and the orientation of one's will. The Apostle Paul stated it this way: "For the kingdom of God is not meat and drink; but righteousness, and peace, and joy in the Holy Ghost" (Romans 14:17). Jesus' parables about the hidden treasure and the pearl show that he thought it was worthwhile for a person to surrender everything else in order to possess the kingdom. Service in the kingdom was to take precedence over even the most sacred and urgent duties. Only those who sought the kingdom with single-mindedness were fit for it (see Matthew 13:46-47, Matthew 8:21-22, Luke 9:59-62).

The kingdom of God seems to contradict the normally accepted values, and shatters human securities. What this means to us, in practical terms, is that we must accept it in humility and trust. In the truest sense, the kingdom of God has never been an achievement of our skill or determination. It is instead the gift of God's grace. As Jesus said to the disciples, "It is your Father's good pleasure to give you the kingdom" (Luke 12:35).

God's sovereignty is not naked power—though it is powerful. It is a sovereignty of grace. Such a divine love liberates us from the limitations of our past, and opens to us the possibilities for our future. The kingdom is in power to the degree that we are transformed in loving God and in acknowledging God's total sovereignty.

The full revelation of the kingdom awaits the final victory over evil, when the will of God shall prevail and divine rule shall extend over all human relations to establish the dominion of peace, justice, and truth.

The kingdom of God is already present. It exists wherever humankind acknowledge in their way of life that God reigns. From our own experience, we too can affirm that we have experienced the reality of the kingdom in the love of the Saints.

At the same time, however, from our own perceptions as well as the message of the scriptures, we know that the kingdom is also "not yet." Its full expression awaits the manifestation of God's kingly rule in the relationships of human society. While Jesus clearly taught that the kingdom has an inner dimension, it is also obvious that this has strong implications for us in our relationships. Sovereign rule does not operate in a vacuum. There must be a realm or community where the practical meaning of God's reign is shown in the habits of people. The symbol of the kingdom of God, by its very nature, stands for the inner personal and social aspects of our life.

In the nineteenth century, it was thought that the kingdom of God would result from the progressive Christianizing of the social order. But, as John MacQuarrie has observed,

> Christianity is too realistic to be carried way by a facile optimism that sees in the expansion of knowledge and technological development the salvation of the human race and the solution of its problems.... The Christian hope is in God's activity and presence in the world.—*Principles of Christian Theology*, p. 309

God's judgment is applied to all social structures and programs. None of our schemes for reform equates with the will of God. The liberal optimism of the nineteenth century, the era of the "social gospel," has been chastened. Of necessity, we have had to reject the confident assumption that the social order would inevitably improve into the kingdom of God.

However, let us not be mistaken about the importance of social reform. In order to realize the kingdom of God, significant social renewal is in order. Indeed, the responsibility of the church in serving the cause of the kingdom is to constantly confront the existing order with the judgment of the law of love. We must forever seek positive ways to establish more just relationships among people. This task is an urgent and proper concern of the Saints. Consequently, in latter-day revelation, the Saints are advised,

> to so conduct themselves in the carrying into operation the details of their organizations as to be in the world but not of it, living and acting honestly and honorably before God and in the sight of all men, using the things of this world in the manner designed of God, that the places where they occupy may shine as Zion, the redeemed of the Lord.—D. and C. 128:8b, c

For us, the kingdom of God has to do with relationships between persons. A private or personal kind of religion is contrary to our Christian experience. The kingdom of God is prophesied in and for and through human relationships. To the degree that Christ's life is in our midst, the kingdom of God exists among us. The kingdom is God's enterprise taking form on earth.

Many of the parables, while looking forward to an ultimate realization of the kingdom, imply that the kingdom is already in our midst. The parables of the mustard seed, the sower, the seed growing secretly, and the leaven, all imply an actual presence of the kingdom here and now. In each instance, however, the process of growth culminates in a climax: a plant, a harvest, a full-grown tree, or the leavening of the whole. This is characteristic of the ultimate yearning sensed in Jesus' teaching, in which the full and complete expression of God's sovereignty is seen at the end of history. But of course, the only way to understand an "end" or the "ultimate" is in the sense of fulfillment that it brings in relationship to all that has preceded. The achievement of the end is of greatest value when seen as a natural result of all of the striving and yearning which has gone before. We clearly see the revelation of the kingdom which is represented in our Lord, Christ Jesus. This vision therefore comes to us both as guarantee and prophecy that the full realization of the kingdom is also in Christ, who is yet to come in power and glory.

To this end the church proclaims the gospel of the kingdom both as present reality and future hope in the midst of a faithless world.

The church also serves as the anticipation of the kingdom. This is partly because it proclaims to the world God's intention for it. It is also partly because the church serves as the community of the Spirit, and as the spearhead of God's presence and action in the world. The church is constantly sensitive to discern the ways in which God is active in the world. It points to those endeavors which are freeing people to achieve the fullness of their stature under God. The church has an undiscouraged faith in the kingdom. Consequently it lives its life in witness of that confident expectation. It points people to look beyond what *is* to what *may be*, and proclaims the hope of the kingdom in the midst of faithlessness.

As a community of disciples, the church calls upon all people to transform the institutions by which their common life is shaped. In this way the church works to guarantee human freedom and the expression of our true humanity under God.

The church points out that the future is open to all kinds of new possibilities under God. A frequent temptation for those who love the kingdom is to look back to the achievement of some previous generation, and try to recapture it. But a past way of life can never be recaptured. In this regard, F. Henry Edwards said,

> Men of the kingdom look for guidance to the past, and yet not without some suspicion. Mere repetition of our yesterdays, even the best yesterdays, would not be enough to satisfy the deeper needs of humanity in an advancing present.—*God Our Help,* p. 232

The kingdom's disciple is converted to the openness of the future. Our commitment is not to some blueprint, set down on a divine scroll waiting to be unrolled. Our opportunity lies in our God-given ability to face the future as co-workers and co-creators with God. Our freedom to be creative in history implies that we also have a freedom over history itself. We may exercise the dominion which God has given us, and thereby manifest God's sovereignty.

The church lives by the hope of the kingdom. This hope is nourished by our living experience of the kingdom. Our hope is not some figment of imagination, nourished by despair. It is instead the sober assurance that our lives "are hid with Christ in God," that we live in a trust and an endurance by which we find ourselves impelled and drawn on (Colossians 3:3).

Because of our awareness of the revelation of God's grace in Christ; of God's participation in our ongoing history; of our experience of the reality of divine love; and of the hope that nourishes our endeavor, we have the most ample reasons possible to affirm "thy kingdom come."

CHAPTER 12
ZION

We believe that Zion is the means by which the prophetic church participates in the world to embody the divine intent for all personal and social relations. Zion is the implementation of those principles, processes, and relationships which give concrete expression to the power of the kingdom of God in the world. It affirms the concern of the gospel with the structure of our common life together and promotes the expression of God's reconciling love in the world, thus bringing forth the divine life in human society. The church is called to gather the covenant people into signal communities where they live out the will of God in the total life of society. While this concrete expression of the kingdom of God must have a central point of beginning, it reaches out to every part of the world where the prophetic church is in mission.

The call to build Zion has been and still is one of the most dominant beliefs of the Reorganized Church of Jesus Christ of Latter Day Saints. In April 1829, instruction came to Oliver Cowdery as follows: "Now, as you have asked, behold, I say unto you, Keep my commandments, and seek to bring forth and establish the cause of Zion" (D. and C. 6:3a). In later weeks similar words of instruction were given to others who were anxious to follow prophetic guidance. It is significant that the call to "bring forth and establish the cause of Zion" was first given while the translation of the Book of Mormon was in its early stages. This was also before the Aaronic priesthood was conferred on Joseph and Oliver on May 15, 1829. No one had yet been baptized by the authority vested in this new movement. In essence every person, from the very first baptized member down to the present time, has been aware of this commitment to build Zion—if we have understood the faith of the church at all. The baptismal covenant involves us in the everyday business of secular life as well as in the religious life of a follower of Christ. As members we have been sustained by the hope that our own efforts will somehow contribute to the development of Zion as a tangible and prophetic expression of the kingdom of God.

We believe that Zion is the means by which the prophetic church participates in the world to embody the divine intent for all personal and social relations.

Our faith is that God has entered into our world through the person of the Son, Jesus Christ. God's purpose was to reveal the truth about the nature of God, the universe, and humankind. Christ did not leave us a book of law, a set of rules, or a charted way into the future. He said, "I am the way, the truth, and the light" (John 14:6). It is the faith of the church that we are called to bring disciples to Christ, the Supreme Revelation. Jesus is the Universal Truth, and he speaks to all people wherever they are and in whatever period of history they may live. Instructions and scriptural records are given by God within the framework of time and to meet a particular need. They should always be interpreted in terms of our understanding of the revelation to be seen in Christ himself. It is indeed as the Holy Spirit has said to the church:

> Instruction which has been given in former years is applicable in principle to the needs of today and should be so regarded by those who are seeking ways to accomplish the will of their heavenly Father. But the demands of a growing church require that these principles shall be evaluated and subjected to further interpretation. This requisite has always been present. In meeting it under the guidance of my spirit, my servants have learned the intent of these principles more truly.—D. and C. 147:7

An interpretation which speaks the divine will for a particular situation or time may not be applicable to other cultures or times. If we are to be truly prophetic, we must always go back to the source of truth. That source is found in the life of the Lord Jesus. If we are to minister for Christ in this rapidly changing age and to the varied cultures of the world, we must understand the Incarnation.

It is our faith that the church is enlivened by the living Christ. The Spirit of Christ is ever present with us. He is willing to guide us as we seek to fulfill the church's prophetic role in the midst of the world. Perhaps our most significant distinctive is our profound faith in the living Christ who today continues to reveal God's will and guide the church in the midst of a fluid world of confusion and conflict.

The church is prophetic in two ways. First, Christ will not leave the church in darkness but will inspire and direct it through the ministry of the Holy Spirit as it struggles to do God's will in the world. Christ guides the church and empowers it to reveal his will to humanity.

Second, the church is prophetic when it lives in the

continuing spirit and culture of the community established by Christ. This heritage is passed on from generation to generation. It guides the church as the body of Christ. The scriptures are one part of this heritage, but the memory of the church about itself, its dealings with God, and its life in Christ is the background out of which the church always views the future. From this same background it makes decisions regarding the way God wants us to live and move in the midst of an ever-changing world. When the church lives in this way, it is prophetic and stands as a beacon to the world.

Sometimes we have thought that the church is prophetic because it has a prophet who speaks for God, or because its ministers or members sometimes exercise the gift of prophecy speaking under the direction of the Holy Spirit. This is not incorrect. Such genuine expressions of divine guidance are a part of the church's prophetic function. But it is a far more limited expression of the prophetic church than the potential which God has in mind for the church. The church is called to "make the word flesh" in the midst of society in such a way that the world can see what it means to live as God intends. We are called to interpret the meaning of the Incarnation found in Christ in terms of the social, economic, political, and other aspects of the total society. Thereby every member is a part of the prophetic ministry of the church. This occurs whenever we find our place in the effective expression of the church as the community of Christ's followers at work.

Zion is the implementation of those principles, processes, and relationships which give concrete expression to the power of the kingdom of God in the world.

We believe that all are called to be stewards under God. Such discipleship involves one's total life and the use of all our powers and resources in service to God.

This is more than individual stewardship: it is social responsibility. The church as members joined together in one body reveals the meaning of the Incarnation lived out in the everyday affairs of life. Because of this, the church in the early days of its existence often found itself in conflict with other denominations which stressed salvation by faith. Salvation by faith was interpreted by many to mean that salvation is guaranteed when one accepts Christ through giving some outward confession of belief in him. However, such salvation was interpreted in terms of life after death in which one escaped eternal punishment and entered into the joys of heaven. Latter Day Saints insisted that religion involved the total life. Therefore they also stressed the necessity of works. Perhaps it would be appropriate to note that they sometimes overstressed the place of works in their reaction to what they considered error in others' beliefs. They did make clear, however, that faith requires a total stewardship of life, and salvation involves our present life in this world as well as that life which is beyond the grave.

In recent decades, greater emphasis has been placed by many Christians on the importance of "secular" Christianity. This is no new idea to members of our faith. It is important to note, however, that the advocates of secular Christianity are in danger of becoming unbalanced also. In stressing the importance of Christian involvement in this world, they may lose sight of that eternal existence which goes beyond the world and which gives meaning to our present life here.

Because the prophetic church is called to embody the divine intent in the world, it is important to affirm that there are no divisions between the secular and the divine. The activities of business, politics, and education are not separate from the realms of religion. Indeed, it is our faith that all of life is of concern to God. Through the Zionic community, the church may live out the will of God in all personal and social relations.

Zion is the means by which the church speaks to society as it participates in the life of the world. It is the fulfillment of the prophecy recorded in both Isaiah and Micah:

> And it shall come to pass in the last days, when the mountain of the Lord's house shall be established in the top of the mountains, and shall be exalted above the hills, and all nations shall flow unto it; and many people shall go and say, Come ye, and let us go up to the mountain of the Lord, to the house of the God of Jacob; and he will teach us of his ways, and we will walk in his paths; for out of Zion shall go forth the law, and the word of the Lord from Jerusalem.—Isaiah 2:2-3; see also Micah 4:1-2

If we wish, we may think of Zion as a community demonstration for the world to see the example of a people who live the will of God in their midst. However, this falls short of the mark in the same way that Christ could hardly be explained as a demonstration of the way God wants people to live. As did Jesus, so also does Zion participate in the world. It takes the problems, frustrations, and injustice of society upon itself as it struggles to reconcile the world to God.

The church lives the truth which is to be found in the Incarnation and in the ever-living Christ. As the Lord directs the church through the Holy Spirit, it moves forward in the midst of the world. There it implements the processes, principles, and relationships which give a concrete expression of God's will. This is the way the church speaks to the world, not in word only but also in power and "in much assurance"—in concrete terms which are understandable. The church speaks through Zion to a world which needs to hear the message and feel the power of God as it relates to the task of finding meaning and purpose in life.

It affirms the concern of the gospel with the structure of our common life together and promotes the expression of God's reconciling love in the world, thus bringing forth the divine life in human society.

God is concerned with the everyday structures of our society. This is one of the amazing truths revealed by Christ. God is not aloof. In Christ, God participated in every aspect of life's processes. Christ was born of a human mother in a stable. He was cradled among other human beings. Because of this, no one can ever feel that the relationships of birth and home and responsibilities of mothers and fathers are anything less than divine. Jesus grew up as other boys and undoubtedly played in the narrow streets near his home. These normal elements of boyhood life must be a part of what is meant when the scripture tells us that "Jesus increased in wisdom and stature, and in favor with God and man" (Luke 2:52).

He participated in the work of the carpenter's shop, shared in the activities of the family, studied, and walked among the common folk of Nazareth. He ate with the lowly and with the rich. He enjoyed and participated in all classes of society. He did not withdraw from others. He was not a hermit or a monk. In order that he should share fully as one of us, he eventually was nailed to a cross and died as all humans die. God did not shield him from any of the pain or deny him the joys of our common existence. Because the Son of God himself touched life in every aspect, no person can ever look upon any of life as if it were mean or common.

Because the church is the body of Christ, it is called to participate in life as he did. It also should involve itself in society, not withdraw from it. In all this the church lives in the world with a sense of the sacramental nature of all creation and power. It brings to bear the witness of God's reconciling love in the world. Jesus gave himself for it. There is no part which should be despised, no godly creation which is not good, no labor which is menial. For when the work we do is sensed as sharing God's purposes, and the material with which we deal is seen as sacred, then every task is sacramental and every "bush must be aflame."

Zion calls for men and women of the church to live together in the world, treating all of life as sacred because it is of God. The scriptures tell us:

> And it pleaseth God that he hath given all these things unto man; for unto this end were they made, to be used with judgment, not to excess, neither by extortion: and in nothing doth man offend God, or against none is his wrath kindled, save those who confess not his hand in all things, and obey not his commandments.—D. and C. 59:5a, b

Zion is concerned with developing all human institutions and relationships with a sense of divine stewardship. It is our Christian affirmation that all things are spiritual. Therefore, it is in the midst of the community that the church lives its faith, revealing the divine life in human society. Such a place may truly then be said to be a Zionic community.

The church is called to gather the covenant people into signal communities where they live out the will of God in the total life of society.

As the body of Christ, we are all members of one body. The church is not merely an aggregate of individuals. We relate ourselves as a living body, an organism, to do the work of Christ on earth. In the body, each member has a function or a role to fulfill. Individual contributions are important to the smooth functioning of the total body. It is as Paul described it:

> But now are they many members, yet but one body. And the eye cannot say unto the hand, I have no need of thee; nor again the head to the feet, I have no need of you. Nay, much more those members of the body, which seem to be more feeble, are necessary; and those members of the body, which we think to be less honorable, upon these we bestow more abundant honor; and our uncomely parts have more abundant comeliness. For our comely parts have no need; but God hath tempered the body together, having given more abundant honor to that part which lacked; that there should be no schism in the body; but that the members should have the same care one for another. And whether one member suffer, all the members suffer with it; or one member be honored, all the members rejoice with it. Now ye are the body of Christ, and members in particular.—I Corinthians 12:20-27

If the church is to function as a body, the members

must be gathered not only geographically but in spirit and understanding. This is the meaning of Genesis 7:23 which describes Enoch's city of Zion: "And the Lord called his people, Zion, because they were of one heart and of one mind, and dwelt in righteousness; and there were no poor among them." It is in order that others may see and understand the nature and will of God that members of the church are called to develop signal communities where they can live the word of God prophetically. Every congregation should be such a signal community where the spirit and understanding of Zion prevails. In such relationships, the Saints may live together in righteousness and be of one heart and one mind. They can see to it that there are no poor among them. The message of the church does not go forth in spoken or written word only, but also in the concrete proclamation in the midst of society.

One person will have a relatively small impact on the tremendous forces and institutions that work in the world. But joined together in a group, the Saints may influence society and their impact can be significant. The signal community unites them in a common body in which their lives send forth a message to the world by the way they live. It is a message of warning, a message of hope, a message of truth. The signal community is the interface by which the word goes to the world, and the world comes into the kingdom of God. We believe the world cannot survive without this message. It is important but not sufficient for the church to send out its missionaries. It is important but not sufficient for each convert to become a disciplined steward. We are incomplete and fragmented as individuals. Unless our gifts and resources can be combined properly with others, we are not effective in dealing with the overwhelming issues of society. The church is challenged to direct its corporate strength to achieving God's will in the world. Unless this is done, the world cannot see the truth of God in the fuller revelation of Zion. And it will not receive the message which Christ brought his church into being to proclaim.

While this concrete expression of the kingdom of God must have a central point of beginning, it reaches out to every part of the world where the prophetic church is in mission.

The center for Zionic development has been designated by divine revelation as Independence, Missouri. As the church moves into all the world, the center provides resources of administration, direction, and power which make possible the organization of the church in signal communities in every part of the world.

All congregational units of the church have a concentration of members in a relatively small geographic area. As the church develops in such centers, their human resources, diversity of skills, competency of leadership, and financial reserves can be mobilized and united into the common purposes of the Zionic community.

The stakes, districts, and regions of the church provide additional priestly resources to give prophetic leadership to the Zionic endeavors of the community. Both spiritual and temporal leadership are provided at every level. The material and physical resources as well as spiritual and intellectual powers are developed as elements in the Zionic endeavor. These basic ingredients are the stewardships of individuals, but they become also the stewardship of the body of Christ, and comprise the Zionic community which God has called into being. In all of this, we recognize our collective stewardship over collective gifts with which the Lord has endowed the church for the Zionic task.

Every congregation is called to be a signal community out of which the message of Zion shall go into the regions round about. Such communities must never be limited to any one area of geography or even to any one nation. God is interested and concerned about the whole world. Therefore, congregations are called into being wherever the people of the church gather together with sufficient members and resources and leadership to function as a community which can move out as a part of the body of Christ. Every congregation may speak a prophetic message and make an impact for Christ within its area of the world.

From the beginning of this movement, the Saints have understood that God is no respecter of persons. One of the strongest arguments for the Book of Mormon is its emphasis upon the international qualities of the gospel. It proclaims that God's loving spirit of revelation is shared with all people throughout the world.

"For I command all men, both in the east, and in the west, and in the north, and in the south, and in the islands of the sea, that they shall write the words which I speak to them. For out of the books which shall be written, I will judge the world, every man according to his works, according to that which is written. For, behold, I shall speak to the Jews, and they shall write it; and I shall also speak to the Nephites, and they shall write it. I shall also speak to the other tribes of the house of Israel, which I have led away, and they shall write it; and I shall also speak to *all nations of the earth*, and they shall write it."—II Nephi 12:65-69 (emphasis added)

The testimony of the Book of Mormon is that God does not intend to deprive any people of the world of the blessings of scriptures which are indigenous to them. Because of this, there is perhaps something no other people have understood so well as Latter Day Saints: God is concerned about and will establish the gospel in every part of the world where people will respond to God's revelation. Under the spirit of inspiration, the prophet Joseph Smith, Jr. said, "And from thence shall the gospel roll forth unto the ends of the earth, as the stone which is cut out of the mountain without hands shall roll forth, until it has filled the whole earth" (D. and C. 65:1b).

The Center Place takes its meaning from the fact that it is the center or the hub. As a wheel requires a hub to support spokes and rim, ministries of the Center Place shall always be important to sustaining the church in all the world. The Center Place is the point of beginning as the church reaches out to every part of the world, for it has a prophetic mission to discharge.

Zion is not limited to one place or to one period of time. It is the expression of the people of God as they live out the divine will here on earth. Zion is the concrete and tangible expression of the gospel of Jesus Christ. It is the way the Incarnation is expressed in the world by the body of the church. As the church, we not only live in the world as a signal community, but we take upon ourselves the burden of the sins of the world and carry that burden as Christ first did for our sake. Zion is the living and tangible expression of Paul's meaning when he said,

I beseech you therefore, brethren, by the mercies of God, that ye present your bodies a living sacrifice, holy, acceptable unto God, which is your reasonable service. And be not conformed to this world; but be ye transformed by the renewing of your mind, that ye may prove what that good, and acceptable, and perfect will of God is.—Romans 12:1-2

CHAPTER 13
PRIESTHOOD

We believe that all are called according to the gifts of God unto them to accept the commission and cost of discipleship. Some are chosen through the spirit of wisdom and revelation and ordained by those who are in authority in the church to serve in specialized ministries. These include ministry to persons, families, and community as well as preaching, teaching, administering the ordinances, and directing the affairs of the church. The authority of all members of the body in their respective callings emerges out of divine endowment to them and their faithfulness in servanthood with Christ.

We believe that all are called...

It seems that all life forms except humankind are unaware of their creator or the obligations of moral law. Yet they respond to the purpose written into their being. It is only humanity, endowed with the ability to perceive and to will, that can discern and accept or reject the call to fulfill God's purpose in creation. Frequently humankind seems bent on being creation's canker. But on other occasions humanity responds to the call and rises to fulfillment that is creative and sublime.

As the prophet has said, "All are called..." (D. and C. 119:8b). A person's role will vary according to the nature and the extent of the endowment. It is further conditioned by the circumstances of life. But we each have our place, and are held accountable to the measure of our capacity. God's calling is not to a few persons who might constitute the elite. Occasionally very gifted people are tempted to think that this is so. With presumed superiority, they may even look askance at others who are less gifted and perhaps unaware. We need to sense that all persons are called by the nature of God's endowment to them. When we read of those whose calling is legendary in the scriptures or elsewhere, we see the point of our own calling. The calling of prophets, apostles, and other men and women from a broad range of circumstances and qualifications is the means by which we are reminded that we, too, are called to achieve and contribute. The fact that all are called places in perspective the worth and contribution of each, whether rich or poor, bond or free, black, white, or other.

according to the gifts of God unto them...

If we are called according to the gifts of God unto us, then the variety of callings is as great as the variety of gifts that God has given to humankind. It also suggests that we need to be humble about who and what we are, for all that we call "our own" are in fact gifts of God to us. The profusion of gifts bespeaks a lavish generosity on God's part. Their diversity proclaims wide variation in skills and abilities. Yet the command to each of us is to magnify the gifts which are entrusted to us. To "magnify" one's calling means to enlarge upon it, to increase it. One's calling may not be magnified by simply replicating what others are doing with their gifts, especially if one has greater capacity than others.

No one is called according to the gifts of others. However, we may each learn from all the others. Each one of us has a stewardship which rests squarely on the dimensions and potential of our own gifts. Therefore, we ought not to expect in others the same skills and competencies we find in ourselves. Nor should we be envious of others because they have gifts which we do not possess. An accurate appraisal of our own giftedness is appropriate for our own self-respect, as well as to an appreciation of others. Moreover it teaches us our responsibility to the source of our endowment.

Such a careful evaluation will help us to understand how the divine gifts are hindered by our indolence, discouragement from circumstances around us, deficiencies of diet, or even by unwise mating. Sometimes God's gifts are commandeered for personal gain with little regard to the welfare of others or to the purposes of God. God's gifts are a sacred trust held by us as individuals for the good of all. This is the basis of all stewardship. Failure to magnify one's gifts is not only an affront to God but a loss to society and a form of self-condemnation.

to accept the commission and cost of discipleship.

One's calling is given purpose in a specific commission. Without it, the calling is nebulous and unfocused. Without commission and commitment, we feel our calling to be useless and without substance. However, a sense of commission may be felt by alert souls who discern their gifts and with perceptive conscience match them against the needs of their time. It is in this sense that baptism is perceived as more than cleansing and enlistment. It is commission—the wedding of the divine command with the divine giftedness. It results in a life disciplined to achieve God's purposes.

Discipleship is essentially a matter of discipline, thorough and even severe. We submit to it voluntarily in order that we can adjust and integrate our life to the divine intent. This is costly, but who regrets paying the price for desirable ends? Sacrifice is not really sacrifice to the one involved. Fasting is seldom noticed by the one who is completely absorbed in doing the Lord's will.

Sacrifice is only considered loss when we move with reluctance from bad to good to better to best. If we feel sacrifice as loss, we are not free from the love of sin. Like the Israelites we cast lingering glances backward to our captivity. But when we are converted to the values of Christ and are intent on learning to do well, then ceasing to do evil no longer seems an exorbitant price.

Discipline and involvement—this is the meaning of discipleship, and it raises a much higher standard than the customary calisthenics of membership.

Some are chosen through the spirit of wisdom and revelation...

All are called; few are chosen. Why? Leadership is the key to understanding, and the best insight is to be gained from looking at Jesus Christ who was himself chosen. As John 3:17 tells us, the purpose of his choosing was that "the world through him might be saved." Every other calling gains in significance and is measured by sharing in this same purpose.

Jesus became "the way, the truth, and the life" (John 14:6). That is, he was in himself the way we are to act. He was the ultimate reality that purges every falsehood.

He was the living that is truly human. He was the Word made flesh to dwell among us that we might see. He was better than all known paths. He was better than all previous heroes. He was, in short, the embodiment of God's wish for humankind.

For such divine purpose and for the sake of those who follow, persons are still chosen. It is only in leading out in the demonstration of the truth that significant leadership can be given. Seeing is still believing. As Jesus said, "I have given you an example, that ye should do as I have done to you.... If ye know these things, happy are ye if ye do them" (John 13:15, 17). In essence, he was saying, "What ye have seen in me, do." Of course, the demonstration must relate to the truth it depicts. Otherwise it is a snare and a delusion.

Those who are deeply involved in prophetic ministry discern the intent of God. They are also given the gift to recognize the potential of those about them. They see how that potential can be realized in developing relationships between their neighbors and God. The gift of discernment helps our natural observation to be improved. Discernment is intensified by prayer, helping us to perceive potential roles to be played. It helps in matching gifts to the needs of people and the purposes of God. It is a risky business and may border on presumption. But it is a necessary task, the calling of persons to perform the ministries of Christ.

If the church is to be the body of Christ, its organs and nerve and tissue need defining and ordering. Jesus and his disciples conceived of the church as an organism, achieving functions appropriate to the Spirit which was to dwell within it (see I Corinthians 12:12). It was to be apostolic and therefore had apostles. It was to be prophetic, and there were those who continued the prophetic role into the New Testament era. It was to teach and shepherd, and there were those ordained to formalize and implement those functions.

and ordained by those who are in authority in the church...

To bring order to the body, and to regulate and direct its functioning, at its nerve centers there must be those who discern divine intent and coordinate organic functions. The church needs to have an essential integrity for wholeness. After all, it is to be the "body of Christ." This description suggests the nature of its life, its submission to divine purpose, and its unity of action in light of that purpose. There may be diversities of gifts, and the variety of functions within the body may be legion. But they are tied together in common function and destiny, bringing the likeness of Christ into the midst of humanity. To such a body the sense of ordered purpose is imperative. Such coordination is appropriately done by specialized centers of direction.

In the church this is achieved by priesthood members who are themselves ordained, and who have been accorded authority to act for the body in selecting others to serve in the various priesthood callings. Acting in wisdom intensified by communion with the Holy Spirit, men and women are designated for priesthood calling. Upon their own willingness and acceptance by the church, they are ordained in worship experiences in keeping with the significance of God's call to serve.

to serve in specialized ministries.

None of us can approximate the total ministry of Jesus Christ. However, the potential is given to most of us to perform some portion of his ministry. Thus

to one is given by the Spirit the word of wisdom; to another the word of knowledge by the same Spirit; to another faith by the same Spirit; to another the gifts of healing by the same Spirit; to another the working of miracles; to another prophecy; to another discerning of spirits; to another diverse kinds of tongues; to another the interpretation of tongues; but all these worketh that one and this selfsame Spirit, dividing to every man severally as he will. For as the body is one, and hath many members, and all the members of that one body, being many, are one body; so also is Christ.—I Corinthians 12:8-12

To some it is given to serve at tables or to assist in other unsung but nevertheless essential tasks. We each have our own ministry to perform for the sake of others. Our lives are never quite complete if that ministry is withheld or is in some way distorted. Moreover we as ministers are ourselves never complete except in the fulfillment of our ministry to others. People need each other and need to be integrated into the body for their own health as well as to make the body of Christ healthy and capable of performing its mission. This is the essential meaning of a favorite passage in Ephesians, as J. B. Phillips translates it:

> His "gifts unto men" were varied. Some he made his messengers, some prophets, some preachers of the gospel; to some he gave the power to guide and teach his people. His gifts were made that Christians might be properly equipped for their service, that the whole body might be built up until the time comes when, in the unity of common faith and common knowledge of the Son of God, we arrive at real maturity—that measure of development which is meant by "the fullness of Christ."
>
> We are not meant to remain as children at the mercy of every chance wind of teaching, and of the jockeying of men who are expert in the crafty presentation of lies. But we are meant to speak the truth in love, and to grow up in every way into Christ, the head. For it is from the head that the whole body, as a harmonious structure knit together by the joints with which it is provided, grows by the proper functioning of individual parts and so builds itself up in love.—Ephesians 4:11-16

These include ministry to persons, families, and community, as well as preaching, teaching, administering the ordinances, and directing the affairs of the church.

There are "diversities of administration." That ministry which is designated as Aaronic has to do with articulating the will of God to the people. Aaronic priests, teachers, and deacons encourage the fundamentals of discipleship. The basic habits of righteousness are so necessary if more complete personal and community expression is to be attained.

Imagine a skilled pianist who has not first achieved habitual and hard-won skill of finger placement and technique and the ability to read a musical score. There is no freedom to interpret the masters or to improvise from the music of one's own heart until bone and sinew can respond to the unseen signals of the mind.

Expression of the kingdom of God in tangible life-style awaits the mastery of the fundamentals of righteous personality and human relationships. Without these disciplines, freedom to develop Zionic community life is impossible.

To believe in priesthood means also to believe in the calling of sufficient numbers of persons to make ministry available to all who participate in the mission of God's people. Doctrine and Covenants 17:11 tells us that those ordained to be teachers and deacons have their primary ministry to persons. Priests have their ministry primarily to family units (see D. and C. 17:10). They bring the influence of forgiving and reconciling love and help with the fundamentals of home life. Such ministry cannot be expressed unless there is involvement with the people where they live. Ministry given in the stead of Christ is never remote. It is here and now, and wins confidence and authority in association, not in aloofness. Priesthood functioning that is limited to formal services in church buildings begs the issue and distorts understanding of the pastoral role.

Elders have a ministry to persons, too. However, by long custom this ministry has become obscured. The intention is that they are to help persons establish a covenant relationship with the Creator. They are to baptize, and this must not be construed as the simple rite to perform an ordinance. Elders are to be the expression of the concern of Christ that the world is to be saved. Thus they go into the world—living the witness where they go, that all may be won to Christ.

All priesthood share responsibility in ministry such as preaching and teaching. Their efforts are pointed toward nurturing persons in Christian life. Priesthood are called to administer the ordinances; thereby people of diverse backgrounds experience the essential oneness which is to be revealed by the church. In all these priestly activities, those of the ministry are to lead others into surrender to God.

From its beginning, the Church of Jesus Christ has been under the leadership of priesthood called of God to direct the affairs of the church. Beyond custom and precedent, however, is the sheer necessity of a body to have a head. Thus there is provision for presidency, expressed at general and local levels. It is provided in such a manner as to guarantee the right of the people to accept or reject that leadership.

Presidency inheres in the Melchisedec priesthood, with particular reference to the high priesthood. Presidency functions through the body in a way that is rather like the nervous system, alert to direction while sensitive to all that influences the body for good or ill. Similarly, the ministry of the Aaronic priesthood is not unlike the circulatory system, nourishing and keeping every part alive, healthy, ready for action and acting.

Everywhere they occupy, priesthood are to nurture the kind of life that makes possible the witness of Christ in every sector of society, so that crucial decisions may be made in a Christian context.

The authority of all members of the body in their respective callings emerges out of divine endowment to them and their faithfulness in servanthood with Christ.

The responsibility of Christian life and testimony is certainly not limited to priesthood members. It is the mission of every believer. All are called, and every one of us is set in our place by the nature of our gifts and our recognition of the lordship of Christ. In a sense, confirmation is our ordination. Our authority is in the measure of our embodiment of the life of Christ. Each person is expected to embody as much of the will of God as we can perceive, and to express it by means of those gifts with which our life has been endowed.

The source of our authority is God; it is God who has endowed, called and ordained us. The Source of life is also the source of the capacities by which we may achieve. The authority we have because of divine endowment may be enhanced by the sharpening of skills and the enlargement of our store of knowledge. But each of us must trace back to our creator the origin and authenticity of our gifts.

Competence should always be graced by humility. It is cherished by being accountable; it is guaranteed by our faithfulness. The work of God among humankind has been too frequently devastated by fitful loyalty. Perseverance and growth in discipleship is the need of every age—especially this age.

CHAPTER 14
THE ORDINANCES

We believe that the ordinances witness the continuing life of Christ in the church, providing the experiences in which God and the individual meet in the sealing of covenant. In the ordinances, God uses common things, even human nature, to express the transcendent and sacramental meaning of creation. God thereby provides the continuing means of investing divine grace in human life for its renewal and redemption.

We believe that the ordinances witness the continuing life of Christ in the church...

We believe in the ever-living Christ. The ordinances of the church are testimonies of Christ's continuing life. They are specific occasions for experiencing the risen Lord.

The importance of the ordinances as means of God's revelation to us can be seen in the record of our failure to keep them vital, even from days of old. As Malachi said in his day, "Even from the days of your fathers ye are gone away from mine ordinances, and have not kept them. Return unto me, and I will return unto you, saith the Lord of hosts" (Malachi 3:7).

In latter-day scripture, the prophet declared:

> The day cometh that they who will not hear the voice of the Lord...shall be cut off from among the people; for they have strayed from mine ordinances, and have broken mine everlasting covenant; they seek not the Lord to establish his righteousness, but every man walketh in his own way.—D. and C. 1:3c-e

Our covenant with God is expressed in all of life. But it is objectified in momentary experiences of shared commitment. These are the ordinances and sacraments of the church. Baptism and the Lord's Supper are universally considered as sacraments by Christian people. We believe there are others such as the laying on of hands in confirmation, ordination to priesthood, administration to the sick, and blessing. There are two ordinances of blessing—the blessing of children by the elders and the blessing of youth and adults by an evangelist-patriarch. Marriage is also an ordinance of the church, and in some nations ministers of the church are authorized by the state to legalize matrimony. All ordinances of the church are sacramental in origin. This means that they are made holy and sacred: the nature of our practice of them must be sacred also.

The ordinances relate to us at times of crisis in our lives. They come at points in the natural rhythm of life involving particular need and special commitment between ourselves and God. These are the determinative moments when the influence of Christ is most needed. Each generation has a need for a specific reminder of the continuing concern of God through experiences which symbolize our covenant with Christ. The remoteness of Galilee is overcome, not in some abstract manner, but in ways which are as close as our human senses.

Through the ordinances God offers ministry to the whole person. God created us as whole beings, and intends to win our allegiance as a total person. This is actually symbolized in the ordinances: for example, in baptism, the whole person is immersed. It is not only the spirit which is subject to the ordinance. Wholeness is the end of baptism. Therefore, both body and spirit are subject to baptism of water and the Spirit, so that oneness and completeness emerge from the ordinance. This appropriately signifies conversion and commitment of the whole person. Intellectually and physically we are brought into covenant relationship. Because the ordinance is experienced in fellowship with the entire congregation, the social aspects of behavior are also committed in baptism. It is a total experience with God.

There are probably no other experiences in worship so complete as the ordinances. There is total immersion in the life of Christ. There is confirmation or ordination of the full person. The nourishment of bread and wine are received in every fiber. Consequently we may be suspicious of any religious experiences which are partial, stressing either intellect or emotion to the exclusion of the physical and social. Such ritual experiences may be expected among others, but it is well to remind ourselves that worship is frequently brought to conclusion short of full commitment of the total personality to the cause of Christ.

The purpose of the ordinances is to point us toward restoration. Left to our own devices, we are partial, fragmented, or double-minded. It is the purpose of the ordinances to bring us to wholeness and integrity, a sense of oneness. Experiences which work against such wholeness are hardly appropriate to the ordinances. It should be the conscious effort of all who administer the ordinances to do so in such a manner as to realize their fullest function.

The most sacred point of worship experience is that point at which we and God are brought together and find agreement. When this happens, we are motivated toward the good life. Consequently, it is not surprising that the Prophet should tell us: "In the ordinances... the power of godliness is manifest" (D. and C. 83:3). Divine power accompanies the newly transformed life into society. It works through that life for the transformation of the environment, gradually re-creating it in the image of the kingdom of God.

Because the ordinances continue from age to age, they represent an ever-present focal point of confrontation wherein we meet God. The ordinances enliven our memory of the transformed lives which have preceded us. The sacraments also bring judgment upon the present. They constantly remind us that we may participate in yesterday and tomorrow by renewing our heritage. By casting us up against the plumb line of Christ, the ordinances give us a necessary and sometimes excruciating experience. We grow accustomed to crookedness, and need a frequent reminder of the straightness which is our calling under God.

providing the experiences in which God and the individual meet in the sealing of covenant.

Ordinances and sacraments are structured experiences of worship. They are in sharp contrast to practices of worship which are passive, or meditative, or ending in themselves. Ordinances do involve meditation but they also involve action, drama, and tangible things. They are kinetic and sensational, enlisting sinew and senses, making the life of Christ immediate and tangible.

How can we participate in Christ's life? The ordinances depict the love of God, and the best dramatization of that love is in the life of Jesus Christ. The sacraments capture crucial moments in the life of Christ and make them available as experiences to be remembered, relived and celebrated. Their form encourages our participation. Each member is permitted to share dramatically and symbolically in that life which was the Word made flesh.

The ordinances contribute to the incarnational quality of the life of the disciple. Therefore at the heart of the ordinance is the covenant. Ordinances and covenants go hand in hand. Covenant is agreement. It is the expressed hope and end result of the ministry of reconciliation. It is the coming together of divine and human wills. This was perfectly actualized in Jesus who was the Incarnation and the Atonement. This was God's drama illustrating in human flesh his hope for humankind. In the ordinances this incarnation, this coming together in agreement and covenant, is reenacted and made personal for each participant.

One of the philosophies of architecture states that "form follows function." This means that the functions which you would want to have occur in a particular structure or building will be greatly influenced by the form or nature of the structure. In a similar way, even the form of the ordinances is important. If we wish to assure that they function as they should, then we are required to adhere to the form of the ordinance in order to keep the function honest in keeping with the divine intention.

In the ordinances God uses common things, even human nature, to express the transcendent and sacramental meaning of creation.

Prophets and poets have perceived in nature's splendor the meanings which require us to explore and bend the knee. The poet Alfred Tennyson phrased it thus:

> Flower in the crannied wall,
> I pluck you out of the crannies,
> I hold you here, root and all in my hand,
> Little flower, but if I could understand
> What you are, root and all and all in all
> I should know what God and man is.

The psalmist expressed it in this manner: "The heavens declare the glory of God; and the firmament showeth his handiwork" (Psalm 19:1).

In the ordinances God uses the commonest elements to express creation's essential meaning. We use song and scripture to give expression to our wonder of God and his love. That is, we use flesh and blood in organs of speech and song. We stand or kneel, all to give expression to what would otherwise remain unexpressed. This is how we communicate. And God has chosen in his Son and in the ordinances to honor and utilize these means which he has provided.

In the person of the Lord Jesus, God has given us the most abundant illustration of the sacredness of common things. He was born as babies are born. He graced the most humble of surroundings. He grew in a family sheltered by a rude hut and worked with his hands by Joseph's side. He attended wedding feasts and walked through country lanes. He was not offended by fishing nets, and spoke knowledgeably of leaven hidden in a lump of bread on the rise. He spoke with strangers and healed the lepers.

No longer can we call ordinary life mean. In fact, all of life was lifted to become the temple of God in the life of Jesus of Nazareth, both a sacrament and a living testament. The Apostle Paul understood this when he suggested that our appropriate offering to God is also our own lives, as common and humble as they are. He said, "I beseech you therefore, brethren, by the mercies of God, that ye present your bodies a living sacrifice, holy, acceptable unto God, which is your reasonable service" (Romans 12:1).

To participate symbolically in the life of Christ, even in

the fleeting moments of the ordinances, is to lift life out of the commonplace. Or rather to make the commonplace speak of God, perhaps, is what occurs in the ordinances. This is that happens with water, bread, and the touch of a hand.

In baptism, water becomes a symbolic grave reminding us that as Jesus laid down his life for our sake, we are now called to lay down our life for his sake. It is also a fitting symbol of cleansing, but it is more than that. It is God's way of receiving symbolically our surrender to life. The minister acts for God in receiving us in an act of faith, whereby we place our life in the hands of someone we believe represents God. We place our trust in the minister who lowers us into a watery grave where we cannot live. Baptism is also our affirmation of resurrection. We depend upon God's agent to raise us up in token of our resurrection into newness of life by the power of God. In our own baptism, we identify ourself with the One who also submitted himself to baptism, "to fulfill all righteousness" (see Matthew 3:41-44).

The ordinances reconcile us to God, and therefore to one another. Peace can be realized only to the extent of our mutual reconciliation with our creator. Every means we have of furthering that reconciliation deserves our attention. This is particularly true of the sacraments which were initiated in the deeds of the life of the Prince of Peace.

In the sacrament of the Lord's Supper, bread and wine symbolize the surrender of Christ to the will of God. Again, the simplest of elements, this time from grain and vine, spell out principles of life. The cup tells us that if we are to be sustained, life must be sacrificed. The bread reminds us that we ought to give our lives willingly for others. Both assure us that we will pass from death to life. They speak not only of the laying down of life but of its transcendence in the risen Lord.

Once again, the ordinance dramatizes surrender to the will of the Father, for Jesus went from the Last Supper to the garden to the cross. When he said, "This do in remembrance of me," it was not a nostalgic hope of recollection. Instead his disciples were to rise to the quiet surrender of Gethsemane in contrast to the self-will of the Garden of Eden.

Because God first loved us, we love God. This is dramatized in the Communion as the presiding officer reaches out to receive the emblems of God's grace, love, and surrender. Having evidenced personal surrender in this symbolic way, the presiding officer goes forth to bring the ministry of those emblems to the priesthood, who, in turn having tokened their surrender, are motivated to go forth to serve the congregation. The congregation, having also received, then go forth to serve beyond the confines of the church building. Neither persiding officer nor serving priest has the right to ask commitment of others until they have registered their own commitment. The token of that commitment is bread and wine. Service which precedes surrender is apt to be self-serving, but service which follows surrender to the love of God is truly to serve in remembrance of him.

The ordinances inspire and equip the believer to express the sacramental meaning of life. God did not intend that life should be profaned by selfishness and violence. By the grace of God and the response of human beings, it may yet become sacramental.

God thereby provides the continuing means of investing divine grace in human life for its renewal and redemption.

In experiencing the ordinances we find a depth and a power beyond our own. It is possible, of course, for the ordinance to have "a form of godliness, but denying the power thereof" (II Timothy 3:5). Long ago Israel was reminded of its tendency toward meaningless acts of worship:

To what purpose is the multitude of your sacrifices unto me? saith the

Lord; I am full of the burnt offerings of rams, and the fat of fed beasts; and I delight not in the blood of bullocks, or of lambs, or of he goats. When ye come to appear before me, who hath required this at your hand, to tread my courts? Bring no more vain oblations.—Isaiah 1:11-13

Lives are changed and redirected and empowered by means of the ordinances. God meets the repentant person with forgiveness. The committing person is met with assurance. God greets the needy one with health. Beyond the measure of our worthiness, we are blessed more in terms of our willingness to receive. Life plagued by sin may be purged and refined. Life agonized by meaninglessness or remorse may become significant. Opportunities given up for lost may be renewed. All of this is because God is still willing to confront us in worship, and has ordained ways appropriate to our need and our capacity to experience.

The ordinances are set in the church to wean us from self-assertion and from personal and social degradation. Their intention is to redeem us. They are to rescue us from bondage, and to overcome estrangement and hostility. Bondage need not be our lot. It was not always so in Egypt or Babylon. God works eternally to free us. This is the good news in Jesus Christ. The ordinances are moments of confrontation, striking us with the fact of our separation, dramatizing our reunion with God, and freeing us for more abundant living. The tangible elements of water and wine and hands are sensational means of dramatizing Christ's love, our surrender, and the wonder of being new creatures in him.

The best definition of the ordinances is Jesus Christ. It is in him that the physical most aptly expresses the spiritual. In him the things belonging to time express eternity. It is the enduring hope of God that we, assisted by the ordinances, shall be able to go and do likewise, re-creating God's will in ourselves and in the chaotic, awesome, and wonderful world in which we live.

CHAPTER 15
GOD'S REVELATION TO HUMANITY

We believe that God reveals God's own personality to humankind. By entering into the minds of persons through the Holy Spirit, God is disclosed to them, and opens their understanding to the inner meaning of divine revelation in history and in the physical order. Revelation centers in Jesus Christ, the incarnate Word, who is the ultimate disclosure of truth, and the standard by which all other claims to truth are measured.

Divine revelation stands at the center of Christian faith. There may be points of difference about how God reveals, or about how any divine event is seen by humankind. Nevertheless, revelation is the fundamental touchstone on which all Christian faith turns. Without God's gracious self-revelation and the expression of divine will, it would be meaningless for us to pretend that God could reconcile the world unto himself through Jesus Christ. Without God's self-revelation, it would be equally foolish to suggest that God restores sinners to a life of redemption because they *know* the Lord Jesus. Consequently a discussion of divine revelation begins with the affirmation that it is so. We can affirm this because we have experienced it.

What is revelation? At the outset we should note what revelation has been traditionally understood to be. For members of the Reorganized Church of Jesus Christ of Latter Day Saints, revelation is a process. But for most Christians throughout the greater part of their history, revelation has been understood as a message or series of messages. Those events were chronicled in the Bible. Whether or not the Bible needed to be supplemented or interpreted by other sources of truth was not in question. The Bible itself was the word of God. For many, it was the very words of God.

More recently, however, especially in the late nineteenth and twentieth centuries, people have begun to read the Bible as they would any other book. They have started to apply to it the same standards of literary and historical criticism and interpretation that any other document would receive.

The merits of such an approach to understanding the Bible have been argued extensively. But it is interesting to note that this critical scrutiny has not eroded either the Christian faith or a belief in the validity of divine revelation. Instead it shifted the place of revelation from literature to history, and from propositional understandings about God to personal experience of God. In fact, Christians have begun to recover the early understanding well known to the apostolic church, that Jesus Christ is himself the Word of God, and that nothing can take his place as the center of revelation—not even the Bible.

The Bible is a record of many of the ways and times in which God pierced the shell of our mortality, causing both the divine nature and purpose to be made known to us. The Bible is not a book of God's words; it is instead a record of human experience with God. We need to take care therefore that we not worship the Bible, lest we fall into the error condemned by Jesus when he chided the Jews for thinking eternal life was resident within the scriptures. In John 5:40-41, the Lord is saying in essence, "Go ahead and search the scriptures, for you think you can find eternal life there. However, the scriptures only testify of me, and you're not willing to come to me to find eternal life."

The Bible is a sacred book containing a record of the people of Israel and early Christianity. That record is especially of those times and ways in which the revelation of God broke in upon them to enrich their history and give spiritual significance to their lives.

The Bible does indeed reserve for us special revelations through which we can become aware of God. These revelations are not in themselves the words of God, but they are words *about* God. Particularly they describe the incarnate Word of God, Jesus Christ, who is himself the fulfillment of God's self-revealing.

We believe that God reveals God's own personality to humankind.

From the liberals on the left to the fundamentalists on the right, most religious leaders are convinced of one central fact. The revelation of God is not initiated by humans. God breaks through from outside the human condition. The poet Wadsworth, on July 13, 1798, with a burst of insight wrote in "Tintern Abbey:"

> And I have felt
> A presence that disturbs me with the joy
> Of elevated thought;
> A sense sublime,
> Of something far more deeply interfused,
> Whose dwelling is the light of setting suns,
> And the round ocean and the living air,
> And the blue sky, and in the mind of man;
> A motion and a spirit, that impels
> All thinking things, all objects of all thought,
> And rolls through all things.

Motivated by the same spirit, thirty-three years later Joseph Smith wrote of the promise to those with a purely motivated devotion:

It is your privilege , and a promise I give unto you...that inasmuch as you strip yourselves from jealousies and fears, and humble yourselves before me...the veil shall be rent, and you shall see me and know that I am; not with the carnal, neither natual mind, but with the spiritual; for no man has seen God at any time in the flesh, except quickened by the Spirit of God.—D. and C. 67:3

In the evidence which surrounds us and in promises made to us, God wills to speak to us. In John's Gospel, Jesus promises, "Verily, verily, I say unto you, He who heareth my word, and believeth on him who sent me, hath everlasting life" (John 5:24). Recognizing this as God's self-revealing and eternal promise, Peter responds to Jesus, "Lord, to whom shall we go? thou hast the words of eternal life" (John 6:68).

The divine will is that we should not only perceive God's life but also participate in it. It is to faithful and committed persons who are able to personalize God's revelation that it is given. In the midst of human life, living people need a living God who becomes personally present and active in their lives. If we were to try to define revelation as being some understanding of some general truth, then the Gospels would be a fraud. For they are not merely chronicles of the life of Jesus of Nazareth. Instead they are monuments to the tremendous fact that the eternal God came into our history and was made known to us as Jesus Christ, the Son. It was God who came to us—we did not perceive God as a consequence of our own powers of reason or intellect. We believe that God is revealed to humankind on God's own initiative, in God's own way and time.

By entering into the minds of persons through the Holy Spirit, God is disclosed to them, and opens their understanding to the inner meaning of divine revelation in history and in the physical order.

Before departing Jesus said,

I will pray the Father, and he shall give you another Comforter, that he may abide with you forever; even the Spirit of truth; whom the world cannot receive, because it seeth him not, neither knoweth him; but ye know him, for he dwelleth with you, and shall be in you. I will not leave you comfortless; I will come to you... [and] at that day ye shall know that I am in my Father, and ye in me, and I in you.—John 14:16-20

That promise, a source of hope for so many, assures us that revelation is not created by human understanding. It is, nevertheless, to human understanding that revelation is given. It is by the gracious gift of God that spiritual people understand the revelation of God which comes to them. Through the power of the Holy Spirit entering into their minds, reason is able to identify revelation. It receives that revelation, comprehends it, explains it, responds to it, and is constantly learning from it and altering because of it.

An unspiritual person can no more judge such a revelation than a deaf person could judge the music of a virtuoso. For it is the mind of Christ that spiritual people *possess* when they are in the presence of God's self-revelation: "He that is spiritual judgeth all things, yet he himself is judged of no man. For who hath known the mind of the Lord, that he may instruct him? But we have the mind of Christ" (I Corinthians 2:15-16).

Unspiritual people do not possess that mind and therefore are unable to participate in the revelation of God which comes to them through Jesus Christ. But to be spiritual is to have the mind of Christ in us, and it is the Holy Spirit which brings that mind to bear upon our reason.

When our reason is brought face to face with God, it will not permit us to rest there. We must go on to obedience and devotion. When we are true to ourselves, our minds are not set aside by faith. Rather they are transformed as a consequence of it. Our judgment is neither predetermined nor discredited. It is instead transfigured when our reason is so "possessed" by the Spirit of God. In this condition we are able to comprehend the exhortation found in Romans 12:2. "Be not conformed to this world; but be ye transformed by the renewing of your mind, that ye may prove what that good, and acceptable and perfect will of God is."

We don't for a moment believe in a naturalistic or a rationalistic religion in which each one of us constructs our own revelation of God in the images we perceive. But reason is at least the faculty by which we understand truth. It is not like God to ignore the equipment that he gave us, which is a part of our human condition. Our model for this relationship of access to truth is Jesus who was himself human. In Jesus' words and works we see God's presence and God's own self. Jesus speaks with the authority of God.

Christ Jesus has the decisive place in an ageless relationship with God. He possessed the same condition and the same human equipment we possess. Consequently, by the power of the Holy Spirit, God can use that same human equipment for our understanding of the inner meanings of God's revelation in history and in the universe about us. By identifying the Lord Jesus with us in our life circumstance, God has shown how communication is possible with us through the human faculties God created in us.

Revelation centers in Jesus Christ, the incarnate Word, who is the ultimate disclosure of truth, and the standard by which all other claims to truth are measured.

Every believing Christian ought to be able to join in solemn accord in the basic truth of the Christian faith: God was perfectly revealed in our history through Jesus Christ. It is as Paul stated in his letter to the Colossians:

For in him dwelleth all the fullness of the Godhead bodily. And ye are complete in him, which is the head of all principality and power.... For it pleased the Father that in him should all fullness dwell; and, having made peace through the blood of his cross, by him to reconcile all things unto himself.—Colossians 2:9-10, 1:19-20

The great focus of revelation in the New Testament is not on the human, historical Jesus as such, but rather on the risen, exalted Lord. The miracle of his existence can be expressed only by the words "death" and "resurrection." That which is hidden in Jesus of Nazareth does not yield its secret to historical or rational inquiry. Nor is that secret even made known to those who share a sympathetic relationship with him. This secret is not released by any subjective process. It is not comprehensible to us through natural means. It is only understandable to God and to those to whom God discloses it. It is a matter of faith, not indoctrination.

How can we see in Christ's death and resurrection the one life which gathered up all the contradictions and frustrations and despair of human life, and produced from it a promise and a glory no previous person had ever seen? How is it possible for natural, rational persons like ourselves to discover in Jesus an actual coming of God into the midst of our lives? How can we see him sharing in our death, our sin, our contradictions of life, and our chance?

The Christ of revelation is little more than a problem and an offense to our ordinary reason and understanding. To meet the Christ who is God's self-revelation, we must in some way share in his resurrection. That of course is irrational and not humanly possible. It is a possibility that lies only in God's initiative and not our own. Only by means of the divine movement of God in the human soul can this divine moment in human history be understood.

It is not an event caused by reason which takes place in us. Instead it is a revelation of God which is centered in Jesus Christ. He is himself the incarnate Word, God's ultimate disclosure of truth. He is the standard by which all other truth is measured. When we share in this event, it is not like the sharing of any other event in our life history.

In summary, we are creatures of God. We have been created that the purposes of creation could be realized. We are known and loved by God. We have been chosen to participate in an everlasting role: we shall be involved with all creation in an experience of divine purpose and self-revelation. We have been created to know, love, and serve God with all our heart and mind and strength—all which our whole soul has power to possess.

The self-revelation of God was evident in Jesus Christ. Therefore, we can echo the words of Joseph Smith and Sidney Rigdon that we, too, have seen him and know "that he lives;...that he is the Only Begotten of the Father; that by him, and through him, and of him, the worlds are and were created; and the inhabitants thereof are begotten sons and daughters unto God" (D. and C. 76:3g, h).

CHAPTER 16
THE SCRIPTURES

We believe that the scriptures witness of God's redemptive action in history and of human response to that action. When studied through the light of the Holy Spirit, the scriptures illumine the minds and hearts of persons, and empower them to understand in greater depth the revelation in Christ. Such disclosure is experience in their hearts rather than in the words by which the revelation is interpreted and communicated. The scriptures are open because God's redemptive work is eternal, and human discernment of it is never complete.

We believe that the scriptures witness of God's redemptive action in history....

We might expect the literature of a great religion to be filled with statements of timeless truth or moral axioms. This is in fact true of many religious traditions. However, the writings emerging from the Judeo-Christian tradition are of a markedly different character. These scriptures also are rich in exhortation, ethical instruction, and theoretical statements. But their most striking feature is that they are essentially narrative in form. They tell a story. The teachings, the moral insights, and the convictions are rooted in the events recounted.

Those events were not selected by accident. Nor were they chosen for the widespread attention they commanded or for their curiosity value. Rather, they are events which the people themselves interpreted as having revelatory significance. The scriptures do not present us with theories or religious exercises, but with historical events and their interpreted meaning. The statements in the Doctrine and Covenants are not random theoretical sayings about religion: they come to us with the conviction that a "great and marvelous work" has broken forth at God's initiative.

Moreover, these events point to a transcendent meaning. That is, their meaning extends beyond the immediate happening and throws light on all of our human existence. People have understood these events as speaking to them at the deepest levels of their experience.

The Judeo-Christian heritage affirms that the knowledge of God is inseparably connected with the understanding of history's meaning. Living within that heritage, we claim that *our* history has a special meaning, because God is in the process of redeeming all history through it. That which has happened carries within it the meaning of that which is to come.

and of human response to that action.

Scripture is *response*. The testimony of the writings exists as a response to God's prior actions. Consequently, it does not try to prove God's existence. The experiences themselves are evidence of God's existence. God's activity, however, is not obvious to everyone or to "all flesh" together. As the one who initiates the action, God is also the one who graces persons with the power to see that action. The nature of this human response is described by Arthur Oakman in this way:

The prophets saw the movement of God in history. It was there before they saw it.... But it became revelation *to them* when they appreciated this divine movement.... For revelation is based upon the intercourse between the mind which guides the event, and the mind which views it.—*Saint's Herald*, January 15, 1951

Our response is twofold. The first stage may be described as perceiving and interpreting. The scripture is not itself the revelation of God: rather it is the record made by someone who perceives that God has acted and revelation has occurred, and who then interprets the meaning of the events. Arthur Oakman further said:

Sacred writings and formulated statements of doctrine are neither the substance nor the reality of revelation. They are records of the divine acts in which the revelation was given.... Statements of belief (such as are found, for instance, in Doctrine and Covenants 17) are not themselves revelation but compilations of *inferences drawn from living experience with God.*—*Saints' Herald*, May 1, 1966

The second stage of our response is commitment. Certainly the scripture may be analyzed and reflected upon. But full response calls for a declaration. The very recording of the experience is itself a declaration that the writer has perceived God's action, and that it has claim upon the writer. Hearing the word of the Lord is not something we do with our ears, but with our whole being. To hear God's word is to feel a demand upon us that requires a total commitment of our lives.

In fact, we mean commitment when we speak of the

authority of scripture. In a sense, the scriptures are a standard for regulating the conduct of our life. But in a deeper sense, authority cannot be measured in such external terms. Certainly there have been times in Christian history when the Bible was used as the absolute authority, externally imposed and dogmatically interpreted. Adherents of the church were even obliged to subscribe to those positions as a test of faith. But inevitably such arbitrary manipulation of the scriptures has failed.

We show our belief in the authority of the scriptures when we acknowledge their claim upon us. We submit to their authority, not because it is commanded or requested, but in response to experiences which we believe with all our soul. We respond because it becomes impossible to make sense of our experience unless we confess the claim made on us, and yield ourselves to it.

Furthermore, if scripture is to have any authority, it must show traces of its human imperfection. Authority does not imply inerrancy in the human interpretations which produce the testimony. Nor does it suggest lack of human error in the processes by which the record is made available to us. Neither the scripture's content nor our interpretation of it can be thought of as possessing infallibility. Only God is infallible, and the scriptures have, after all, passed through human hands.

Roy Cheville wrote:

We can consider that the most significant authority in scriptural writings is to be found in their influence and effectiveness in changing the lives of persons who read and use them, making them guides for criteria for daily living.—*Scriptures from Ancient America,* page 48

This is the experience of those who have acknowledged an authority in the scripture which addresses them directly. It commends itself by its own inherent worth. It persuades them that they have been confronted by a Truth greater than they themselves. C. H. Dodd, speaking of the Old Testament prophets, said:

Their words convey a personal experience of reality, and our aim is to participate in it, rather than merely to assess the logic of their arguments. If they can make us do that in any measure, then their authority has established itself. It is the only sort of authority they need claim.—*The Authority of the Bible*, page 39

Once again, we see that the character of the response may be best understood in terms of *covenant*. This key gives meaning to human existence. The scriptures testify that we are not made for the moment, nor for futility, but to fulfill purpose. We ourselves participate in working out that purpose in a covenant bond with God who persuades us of the meaning of life. We are not our own. Thus the characteristic theme of the scriptures from first to last, is that "All are called according to the gifts of God... [to] labor together with God" (D. and C. 119:8).

When studied through the light of the Holy Spirit, the scriptures illuminate the minds and hearts of persons...

In medieval times, the church as guardian of the faith and custodian of the Book assumed the responsibility for interpreting scripture. The Reformers reacted against what was felt to be an unwarranted imposition. Especially Luther and Calvin rejected tradition as a sufficient source for understanding. They asserted the work of the Holy Spirit in facilitating insight. They affirmed that neither churchly tradition nor scholarly expertise could alone unveil the revelation of God. Rather, the human mind was illumined by God's gracious and mysterious gift of faith, which brought forth a response and insight.

God's revelation is essentially personal and particular. God's mighty acts could be brought to the attention of humankind, but the kind of revelation which makes God's unveiling a present experience is intensely personal. On one occasion, Jesus had drawn forth from his disciples the opinions of people generally about his identity. He then asked the crucial question, "But who do *you* say that I am?" (Matthew 16:16 RSV). In effect, revelation is essentially only revelation when it is for *you* or for *me*. Each one of us may be addressed by the Holy Spirit in such a way that God's action becomes part of *our* history, unveiling its meaning and summoning us to participate in its fulfillment.

We are not, however, excused from the necessity of the most responsible study of the scriptures, using all the resources available. The command is to "seek learning even by study, and also by faith" (D. and C. 85:36). It is a shame that many people pass by valuable tools to understanding. There is a commendable body of research based on devoted scholarship. Biblical scholarship during the last century has been a remarkable achievement and commands respect. Many unsound and naive interpretations arise from the failure to take such scholarship into account. In recent years, considerable research on the manuscripts of the Restoration scriptures has provided an invaluable tool in helping us understand the processes involved in their coming forth.

Of course, not every theory or conclusion of scholars should be accepted uncritically. But we should accord their work our serious attention as an important element in understanding the nature and process of scripture.

It is important for us to *listen* if the Holy Spirit is to function in illuminating our study of scripture. We may become so intent on pressing our own interpretations and arguments on the text that it cannot speak to us. We must not be so busy speaking to it, or manipulating texts, or constructing arguments to support our point of view that the channel of communication is impeded. The whole history of hermeneutics (the study of interpretation) bears witness to the dangers of such a preoccupation. Careful study is necessary; and we do well to maintain a certain modesty and openness in the event that we, like Moses, need to discover something which we "never had supposed" (D. and C. 22:7b).

and empower them to understand in greater depth the revelation in Christ.

In a sense, all scripture is commentary on the revelation in Christ. Christian faith declares that Jesus Christ is the "Last Word." This is not because God ceased to participate in human history after this revelation in the flesh, but because Jesus is held up as the ultimate sharing of truth. He is the One against whom all claims to revelation and truth must be measured. (See Hebrews chapter 1.)

The scriptures themselves are evidence that every response to the revelation of God is undertaken in the light of the revelation which is in Christ Jesus. Made known to us in the Incarnation and in the continuing life of the church, Jesus is the standard of all claim to truth.

Once again we confess that God is revealed not in abstract truth or religious tenets but through concrete acts. The gospel is not primarily a message about Jesus or a set of doctrinal propositions. It is Jesus himself, the Word or action of God made flesh. This is the central revelation without which all other claim to revelation is incoherent.

Such disclosure is experienced in their hearts rather than in the words by which the revelation is interpreted and communicated.

At certain times since the sixteenth century, with great intensity many people have regarded the Bible as literally the *words* of God, inerrantly given and preserved. Even some Latter Day Saints have held a similar view regarding the Book of Mormon and the Doctrine and Covenants. This point of view implies that scripture *is* itself the revelation of God. It also implies that the scriptures are equally true in all their parts, and completely free of error except for the incidental errors of transmission. Such a view is difficult to hold in light of the doctrine of revelation. But it is virtually impossible to maintain in the face of a knowledge of the processes through which the scriptures have reached their present form.

In a series of articles in the *Saints' Herald,* F. Henry Edwards commented on the difficulties encountered in holding to plenary inspiration (that is, the belief that the scriptures are literally the words of God). Edwards first cited Joseph Smith III's evidence concerning the Inspired Version in the Temple Lot suit (*Abstract of Evidence,* pp. 491-494): "We do not consider it infallible...we do not consider anything that passes through human hands to be infallible." Edwards then summarized the matter in this way:

The idea of plenary inspiration was accepted for a long time by a great majority of Christians. It was an attempt to explain what is undoubtedly true...that the Bible does indeed contain the word of God....But the theory itself—this particular way of explaining what Christians know to be true—no longer stands the test of careful scrutiny.—*Saints' Herald,* December 15, 1967

Therefore when we confess that the scriptures are the word of God, we do not mean that the words of the record are literally the words of God. They refer instead to the action of God and they are the words about God. In sequence, here is what happens. The revelatory act of God occurs in some spiritual experience. The person or persons who receive that experience commit their witness to writing, sometimes years later. The testimony will be shared in some literary form of the author's choosing, and it may eventually be accorded the status of scripture—or it may not. But to identify the word of God with the words which are used to interpret and communicate the experience ascribes to those words a finality and inerrancy which does not exist. The words used to communicate the insight of revelation are subject to the limitations of language. They are also subject to the partiality of human understanding, and the cultural limitations of the writer.

The writers have at their disposal all the literary methods for communicating truth. These vary according to the disposition of the writer, the nature of the ideas being treated, or the literary conventions of the times. The Bible includes such widely diversified forms as poetry, sermons, chronicles, letters, testimony, riddles, drama, parable, song, and legend. The Book of Mormon and Doctrine and Covenants also contain examples of many of these literary forms. Truth may be conveyed in different modes, each appropriate in its particular setting.

Regardless of what literary vehicle is employed, the primary concern is to witness of God's action in human experience. On occasion, such forms as parable or myth or legend have been considered in a derogatory sense. Some people seem to think that these forms are incapable of conveying truth as effectively as a historical description. Yet in a unique way symbolic language may become the bearer of meaning and truth. As the prophet said in Doctrine and Covenants 85:12, "Unto what shall I liken these kingdoms, *that ye may understand?*" Unhistorical stories have often been used in scripture to explain a concept which otherwise would be difficult to understand. The greatest storyteller of all, Jesus, frequently used parables that described both the simplicity and the complexity of the intersection of the gospel with human life in terms that even a child can understand.

The scriptures *contain* the word of God. This insight is reflected in one of the earliest statements of belief produced in the Restoration church. Against this background we may speak of the scriptures as being both divine and human. On some occasions, someone may ask us if we believe the scriptures are divine. What is really being asked is *how* we believe them to be of divine authority. (After all, the scriptures are not divine in the sense of being deity. If so, they would become idols.) If our opinion coincides with their own opinion, they usually are satisfied. It is an easy temptation to oversimplify this question. We should keep foremost in our thinking the idea that scripture is our human interpretation of the acts of God which we have experienced. The scriptures openly show their human authorship. But they also testify of God, and through them God speaks to the hearts of men and women.

The scriptures are open because God's redemptive work is eternal...

In a way, the scriptures are open because we who read them today may still enter into the experiences of others in former times. The revelatory events to which our ancestors responded are not closed to us who follow after. The scriptures are a *living* testimony because the Word breaks out afresh in every age and for every person responding to that Word.

There is a second sense in which the scriptures are open. Alan Richardson writes:

The inspiration of the Holy Spirit... did not cease when the New Testament books were all written, or when the canon of the New Testament was finally drawn up; there is a wide range of Christian literature from the second to the twentieth century which can with propriety be described as inspired by the Holy Spirit in precisely the same formal sense as were the Books of the Bible.—*Christian Apologetics,* page 207

Certainly the Restoration movement has insisted that God's redeeming activity continues, and that people have been called to interpret and proclaim it. The scriptures do not and cannot constitute the whole revelation of God. Neither one book, nor three, nor any finite number could compass that revelation. The Book of Mormon illustrates this principle.

"I am the same yesterday, today, and forever.... And because I have spoken one word, ye need not suppose that I cannot speak another; for my work is not yet finished; neither shall it be until the end of man; neither from that time henceforth and forever.... For I command all men, both in the east, and in the west, and in the north, and in the south, and in the islands of the sea, that they shall write the words which I speak to them... and I shall also speak to all nations of the earth, and they shall write it."—II Nephi 12:62-63, 65, 69

Nonetheless, the church must exercise its judgment in

deciding which writings serve a valid purpose. This is not for the purpose of limiting the revelation of God but to provide some guidance for the church and regulation for its life and mission.

Various procedures have been followed in the canonizing, or selection, of writings to go into the body of scriptures. The biblical canon developed over a long period of time based on criteria of usage, availability, and value. The contemporary canon of our church rises from a more immediate process of evaluation and judgment, though initially this selection came after a period of several years. In all cases, however, it is the body of the church which, in one way or another, acts in the canonizing process.

This is true for all three standard books of scripture. Both the Bible and the Book of Mormon have stood the test of time, so that many millions of people bear witness that these two volumes minister to them as scripture inspired of God. The Doctrine and Covenants is too immediate in its acceptance section by section for the test of time to work. There is value in both approaches. An early acceptance by the general officers, councils, quorums, and orders, and by the delegates of the World Conference removes a new revelation from the political arenas of debate. Both formal and informal disputing of issues could only be enhanced if the period of consideration were extended over decades of time. Nonetheless some have suggested that the selection process might well undergo further refining including the test of time. But that remains for future consideration.

We ought to be cautious about arbitrarily dividing literature into two sharply defined classes of "inspired" and "uninspired." Canonization does not imply limiting the spirit of revelation to those materials only which are identified as "scripture." It is true that scriptures are selected on the basis of their value to the community of faith. While according them priority, respect, attention, and authority, Latter Day Saints have always been careful not to set them aside as different in kind from all other writings. Plainly put, we do not understand scriptures to be "divine" while all other writings are "human." Divine truth is divine wherever it is found. God's truth is true and godly no matter what the source.

and human discernment of it is never complete.

There was a time when Jesus was confronted by men who supposedly were very learned. They said, "We know that God spake unto Moses; as for this man we know not from whence he is" (John 9:29). Thus they closed their minds to the supreme revelation of God in their own time. Latter Day Saints have confidently affirmed, "The Lord hath yet more light and truth to break forth from his word." This hymn by George Rawson (*Hymns of the Saints*, No. 309) has long been a favorite among the Saints of the Restoration. We recognize both the inexhaustible riches of God and the partiality of our own insights and achievements. Our most appropriate action is to "wait on the Lord." In so doing, we soberly confess the awesome responsibility of recognizing God's redeeming activity in this world. Others in other times and other places have preceded us in this duty. In our task of discernment and commitment, we are enlightened and enriched by the testimony of the scriptures.

CHAPTER 17
THE RESURRECTION

We believe in the Resurrection. This principle encompasses the divine purpose to conserve and renew life. It guarantees that righteousness will prevail and that, by the power of God, persons may move from death into life. In resurrection, God quickens and transforms the soul, i.e., the body and spirit, bringing persons into communion with the Son.

We believe in the resurrection.

We join all Christians in the belief that Jesus Christ arose from the tomb and that he lives. The word "restoration" implies, at least in part, that this church is moved by the same spirit which moved the early disciples. Whether by the testimony of the New Testament, or the Book of Mormon, or the Doctrine and Covenants, Christ's resurrection is affirmed. That he arose from the dead is part of the evidence that Christ was God in the flesh. While some who walked with Jesus may have thought was a man of unusual powers, it was the Resurrection that brought the revelation of his divinity. Even Thomas the doubter confessed this when he said, after the Resurrection, "My Lord and my God" (John 20:28). Until that time the early disciples were confused about who Jesus was. But this event brought new meaning to all that Jesus had done and said before his crucifixion.

In the Book of Mormon narrative is the account of Jesus appearing to the Nephites in a manner similar to his appearance to the disciples in Jerusalem after his resurrection.

"Behold, I am Jesus Christ, of whom the prophets testified should come into the world.... Come forth to me, that ye may thrust your hands into my side, and also that ye may feel the prints of the nails in my hands and in my feet, that ye may know that I am the God of Israel, and the God of the whole earth, and have been slain for the sins of the world."... When they had... witnessed for themselves, they did cry out with one accord, saying, "Hosannah! Blessed be the name of the Most High God!" And they fell down at the feet of Jesus and worshiped him.—III Nephi 5:11, 14, 17

With such founding experiences the Restoration set its course firmly in the belief that the Resurrection was designed by God for all humankind.

This principle encompasses the divine purpose to conserve and renew life.

The chemistry of life is even now only dimly understood. The nature of the soul of man remains a mystery. Scientists keep searching for that essence which makes physical beings alive. We have been aware for centuries that there are emotional and spiritual forces which influence our physical lives, but what is it that makes us live? What is that gift of life?

The Genesis story of creation simply says, "God... breathed into his nostrils the breath of life; and man became a living soul" (Genesis 2:8). Our beginning was a miracle, as was the creation of every other thing. But even more unique was our gift to transcend ourselves in thought and to become self-conscious, aware of ourselves. How could God create such a being with such powers, and fail to provide a destiny far greater than our own power to conceive?

Through the ages many different people have believed in some kind of continuation of life after death. Many of the Jews at the time of Jesus believed in the Resurrection. When Jesus told Martha that her brother, Lazarus, would rise again, Martha agreed by saying, "I know that he shall rise again in the resurrection at the last day." Jesus took this occasion to make the statement, "I am the resurrection, and the life; he that believeth in me, though he were dead, yet shall he live; and whosoever liveth and beliveth in me shall never die" (John 11:24-26).

Who knows the full meaning of this statement? It is unfathomable. But it is related to the quality of love revealed in him and relates to other statements he made about the "abundant life" he proposed for us. Therefore we sense that Christ would take our life as it is, conserve it, cleanse it, and give it a quality that is glorious and indestructible. This hope in Christ brings to us a vision of our destiny in terms of eternal values which are without end. And this hope releases in us a newness of life and a vitality we have not known before.

In Jesus' day, life after death was not a new idea. But

for many of his disciples, it took on new meaning when they saw it in the light of God's coming to us in the flesh as the man Jesus Christ. This God/man testified by being in the flesh that mortal humans are related by purpose to God. By his resurrection, Christ testified that the same power which raised him from the dead will operate in us, relating us to God eternally. It is as Paul stated it in Romans 8:11, "And if the Spirit of him that raised up Jesus from the dead, dwell in you, he that raised up Christ from the dead shall also quicken your mortal bodies by his Spirit that dwelleth in you."

Jesus was a person, an individual personality. As he ministered he showed his concern for people as persons. His intimate attention to persons gave worth and value to the individual personality. The tenderness of his solicitations for persons, regardless of whether they were young or old, rich or poor, testified of God's reaching out in intelligent love for them.

This kind of love is timeless. It does not end with death. One of the best supports to the Christian faith in the principle of the Resurrection is the conservation of matter and energy in the physical world. From objective scientific research, we know that matter and energy are never lost, but are conserved or preserved in one form or another. It is beyond normal credence to believe that such a God who would preserve the tiniest minutia of matter or electrical particles would carelessly build into the structures of life an ultimate death beyond which there could be no continuing life. Because we can observe the continuation or conservation of matter and energy, we have reason for our faith in the continuation or conservation of human life.

The resurrection in Christ can be understood only in terms of a God whose individual children are cherished with an infinite love that preserves the individual personalities which God brought into being. Paul was so convinced of this that he wrote, "Neither death, nor life,... nor things present, nor things to come... shall be able to separate us from the love of God, which is in Christ Jesus our Lord" (Romans 8:38-39).

It guarantees that righteousness will prevail...

As we look out upon our world and see chaos, suffering, and death, we wonder: Is this the meaning and purpose of life? Is there no other way—no other life to live? The prophets struggled with this question and they found their answer in the God of their creation. In the words of Isaiah, we find this promise and comfort:

> Hearken unto me, ye that follow after righteousness; ye that seek the Lord, look unto the rock from whence ye were hewn.... Hearken unto me, my people; and give ear unto me, O my nation; for a law shall proceed from me, and I will make my judgment to rest for a light of the people.... Hearken unto me, ye that know righteousness, the people in whose heart I have written my law; fear ye not the reproach of men, neither be ye afraid of their revilings. For the moth shall eat them up like a garment, and the worm shall eat them like wool; but my righteousness shall be forever, and my salvation from generation to generation.—Isaiah 51:1, 4, 7-8

The prophet was telling the people that the way of righteousness is the way of deliverance, because it is God's way. It is the eternal way that endures forever. Evil is of the earth. It has its origin in carnal humanity whose attention is focused on their own lusts and greed. When they try to stand alone without God, they are so possessed by their animal nature that they are always self-seeking and thus become a destructive force. Out of their carnal nature comes chaos, suffering, and death.

In the closing verse of the quotation above, the prophet equates righteousness and salvation. Righteousness is of God. The way to salvation or deliverance is indeed God's righteousness. Jesus came as God in the flesh saying, "I am the way, the truth, and the life" (John 14:6).

The ways of righteousness are eternal. People who give themselves to righteousness belong to God. As the Apostle Paul said,

> Know ye not, that to whom ye yield yourselves servants to obey, his servants ye are to whom ye obey; whether of sin unto death, or of obedience unto righteousness?...For the wages of sin is death; but the gift of God is eternal life through Jesus Christ our Lord.—Romans 6:16, 23

The followers of the resurrected Christ carried the conviction that the divine energy which raised him from the dead was a power without limits. His cause—the cause to which they were committed—could not be defeated. They had seen their Lord put to death. They had seen their enemies rejoice thinking that they had put an end to this movement. Having seen the resurrected Lord and having received power at Pentecost, the disciples went out with new life. They had the assurance that his way, the kingdom-of-God way, would be victorious. There is no evidence of God's guarantee that is so powerful and unmistakably clear as this. Righteousness must always prevail over evil. The Resurrection is victorious over the forces of evil, vested interests, cowardice, and the death on the cross.

and that, by the power of God, persons may move from death into life.

Jesus said to his disciples, "He who heareth my word, and believeth on him who sent me, hath everlasting life, and shall not come into condemnation; but is passed from death into life" (John 5:24). When Jesus made this statement it is doubtful that those around him understood the meaning of it. He was stating a principle that became more clear to his disciples after the Resurrection. He was speaking of a rescue from a death caused by destructive values, such as hatred, lust, and self-centeredness.

Paul described this new life thus:

> And you hath he quickened, who were dead in trespasses and sins....But God, who is rich in mercy...even when we were dead in sins, hath quickened us together with Christ...and hath raised us up together, and made us sit together in heavenly places in Christ Jesus.—Ephesians 2:1, 4, 6

The life spoken of here is something more than being alive forever. To sit in heavenly places with Christ means that we possess the quality of life which enables us to enter into the intelligent fellowship of the saints with God. In some measure, Jesus' parable of the prodigal son has called attention to the meaning of life with God. "This my son was dead, and is alive again; he was lost, and is found" (Luke 15:24).

In resurrection, God quickens and transforms the soul, i.e., the body and spirit...

All our joy and hope is based on the reality of the Resurrection. The power of the Resurrection is God's power. As Paul says, "He who raised the Lord Jesus will raise us also with Jesus" (II Corinthians 4:14 RSV). The resurrection of Jesus is evidence that this power is operative. It gives proof to the authenticity of Christ's teaching and his being. He had predicted that he would arise on the third day. When this prediction came true, it was the climax of God's revealment in Christ. If his predictions had not come true—if he had not risen and shown himself in bodily form—the Christian gospel might very well not have been known to us today.

Our belief is that all humanity will be quickened and resurrected. This means that our soul—body and spirit—will be made "alive" and will function with capacities beyond that of our present natural state. The testimony of the early disciples was that they had seen Jesus, and they had faith in him and his promises. They went forth with confidence to testify that the Lord had risen, and that this was the beginning of a new life of glory. He was the firstborn in a new creation (see Colossians 1:18 and Romans 8:29).

The significance of the Resurrection is not merely that we will live again. What is important is that the gospel is vindicated in the resurrection of Christ. In this mighty act of God, we see more clearly, more forcibly, more undeniably what kind of God Christ was revealing to us. This was the climax of the revelation of God in Christ. We may put our faith in God's redemptive purpose for all humanity in this demonstration of his mighty power. The giver of life was moving creatively with power to show his love for humanity.

He was the conqueror of death. His compassion, intelligence, wisdom, and power were all revealed as evidence of the value and worth which God placed on us. We can with assurance put our trust and faith in this kind of God. We know that life is not purposeless, and that God is directing our affairs toward a glorious destiny of justice, love, truth and beauty.

The Resurrection is a mighty creative act of God in our redemption. Paul helps us to understand the nature of the resurrected body in his writings to the Corinthians. The first letter to the Corinthians probably was written ten or more years before the first Gospel. Some scholars consider the fifteenth chapter dealing with the Resurrection to be one of the most important in the New Testament. Evidently there were some in the church in Corinth who did not believe in the Resurrection, and this was the reason for Paul's essay. He started by telling of the death and resurrection of Christ, presenting as historical fact that Jesus was seen by a number of people still living. His point was that there could have been no gospel to preach nor churches founded had not these people witnessed the risen Lord. He said,

If there be no resurrection of the dead, then is Christ not risen; and if Christ be not risen, then is our preaching vain, and your faith is also vain.... If in this life only we have hope in Christ, we are of all men most miserable.—I Corinthians 15:13-14, 19

Paul continued by saying that Christ was the first to be raised from the dead, and that after him would come those that belong to him. In responding to questions about how they would be raised, Paul made four points:
1. The body which we lay down in death will not be the same body that comes forth in the Resurrection. He

used an illustration of the planted seed to make the point that the body given by God will be transformed but still recognizable.
2. The body which goes to the grave is mortal and perishable. The new body will be immortal and imperishable.
3. The mortal or natural body is raised a spiritual body.
4. The resurrected body shall be like the body of the Lord Jesus Christ (see I Corinthians 15:35-50).

Latter Day Saints believe that the kingdom of God will become an earthly reality symbolized in the word Zion. We believe that eventually those who dwell on the earth will be the redeemed whose bodies will be complete and free from the disabilities of mortal life. As the prophet has said in Doctrine and Covenants 85:4a, b: "The spirit and the body is the soul of man. And the resurrection from the dead is the redemption of the soul; and the redemption of the soul is through him who quickeneth all things."

bringing persons into communion with the Son

What is meant by "communion with the Son"? If we can catch a sense of what happened to the disciples of Jesus after his resurrection, perhaps we can understand something of the meaning of this communion.

Some who read of the events which followed the Resurrection become critical of the people who lived then. Still others gloss over this whole series of events and describe them as fables. But let us go back in time and put ourselves in their place.

They had seen this man Jesus put to death. They knew where he was buried. They were in a hostile social environment without protection. This great personality had opened their mental and spiritual eyes to truths they had not comprehended before. They had seen him do many miraculous things. Now he was dead! Even though he had told them he would rise again the third day, somehow his death seemed as final to them as the death of any other person. They were in despair—this communion with him had come to an end.

Luke then tells of Jesus walking with the two disciples on the road to Emmaus. Why did it take them so long to recognize him? These two returned to Jerusalem to tell the others they had seen Jesus. While they were all talking about him, Jesus appeared and spoke to them, saying, "Peace be unto you." And the account says some of them were terrified, thinking they had seen a ghost. Speaking quietly, Jesus said to them,

> Why are you troubled, and why do thoughts arise in your hearts? Behold my hands and my feet, that it is I, myself. Handle me, and see, for a spirit hath not flesh and bones, as you see me have. When he had thus spoken, he showed them his hands and his feet. And while they yet wondered and believed not for joy, he said unto them, Have ye here any meat? And they gave him a piece of a broiled fish, and a honeycomb. And he took it and did eat before them. And he said unto them, These are the words which I spake unto you while I was yet with you, that all things must be fulfilled which were written in the law of Moses, and in the prophets and in the Psalms, concerning me. Then opened he their understanding, that they might understand the scriptures.—Luke 24:37-44

Why did he appear to them at all? What was the nature and purpose of this association? If we had seen a man die on Friday, and then he appeared before us as alive on Sunday, would we not be shaken? Some events are just too great for us to understand, and we tend not to accept them.

The story goes on to tell us that Jesus made numerous appearances over a period of forty days (see Acts 1:3). How many we do not know, because as John indicates (John 20:30), they are not all recorded. During this period, however, Jesus taught and showed them many things. There seems little doubt that he wanted to convey to them in this communion that God, through him, had conquered death.

Furthermore, this power over death was related to God's love for them and for all people. Those who responded to God through Christ would live in this kind of communion. During the time between the Resurrection and the Ascension, Jesus was helping them to get accustomed to the idea that he was with them. He was preparing them for his day of departure, and reassuring them that even though he would not be visibly in their midst, yet he would be *in* them. On the day of ascension, after days of fellowship and association with Jesus, "they were assembled together." While he was teaching, instructing, and blessing them, "he was taken up...out of their sight" (Acts 1:9). He had promised them that he would be with them always. Their communion, their fellowship, would not be dependent upon a physical presence.

This small band of disciples returned to Jerusalem having been instructed by Jesus to wait there until they received the Holy Spirit before starting out on their mission. They knew something of the power of their communion with Jesus. Today, disciples are caught up in a similar communion when they are moved by the same purpose as Jesus, and are committed to the same cause—the redemption of humankind. After the early disciples experienced Jesus, they moved out in assurance that his cause would be victorious. They knew that God had become a human being in the form of Jesus. They knew that through the Resurrection he had overcome death.

Of necessity we accept the testimonies of the early disciples regarding their experience with the resurrected Jesus, and their association and communion with him. But our communion with him is not restricted to this kind of experience only. In the same way that Paul sensed the communion of Christ by the indwelling of the Holy Spirit, so can we and people of every generation. Christ meant this to be so. It was the central theme of his heart's outpouring to the Father when he said,

Neither pray I for these alone, but for them also which shall believe on me through their word; that they all may be one; as thou, Father, art in me, and I in thee, that they also may be one in us; that the world may believe that thou hast sent me. And the glory which thou gavest me I have given them; that they may be one, even as we are one; I in them, and thou in me, that they may be made perfect in one; and that the world may know that thou hast sent me, and hast loved them, as thou hast loved me.—John 17:20-23

CHAPTER 18
ETERNAL JUDGMENT

We believe in eternal judgment. It is the wisdom of God bringing the whole creation under divine judgment for good. This judgment is exercised through persons as they are quickened by the Holy Spirit to comprehend the eternal implications of divine truth. Through the judgment of God their eternal destiny is determined according to divine wisdom and love, and according to their response to God's call to them. The principle of eternal judgment acknowledges that Christ is the judge of all human aspiration and achievement, and that he summons persons to express the truth in decision until all things are reconciled under God.

One of the most pious notions treasured by Christians is their expectation for their future state. Where will it be? Under what conditions? And what differences will mark the boundaries between the righteous and the unrighteous? What will be the terms for entry into the future state? All these have been subjects of endless discussion, conjecture, and perpetual longing.

To many Christians, to be mortal is to bear God's curse. To escape mortality means to rise above the indignities of pain and loss, of suffering and ambiguity. They believe it implies finding an unending happiness presided over by God for those who are good. The "good," for them, are usually members of the church's communion who valiantly testify of their faith and hope. This is a part of the condition upon which they believe the promised future is based.

Others, not so devout, may or may not be members of the communion. Because their lives exhibit an unsteadiness in allegiance to Christian values, they are faulted for their trifling. A future state of considerably less promise and reward is reserved for them.

Outright sinners, whose manner and deportment mark them off as persons opposed to Christian principles, are usually seen as candidates for a different environment. They are assigned to a place where past offenses can no longer be ignored but must be faced up to and repudiated. Even there the future is bleak for these souls, for "where God and Christ dwell they cannot come, worlds without end" (Doctrine and Covenants 76:7v). However, even they shall receive the ministry of the Holy Spirit.

For those who do not repudiate their past misdeeds, the future is not merely bleak, there simply is no glory at all. Though this is an extremely oversimplified recitation, it sums up in general the prevailing beliefs about ultimate events held by many Christians.

What we are primarily concerned about, however, is the principle of eternal judgment itself. This is much more than just a principle of punishment and reward.

The revelations in the Inspired Version of the Bible, the Book of Mormon, and the Doctrine and Covenants provide the data which give our Restoration theology its substance.

We believe in eternal judgment.

Most persons who talk easily about judgment and the future state of the dead do so because of a kind of wonderful innocence. They frequently lace their statements with aggressive feelings, dogmatic convictions, and pious certainties which have a kind of static quality. It is likely that additional information will not change their understandings.

Usually the way they are to be judged is directly related to the way life has been for them. If they were charitable or patient or virtuous in life, observers would ascribe to them the rewards of charity, patience, or virtue. If the person facing judgment had been known to be a good-for-nothing in life, then judgment would certainly bring a reckoning for such frivolity and wasted opportunities. "For whatsoever a man soweth, that shall he also reap. For he that soweth to his flesh shall of the flesh reap corruption; but he that soweth to the Spirit shall of the Spirit reap life everlasting" (Galatians 6:7-8).

And so he *shall!* But it is at this point that most "judgment specialists" are in danger of making their first error. Eternal judgment is not properly described as an *event* but as a *quality*. It is not correct to say that eternal judgment is an event which occurs because of earlier events. Rather, eternal judgment is a kind or quality of judgment. In latter-day revelation, we read, "Behold, I am God... and Endless and Eternal is my name, also" (Doctrine and Covenants 36:7d). What this means is that endless and eternal are synonyms for the name of God. Thus endless or eternal judgment is God's judgment.

If we focus our eyes on events, it is easy to get lost in the shallow and trivial differences which are frequently apparent in events. This was the sin which Jesus so soundly condemned among the Pharisees. To break them from the chains of such narrow vision, he often used events just to illustrate that God's judgment was not visited in such. Eating with the sinners, healing on the Sabbath, feeding his disciples with grain plucked during a prohibited time—all these were examples to which Jesus turned to show that events do not have judgmental characteristics in themselves. The eyes of the disciples needed to be upon God, not things.

Eternal judgment then is a kind or quality of judgment. It is God's judgment. Latter Day Saints believe in eternal judgment. By this we mean that all the circumstances and conditions of our lives are known to God. In his beneficent mercy and unwavering justice, God deals with all these circumstances and conditions in a way that preserves all that is worth preserving: the interests of the person whom God judges, and the whole of creation which is also affected by the judgment.

It is the wisdom of God bringing the whole creation under divine judgment for good.

Judgment is never a singular event. Yet here is where people frequently make a second error. They tend to think that a person passes through judgment alone. But this is not so. Instead, the whole creation participates at every point in the judgment process. Doctrine and Covenants 85:22 states, "Behold, I sent you out to testify and warn the people, and it becometh every man who hath been warned, to warn his neighbor; therefore, they are left without excuse, and their sins are upon their own heads." The implication of this statement is that the people who have been warned are left without excuse. But the reverse is also true, that if they had not been warned, we are without excuse for leaving unloved and unwarned people to exist around us. The commandment to us is to testify and warn. We share then in the guilt or blame to be assessed to those whom we have not warned.

No one goes to the judgment bar alone. Instead, that person is accompanied by every other person whose life he or she has touched, and every other person whose life he or she might have touched effectively. Whether one person has touched another to bless or to injure, their lives are both interconnected in judgment. In this way all creation is bound together even as we have all been "made of one blood" (Acts 17:26).

Judgment is not an experience through which only human beings pass. All of creation has been formed to answer the ends for which it was created. As the prophet Joseph Smith said, "The earth abideth the law of the celestial kingdom, for it filleth the measure of its creation, and transgresseth not the law" (Doctrine and Covenants 85:6a). In the wisdom of God, the earth was formed to provide an appropriate dwelling place for humankind. Moreover, the life forms which exist were designed to enrich the earth and to provide us with food and the resources that would sustain human life.

When humanity was at its worst, as at the Crucifixion, "All the creations of God mourned, and the earth groaned" (Genesis 7:63). The Apostle Paul bore the same testimony: "We know that the whole creation groaneth and travaileth in pain together until now. And not only they, but ourselves also...even we ourselves groan within ourselves, waiting for the adoption, to wit, the redemption of our body" (Romans 8:22-23).

This is not merely a matter of the earth suffering in some mystical way because of human misdeeds. The earth literally suffers the results of human pollution of the environment. Sins of humankind are visited upon the environment, which in turn affects the quality of life of humankind. We and creation are linked together in the judgment which operates. Not alone do we look toward the redemption which is before us. But even the whole of creation anticipates the marvelous day when we shall all be redeemed, and answer the end of our creation.

When that redemption comes, not only will all humankind have joy, but also the living forms which God has created. "Make a joyful noise unto God, all ye lands," says the psalmist. "Sing forth the honor of his name;... [for] all the earth shall worship thee" (Psalms 66:1-4). And bursting out with praise for all the things God created, the psalmist added, "O Lord, how manifold are thy works! in wisdom hast thou made them all; the earth is full of thy riches" (Psalm 104:24).

Judgment is an experience in which all life forms share. Together they acknowledge the ends for which they were created and the Creator who fashioned them. There are two things which reveal the wisdom of God and testify of his loving purposes: the totality of judgment, and the eternal purposes for which all were created.

This judgment is exercised through persons as they are quickened by the Holy Spirit to comprehend the eternal implications of divine truth.

Even when we are at our best, God's wisdom and purpose are only dimly seen by us. The mysteries of eternity almost always remain mysteries. This does not mean that we cannot comprehend God. It simply means that we are never able to comprehend God fully. What we do understand, moreover, comes to us only as we are quickened by the Holy Spirit and participate in the process of revelation. We are not at all able to see God except as the Holy Spirit quickens our faculties. It is the Spirit that enables us to understand what in the world God is doing, and how in the world he is doing it.

Through the indwelling of the Holy Spirit, we can perceive the ends toward which all existence and all eternity are bent. Then are we able to freely and fully submit to the divine forces at work within us and around us. We can then participate redemptively in the judgment which is even now being exercised through us. Our normal inclination is to value the standards of the world and to judge ourselves by others' behavior. But under the influence of the Holy Spirit, we are able to see with our spiritual eyes the true nature of life around us. In the light of that divine truth, we then are permitted to judge ourselves and our neighbors with divine clarity.

The inclination to feed the stranger at our gate, the patience we learn to apply to the problems of life, the loving regard we are learning to have for the associates before our eyes—these are evidences of the work being done in us and through us by the Lord and Judge whom we do not yet clearly see. In the words of John, neither the sons of God nor the children of the world have clearly perceived what God is like. The children of the world do not yet know him. But for those of us who do, we still "look through a glass darkly," and confess that "it doth not yet appear what we shall be; but we know that, when he shall appear, we shall be like him; for we shall see him as he is" (I John 3:2).

Through the judgment of God their eternal destiny is determined according to divine wisdom and love, and according to their response to God's call to them.

It is apparent that God is at work in our midst. Jesus says, "My Father worketh hitherto, and I work" (John 5:17). His work is to bring to pass "the immortality, and eternal life of man" (D. and C. 22:23).

God's method is to bring the enormous energies available to God to bear upon human beings, inviting and encouraging them to do good continually. In the words of Moroni 7:11, " 'Behold, that which is of God invites and entices to do good continually; wherefore, everything which invites and entices to do good, and to love God, and to serve him is inspired of God.' " In this method, God suffers us to be confronted with the alternatives of good or evil while never withdrawing the persistent and redemptive forces which entreat us to spurn the evil and respond to the good.

When we stand in judgment before God, it probably will not be observed that on such-and-such a day, in such-and-such a place, we did thus-and-so. Instead, our God will more likely read the volume of character we have written into our own Book of Life, and our souls will bear witness to the kind of persons we are.

As we respond to the options which confront us, we are clearly describing our particular strengths and weaknesses. As F. Henry Edwards has said, "The character and personality of Jesus are the ultimate standards of humanity; and we must be judged by our approximation to those standards" (*Fundamentals*, page 346). How well we approximate Jesus' standards describes the eternal destiny which awaits us.

We must remember that our eternal destiny is in God. The standards set by Jesus are the measuring rod by which we are judged. Herein is both God's wisdom and love. In such a judgment God does not take from us our right to "do according to [our] own will." Nor does God's mercy relieve us of the consequences of our actions. The ends of justice must be served as well as mercy, or God would be partial.

This does not by any means imply that we are all to become carbon copies of Jesus. This is another place where dogmatists make serious error. Thinking of Jesus as the model by which we should live, they suppose that our best response would be to think and behave exactly as Jesus would if he were in our situation. Such persons frequently support this view by quoting, "Ye are therefore commanded to be perfect, even as your Father who is in heaven is perfect" (Matthew 5:50). In effect, they want us to believe that God is perfect; therefore, we are epxected to be as perfect as God. They believe that Jesus has said that we must do this.

But that is not at all what Jesus is saying, nor what God expects of us. The biblical text does not say, "Ye are therefore comannded to be *as* perfect, even as your Father who is in heaven." It says, "Ye are therefore commanded to be perfect, even as your Father who is in heaven is perfect." In fact, the Greek word which is here translated "perfect" is translated elsewhere in the King James and Inspired Versions of the Bible to read "of full age," or "mature" (see Hebrews 5:14). It is also translated "men" in comparison to "children" (see I Corinthians 15:20). The Greek word most often translated "perfect" in English actually carries the meaning of maturity rather than the idea of being without fault. While God expects us to strive toward perfection, the commandment is that we shall be mature, grown up, adult in our stewardship over life. We cannot be as perfect as Christ, but we can be as perfect as possible under the leading of Christ's Spirit.

This means that we are commanded to be as perfectly and completely and fully human as God has created us to be. Moreover, we are expected to bring all of the resources and insights we possess to every situation in life, just as Jesus did. By so doing we may approximate the same standards which Jesus applied to his life situations.

Our stewardship is to bring to bear on our lives all of the truth and worth and love and divine purpose that we possess. This is what Jesus did. But the understanding which Jesus had of these things may be enormously different from the understanding which any of us may hold at any given moment in time. God expects us to respond as fully to the divine invitations and enticements as we can. As we do this, on whatever levels we respond, our agency is respected and our eternal destiny is described.

The principle of eternal judgment acknowledges that Christ is the judge of all human aspiration and achievement, and that he summmons persons to express the truth in decision until all things are reconciled under God.

All human aspirations and achievements are reconciled in Jesus Christ. He alone provides the bridge between mortality and immortality over which we all must pass who move from death to life. As Jesus said, "He who heareth my word, and believeth on him who sent me, hath everlasting life, and...is passed from death into life" (John 5:24).

It is Jesus alone who can say, " 'I am the light and the life of the world...and have glorified the Father in taking upon me the sins of the world" (III Nephi 5:12). The Apostle Paul suggests that it was the Lord Jesus who accepted the responsibility for reconciling the ambiguities of life which alienate us from one another and from God. Paul said,

For it pleased the Father...by him to reconcile all things unto himself; by him, I say, whether they be things in earth, or things in heaven. And you, that were sometimes alienated and enemies in your mind by wicked works, yet now hath he reconciled, in the body of his flesh through death, to present you holy and unblamable and unreprovable in his sight.—Colossians 1:19-22

Our Lord loves us and respects the nature of God in us. He sees each separate person as a unique creation of God, and will not take from us the right to make our own decisions about how we shall respond to truth.

Nevertheless, Jesus exercises a persistent love that will not leave us alone to struggle. He calls after us and bends all the great energies at his disposal to stir us to freely choose the good and the true. By him and through him all things coexist and have eternal meaning. Apart from Jesus there is no life worth possessing. When at last all knees are bent and heads are bowed, all humanity will recognize Jesus as the one in whom God has been "reconciling the world unto himself" (II Corinthians 5:19).

CHAPTER 19
CHRIST WILL COME

We believe that the inner meaning and end toward which all history moves is revealed in Christ. He is at work in the midst of history, reconciling all things unto God in order, beauty, and peace. This reconciliation brings to fulfillment the kingdom of God upon earth. Christ's presence guarantees the victory of righteousness and peace over the injustice, suffering, and sin of the world. The tension between the assurance that the victory has been won in Christ and continuing human experience in this world where God's sovereignty is largely hidden is resolved in the conviction that Christ will come again. The affirmation of his coming redeems humankind from futility and declares the seriousness of all life under the unfailing and ultimate sovereignty of God.

We believe that the inner meaning and end toward which all history moves is revealed in Christ.

It is our faith that God is the source of all creation and the power which sustains it. All life and existence arise from God, and are dependent upon God. Such a faith as ours must confess that all truth is in God, for whatever is, is of God. Only God can reveal that truth to us.

When God entered history in the person of Jesus Christ, truth was revealed in terms which we can understand. God was that truth. The same Deity who is unlimited by our time and space, who created and sustains all things that exist, took our flesh and became one of us in Jesus Christ, in order to be the truth in our midst.

It is not enough to say that Christ is our example. He is profoundly more than that. Matthew 2:6 states: "They shall call his name Emmanuel (which, being interpreted, is, God with us)." In this spirit, John was impelled to say of him, "And the same word was made flesh, and dwelt among us, and we beheld his glory, the glory as of the Only Begotten of the Father, full of grace and truth" (John 1:14). These testimonies from the scriptures remind us that the meaning of all life which is revealed in Jesus is not merely in the form of an example or a list of statements to guide us. Jesus is in himself the truth, and the inner meaning of existence.

From our human point of view, God is always revealed through the mighty acts of human history. Some of them have been recorded and interpreted for us in the scriptures. These scriptures are not merely a record of the past. They open to our eyes the inner meaning of the present and the very nature of our own being. Whatever knowledge past or future revelation yields to us, it is validated in Jesus Christ. In fact, it serves only as windows of experience through which we see more clearly the depth of truth revealed in Christ.

In Jesus both the beginning and the end of truth and revelation are experienced. In this light we can understand what Jesus meant when he said, "He who believeth on him is not condemned; but he who believeth not is condemned already, because he hath not believed on the name of the Only Begotten Son of God, which before was preached by the mouth of the holy prophets; for they testified of me" (John 3:18). A similar testimony is found in the Book of Mormon: " 'Behold, I say unto you that none of the prophets have written, nor prophesied, save they have spoken concerning this Christ.' " (Jacob 5:19).

Jesus' truth does not speak merely to some aspect of our life, but speaks instead to all of life. If our minds are open to him, he will illumine every facet of life, and will disclose its inner meaning and purpose. In this light, we can understand and interpret history more truthfully, because we are permitted to see it from Christ's perspective. But Jesus is also the revelation of God's purpose for our future. It is not as if all of the future events have been prophesied and will transpire. Rather, we have a firm assurance of the end and purpose toward which creation moves.

Because of Christ, we know that God will succeed. Without Christ we could not have such faith. Without Jesus as the fully revealed model of human life, we would not be able to understand the purpose and destiny which God has written into our universe. Truthfully, without Christ there is no hope. Human beings hunger and search for meaning and a sense of destiny. Left to their own devices, they will attempt to provide for themselves such imaginary hope as their own mental powers can create. But Christianity speaks out of the solid ground of God's action in history! Through Christ the truth is revealed to us so we are not left to speculation. We have historical and rational undergirdings that give meaning to life, both past and future.

He is at work in the midst of history, reconciling all things unto God in order, beauty, and peace.

There is a popular idea held by well-meaning people that God judges and condemns sin—but never the sinner. This casual view of sin fails to acknowledge it as rebellion against God. It is not something external to the sinner, for sin is a part of the sinner. God's judgment on a person's sin is a judgment upon that person. But it is while we were yet in sin that God has loved us. The Apostle Paul stated it so beautifully:

Scarcely for a righteous man will one die; yet peradventure for a good man some would even dare to die. But God commendeth his love toward us, in that, while we were yet sinners, Christ died for us.... For if, when we were enemies, we were reconciled to God by the death of his Son; much more, being reconciled, we shall be saved by his life.—Romans 5:7-8, 10

God both loves and judges us while we are yet in sin. The disruptive forces of evil war against the purposes of God and are subdued in Jesus' own being. This divine agony demands our attention. The heavens cannot weep without our standing in awe and amazement. We begin to recognize how great is God's grace and love when we realize that such a great One can care so much for us.

In this life we see all about us the disharmony and suffering which we know is at variance with God. Sin is disruptive and destructive. Death is written into its very structure. It is the opposite of order, beauty, and peace. Though we see evil and strife around us, we find in Christ the revelation and power which will conquer evil and bring harmony. We know that the day will come when "at the name of Jesus every knee should bow, of things in heaven, and things in earth, and things under the earth; and that every tongue should confess that Jesus Christ is Lord, to the glory of God the Father" (Philippians 2:10-11).

Christ's reconciliation is not reserved for humankind alone. The scripture just quoted suggests that his reconciling ministry affects the world: "things in heaven," "things in earth," and "things under the earth." Such reconciling power that affects the harmony of the universe is described scripturally as the millennial reign. This means that the day will come when Christ shall rule on earth, as people of all ages have yearned for. Isaiah spoke of such a time—depicted in our church seal—when "the wolf also shall dwell with the lamb, and the leopard shall lie down with the kid; and the calf and the young lion and the fatling together; and a little child shall lead them" (see Isaiah 11:6-9).

Although our hearts and thoughts and emotions respond with excitement and yearnings and hopes for such a time, our honest attempts to understand the millennium fall short of our own yearnings. Whatever interpretations we place on the scriptures that describe God's marvelous reconciliation of all things in universal harmony, we must confess that those symbols are only a foretaste of the reality that God holds in store for us.

This reconciliation brings to fulfillment the kingdom of God upon earth.

The end toward which God's work of reconciliation moves is the reality of the kingdom of God. God's kingdom is to come on earth. Sometimes, we humans have thought that it would be up to us to take charge of God's kingdom and bring it into being. Usually such attempts have been attempts to establish our own kingdom based upon some economic plan or social structure that we have thought to be ideal. God's kingdom, however, is found in God's reconciliation, worked by God's own Spirit, and not achieved by some external manipulation of ours.

It is therefore extremely important that we, who are the followers of Christ, should be at work with God in achieving these ultimate divine and eternal purposes. The church yields itself to Christ's direction so that it may become his body on earth, that his ministry may continue to go forth to the world through the church. But the kingdom is God's! We are called to be God's ambassadors of reconciliation. As the Apostle Paul wrote, "Now then we are ambassadors for Christ, as though God did beseech you by us; we pray you in Christ's stead, be ye reconciled to God" (II Corinthians 5:20).

Christ's presence guarantees the victory of righteousness and peace over the injustice, suffering, and sin of the world.

It is because we have faith in God that we have faith that righteousness will ultimately prevail. Creation's victory is guaranteed through the Creator. The future is secure in God. As the latter-day prophet has said,

The works, and the designs, and the purposes of God, cannot be frustrated, neither can they come to naught, for God doth not walk in crooked paths; neither doth he turn to the right hand nor to the left; neither doth he vary from that which he hath said; therefore his paths are straight and his course is one eternal round. Remember, remember, that it is not the work of God that is frustrated, but the work of men.—D. and C. 2:1-2

The seeds of death are written into the nature of sin. Isaiah described the distortion of soul which makes a rebellious person feel that evil works will achieve their goal. If we take that pathway, we are doomed to failure. We are following a phantom which has no substance. Isaiah compares us to "a hungry man who dreameth, and behold, he eateth, but he awaketh and his soul is empty; or . . . a thirsty man who dreameth, and behold, he drinketh, but he awaketh, and behold, he is faint, and his soul hath appetite" (Isaiah 29:8). Isaiah was not suggesting that sin is unreal. Instead, he was pointing out that failure is written into sin's very structure. Those who serve evil, he says, must see their designs come to naught.

It is in the crucifixion and resurrection of Jesus Christ that we see God's ultimate victory revealed. All other evidences of God's victory over sin and evil come to focus in the Resurrection. It was there that humankind's vested interests, political power, intrigue, and selfish lusts combined in one horrifying effort to gain the victory. Cowardice and fear did their work even among the disciples, and Pilate gave way to the threatening persuasion of the mob, thinking to be rid of responsibility by washing his hands of the affair. In this one act we see our own evil desires, lusts, and weaknesses playing their part in the drama of the Cross. All of us look at the Cross and see ourselves condemned. This is not only a personal judgment on our lives. It is a judgment also on our society and institutions. The sin we would never do alone, we conspire to do together in the institutions of society which we have fashioned. All of our own sin, self-interests, lethargy, and cowardice are revealed in bold relief in the Crucifixion.

While the Cross is a revelation of the truth about our sin, the Resurrection is the truth about God's victory. Once and for all, here we find victory written in such large letters that it staggers our imagination. God has been able to take even the evil within us as a means of revealing divine power and glory and righteousness in which we may also participate. Surely we can trust such a God with our faith, and with our life! Our Lord has paid such a price to save us from ourselves! Such a depth of love demands from us a response in love. We can trust such a God and offer our worship and total allegiance.

Christ's Spirit works reconciliation in us, both to God and to our neighbors. That same Spirit endows us with the powers of praise and worship. Working within us, the Holy Spirit brings justice and healing to others. The Spirit of the Lord always moves us to do the works of the Lord. It is as Jesus himself said,

The Spirit of the Lord is upon me, because he hath anointed me to preach the gospel to the poor, he hath sent me to heal the brokenhearted, to preach deliverance to the captives, and the recovering of sight to the blind; to set at liberty them that are bruised; to preach the acceptable year of the Lord.—Luke 4:18-19

Christ not only lives, he lives in our hearts and our

world. The victory of righteousness is guaranteed!

The tension between the assurance that the victory has been won in Christ and continuing human experience in this world where God's sovereignty is largely hidden is resolved in the conviction that Christ will come again.

There is tension in our world. This is unmistakably clear from what we have been saying. We are compassed about by sin and evil on every side, and even within. Yet we live by faith that the victory is already assured in Christ. The end toward which we and all creation move is already revealed in Christ.

But while we wait for that end, our whole being seeks communion. We long for the presence of our loved ones. When Jesus prepared the disciples for his departure, he assured them that although it was expedient for him to leave, he would come again (see John 16:7).

And he does come. First of all, Christ comes again to all who will receive him in the Comforter or the Holy Spirit. Jesus referred to the

> Spirit of truth; whom the world cannot receive, because it seeth him not, neither knoweth him; but ye know him; for he dwelleth with you, and shall be in you. I will not leave you comfortless; I will come to you. Yet a little while, and the world seeth me no more; but ye see me; because I live, ye shall live also. At that day ye shall know that I am in the Father, and ye in me, and I in you.—John 14:17-20

From very early times, the saints recognized the unity between Christ and the Holy Spirit. They naturally referred to this Holy Spirit as the Spirit of Christ (see I Peter 1:11). Sometimes they spoke of the Holy Spirit functioning in them as being the mind of Christ (see I Corinthians 2:16, Philippians 2:5). For them, although Jesus had gone, he had returned in the Spirit. His presence was with them in ways that far exceeded what he did while here in the body.

Although the early saints enjoyed the presence of

Christ which they felt in the Holy Spirit, they looked forward to the day when Jesus would return. The scriptures are quite clear: they expected him to return within their own lifetimes. They, like preceding generations, did not fully understand God's intention or the timing of events. Jesus himself had cautioned them against unneccessary speculation about ultimate events. He had said, "But of that day and hour no one knoweth; no, not the angels of God in heaven, but my Father only" (Matthew 24:43). Nevertheless, Jesus reassured them by giving them many signs of his coming, particularly warning them, "Watch, therefore, for ye know not at what hour your Lord doth come.... Therefore be ye also ready; for in such an hour as ye think not, the Son of man cometh" (Matthew 24:49, 51).

Nearly two millennia have passed since Christ's ascension. Yet the church still cherishes the promise of the two heavenly messengers who spoke to the disciples on the day Christ left them. They said, "Ye men of Galilee, why stand ye gazing up into heaven? this same Jesus, which is taken up from you into heaven, shall so come in like manner as ye have seen him go into heaven" (Acts 1:11).

Christ's followers continue to believe that the coming of Christ's kingdom on earth will be accompanied by his physical return as well. Then will the earth recognize him as Lord of Lords. The word "millennium" means a thousand years. The "millennial reign" refers to Christ's rule over the earth during a period of a thousand years. This is the condition foretold by prophets in ages past when Christ shall reign in a world responsive to his love and power. Much of the language which describes the millennium in our scriptures is symbolic. It surpasses our human understanding in much the same way as other concepts, such as "paradise" or "eternal life." But the nature of creation as well as our own longing combined with the promises of the scriptures do assure us that we are created for communion with God.

For its full expression, our spirit requires our body. If it were not so, there would be no need for the Resurrection (see Doctrine and Covenants 85:4). Our spirit and element (or spirit and body) "inseparably connected" in resurrection "receiveth a fullness of joy." So also in a similar manner do the human in us and the divine in God find communion as we offer our worship and obedience (see Doctrine and Covenants 90:5e).

The affirmation of his coming redeems humankind from futility and declares the seriousness of all life under the unfailing and ultimate sovereignty of God.

The fact that we look for Christ's coming transforms and redeems our life. No act done for God can be futile. God is able to keep and use that which is a part of God's purpose. No thought or act or worship is lost. The truth and assurance of victory in Christ make our life both joyful and serious. Although the victory is assured, it is clear to us that all we do will be judged by the end result of the divine enterprise in which we are engaged. No relationship is casual. No activity is unimportant. No creation of God is bad, for God pronounced them "good" in the very beginning (see Genesis 1:33).

Our frustrations in this life, even the ravages of age and the fear of death for ourselves and our loved ones, are all transformed by our faith. Hebrews 2:15 tells us that by his death Christ destroyed the one who had the power of death, and delivered us all "who through fear of death were all their lifetime subject to bondage." Our deliverance is not merely the achievement of a life which never ends. It is instead the assurance of *eternal* life. Eternal life is life linked with God in God's eternal purposes. It is guaranteed by the divine nature expressed in all creation.

Christ will come, and we shall be with him. It is as the New Testament affirms: "Beloved, now are we the [children] of God, and it doth not yet appear what we shall be; but we know that when [Christ] shall appear, we shall be like him; for we shall see him as he is" (I John 3:2).

CHAPTER 20
TESTAMENT

Although this is the final chapter in this book, it is not the final chapter in one's statement of belief. It is only the end of another beginning. From the start the writers of this book have known that no complete appraisal of faith could be given. We are neither wise enough nor good enough to perceive fully the nature of God and the divine purpose in humanity. Wherever we stand in our doctrinal understandings, it is merely a point in a larger process.

A puzzle now faces us. No two persons exploring their common faith, either with or without a study of this book, are likely to come to the same identical conclusions. How can we allow honest divergence of opinion and still be unified in our faith? The truth is, it is only in our trust in God that we *can* be united. Unity of opinion is only a mirage that seems always to elude us. It is in Christ alone that we are united. With that fundamental unity we are able to establish mutual confidence and devotion that enable us to work together for the sake of our Lord.

Unity in Christ is possible, but it does not come from prescriptions of belief. If we were to have to adhere to some set statement of belief, we would be denied the freedom to learn more of the nature of God. There can be no statement of belief to which all must submit. Truly enough, we are to surrender, but that surrender is to God and not to some formula of belief. Frozen formulae require no faith, only allegiance—sometimes thoughtlessly and grudgingly given. But faith leads to adventure, and adventure to discovery. The object of our search is the discovery of One who is willing to disclose more and more of truth about all things to those who are open of heart and mind.

This book, then, should not be taken as one more formula among all the other formulae. Instead, it illustrates the fact that the church through years of testing and experience has come to this present understanding of the way of God with humankind. All the while, we confess that the Holy Spirit has endeavored to enlighten and correct. It is the testimony of those who have written this book that the Holy Spirit is still at work bringing clarity of insight, and enlarging the scope of understanding. We must seek and heed the direction of that Holy Spirit.

Every student who studies the contents of this book should seek the additional revelation which is beyond anything expressed here. Rather than accept as your own these attempts at explanations of the gospel, it is much better to create new occasions and climate for experiencing with God your own basic beliefs. This should be done both as an individual and also in the company of your brothers and sisters of the faith. Frequently we go beyond private devotions to public worship that is immeasurably enriching to us. We can have the same experience in our studiies with one another.

In many dispensations of human history, those of prophetic spirit have sensed the urgency of God's word. Has there ever been a time when the urgency was greater than now? We, and all humankind, need not only hear the word of the Lord but see it lived incarnately. In this we are confronted by God. What we hear now is as direct and unmistakable as the word to Ezekiel: "Son of man, stand upon your feet, and I will speak with you." If we will permit it, our experience can be similar to that of Ezekiel's: "When he spoke to me, the Spirit entered into me and set me upon my feet...and took me away...the hand of the Lord being strong upon me" (Ezekiel 2:1-2; 3:14 RSV).

We have long been a people who believe that God speaks. We must now become a people who hearken to what God says. We must re-create the divine word in ourselves and in our situation. We are to be the body of

Christ, the means by which Christ is kept visible among humankind. The Incarnation lays demands upon the believer.

We can be empowered by the Holy Spirit to become God's message, shining with a Christlike splendor wherever we go. If we can do this, Zion and the kingdom of God will become more visible among humankind.

No matter which way we turn, the demand of the gospel is there: Let the Word become flesh! This is the truth about theology, too. In the final analysis, theologizing is not just thinking: it is active. Belief is more than thought—it is deed.

NOTES

NOTES

NOTES

NOTES

NOTES

NOTES